VICTORIA
AND ALBERT
MUSEUM
YEARBOOK
1969

VICTORIA AND ALBERT MUSEUM YEARBOOK 1969

Number one

Phaidon

© CROWN COPYRIGHT 1969

PUBLISHED BY PHAIDON PRESS LTD, 5 CROMWELL PLACE, LONDON S.W.7

PHAIDON PUBLISHERS INC., NEW YORK

DISTRIBUTORS IN THE UNITED STATES: FREDERICK A. PRAEGER INC.

111 FOURTH AVENUE, NEW YORK, N.Y. 10003

LIBRARY OF CONGRESS CATALOG CARD NUMBER: 77-83519

SBN 7148 1384 2

MADE IN GREAT BRITAIN

PRINTED BY THE CAVENDISH PRESS LTD., LEICESTER

CONTENTS

FOREWORD

One of the difficulties that confront museums is that they must appeal on many levels simultaneously; they are not directed solely to one public or one class of visitor. Their galleries may, like the galleries of this Museum, be consciously designed to arrest the eyes of those who are not interested, but the collections that they house offer unrivalled opportunities for specialised research. This aspect of their work is often concealed under the rather pretentious term "scholarship". In the public mind "scholarship" connotes study that is pedantic and superfluous, but the research that has been undertaken in this Museum in the past and that is still being vigorously prosecuted now, is practical. It aims first at increasing knowledge in the areas covered by the Museum collections, and then at promulgating the results so that they are accessible to anyone who chooses to avail himself of them. The great catalogues of Rackham on Italian majolica and of Kendrick on Early Medieval Woven Fabrics and Tapestries and Mohammedan Textiles, and Long's *British Miniaturists* and catalogue of Portrait Miniatures are works of this kind. Through more than a century a great part of the basic study of Italian sculpture has been prosecuted within this Museum, and recent years have seen the issue of standard catalogues of Hispanic silver, of works by Constable and of Indian paintings. This is the background of the present publication.

The *Bulletin of the Victoria and Albert Museum*, which was launched in 1965 and discontinued in 1968, had the disadvantage first that it was geared in the main to recent acquisitions and second that the articles printed in it were necessarily short. In the *Yearbook* recent acquisitions will also be discussed, but the main emphasis will rest on works acquired for the Museum in the past which have not hitherto been properly investigated. One of the articles of the present volume deals with the largest single exhibit in the Museum, the rood-loft from Bois-le-Duc, a masterpiece of Netherlandish sculpture which has been all but ignored since its purchase in 1871. Another is devoted to a work acquired in 1962, Canova's *Theseus and the Minotaur*. A third reviews the jewellery of Pugin and a fourth deals with a painting presented in 1857, Turner's *East Cowes Castle*. When the first number of the *Bulletin* appeared, its expressed intention was "to publish articles learned enough to satisfy the most exacting scholar and yet lucid enough to be read with pleasure by any intelligent member of the public." The purpose of the *Yearbook* is likewise to enhance the usefulness of the Museum.

The present volume includes articles from three scholars outside the Museum. It is our earnest hope that these will be no more than the first of many contributions of the kind.

JOHN POPE-HENNESSY

1–4. THESEUS AND THE MINOTAUR by Antonio Canova (1757–1822). Victoria and Albert Museum. Height 4 ft. 9¼ in. (145·4 cm), Length 5 ft. 2½ in. (158·7 cm), Width 3 ft. (91·4 cm). (A. 5–1962).

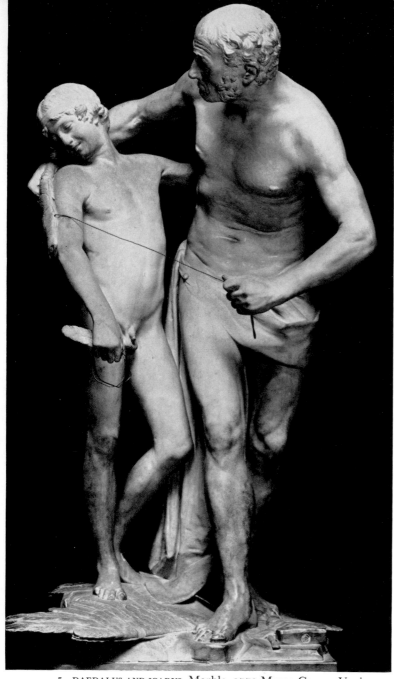

5. DAEDALUS AND ICARUS. Marble. 1779 Museo Correr, Venice. Height 5 ft. 7 in. (170 cm).

exact imitation of nature: one could only wish for a little more *di gusto antico*".[10] An anonymous biographer writing in about 1804 records Zulian asking Hamilton what he should do to encourage Canova and being told: "Nothing but give him a stone and leave him at liberty to make what he will of it".[11] Missirini's much longer account is no more than a "written up" literary version.[12]

Having agreed to finish the statue of Poleni for the Prato della Valle, Canova was unable to take immediate advantage of Zulian's offer. He returned to Venice on June 25, 1780 and appears to have completed the figure as quickly as he could. Later he expressed deep dissatisfaction with it and in the list of his works that he wrote seven years later he said that he would gladly pay the double of what he had originally received

if the statue could now be destroyed and replaced—"perchè non merita di esistere".[13] And in 1793 he told Roberti that it was *cattiva*, like all works he had executed before settling in Rome.[14] Nevertheless, the anonymous biographer of about 1804 was surely correct when he remarked that "in this work one begins to see a type of drapery different from that carved by other Venetian sculptors of the time".[15] The toga is, indeed, copied fairly closely from the Ludovisi *Zeus*, of which Canova had made a drawing in Rome.[16]

Canova returned to Rome in late November or December 1780. He was provided with a room and a studio in Palazzo Venezia and promptly began on the *bozzetti* for the work he was to execute for Zulian. According to Missirini,[17] he at first intended to represent the combat between Theseus and the Minotaur but, on Gavin Hamilton's advice, decided to show Theseus seated triumphant on the body of the dead monster.[18] He had finished a *modello* for the group by June 2 when he wrote to Giovanni Falier saying that he was sending a cast of it to him.[19] Zulian was apparently satisfied and obtained a block of marble costing 200 scudi.[20] With a single assistant, to help him rough out the statue from the pointed *modello*, Canova then began work on the marble.[21]

On December 29, 1781 Canova wrote to Giovanni Falier, expressing his gratitude for a pension which the Venetian Republic had granted him for three years.[22] He also referred to a small statue of Apollo crowning himself which he was carving for Senatore Rezzonico as a pair to a statue of Minerva Pacifica by Giuseppe Angelini. This statue, which he appears to have begun while waiting for the marble for the *Theseus* to arrive, seems—from a damaged cast at Possagno and a photograph taken when it passed through a Paris sale-room in 1951 (fig. 6)—to be an attractive and delicate little work inspired by the Apollo in Mengs' *Parnassus* ceiling as much as by the antique.[23] But the greater part of the letter to Falier is about the statue for Zulian. He promised to send a *gesso* of the head of Theseus *in grande* as soon as it had been cast, also another *picciola* (sic) to put on the body of Theseus in place of that already sent—presumably for a *bozzetto* he had given to Falier. This suggests that between executing not merely the *bozzetto* but also the full-scale *modello* and the marble, Canova had changed his mind about the representation of the head. There were other changes as well. "I did not make the body of the Minotaur hairy *(peloso)* in the *modello*," he continued,

4

6. APOLLO CROWNING HIMSELF. Marble. Signed and dated 1781. Sold from the M. R. d'H. collection on April 27, 1951, Lot 73, (Galerie Charpentier, Paris). Height 33 in. (84 cm).

the text of Ovid and if the club is mentioned I will more willingly make one than a sword in as much as I have kept enough stone. I have found no reference to the Minotaur carrying a club; I know well that this weapon is always carried by centaurs and satyrs. If your Excellency can ascertain from some passage that the Minotaur should carry a club I shall be most grateful."[24] Canova also told Falier that he hoped to finish the group within twenty months—that is to say by August 1783.

In fact the *Theseus* must have been completed several months earlier—before April 1783, when he began work on the monument to Pope Clement XIV for the church of the SS. Apostoli. In his own list of his works executed in Rome, compiled in 1793, he mentioned the *Theseus* under the date 1782.[25] When he had completed the group, Canova asked Zulian where he wanted to have it placed. According to Antonio D'Este, the ambassador replied: "I did not carve the group, you did, therefore make of it what use you think best: I wish you well and good luck."[26] Canova himself wrote that Zulian "gave it to me as a gift, which amounted to 1000 zecchini because it was for that sum that I sold it to Count Fries of Vienna".[27] The precise date of the sale is not recorded. Tiberio Roberti said: "non passano mesi ma giorni che il Conte Fries di Vienna lo acquistò",[28] but the anonymous biographer mentions the sale as in about 1786, which is more likely to be true. Fries had certainly bought it before 1787, when he commissioned Raphael Morghen to make an engraving of it (fig. 7).[29] In the following year Guattani commenting on Morghen's print said that he had sorrowfully seen the group leave Rome 'where someone could and ought to have bought it".[30]

The purchaser, Graf Josef von Fries, was a man of some interest. He was the son of Johann Fries, a very rich Viennese banker who had been ennobled. The father was a patron of the arts and commissioned Ferdinand von Hohenberg to build him, in Vienna, a large and rather severe palace (now called the Pallavicini-Fries Palais) in the Josefsplatz, looking on to the Hofburg. He died in 1785 and Josef von Fries, who then became head of the family, appears to have gone to Rome later that year or early in 1786. Angelika Kauffmann painted a portrait of him in Van Dyck costume with Canova's group in the background in Rome in 1787 (fig. 8).[31] He became a friend of Goethe, who referred to him on several occasions in the *Italienische Reise*. On July 16, 1787 Goethe said that

"as it was useful for me thus to see all the parts, but in the statue I had always intended to represent him with hair." Another problem was presented by the instrument Theseus was to hold in his hand. "I dare say that Theseus ought to have a club instead of a sword, having always carried one with him as a trophy of the first exploit he undertook. Ovid, whom I have read in translation, says that Theseus chastised, wounded and then cut off the head of the Minotaur, therefore I made a sword; but as your Excellency advises, I will look at

5

7. THESEUS AND THE MINOTAUR. Engraving by Raphael Morghen after Canova's group. Inscribed 'Bonav Salesa delin. Raphael Morghen sculp'. Executed in 1787.

9. Canova's Theseus group in the Fries Palais, Vienna. Coloured print by J. Gurk.

Fries was buying many works of art including a famous *Madonna* by Andrea del Sarto.[32] But in another passage he remarked that it was a pity that such a rich and well-intentioned young art-lover was not served by more reliable men: he had recently acquired a poor gem but a good antique statue of Paris. When Josef von Fries died in 1788, shortly after returning to Vienna, his collection was inherited by his brother Moritz, to whom Beethoven was to dedicate his String Quintet Op. 29, in 1802, his Violin Sonatas Op. 23 and 24 in 1801 and his Seventh Symphony in 1816.

Canova's *Theseus* was transported from Rome to Vienna and placed in the centre of a circular room in the Fries Palais: a contemporary print shows it *in situ* (fig. 9). But it was later acquired by the Marquess of Londonderry, half-brother of Lord Castlereagh, who was British Ambassador in Vienna from 1814 to 1822.[33] The group remained at Londonderry House until 1962, when it was bought by the Victoria and Albert Museum. Weathering suggests that it may have been placed in a garden at some time.

So much for the documented history of the group. What of its artistic conception? The subject is a very unusual one, perhaps unique at that date.[34] As Fausto Tadini wrote in 1795, it was "an entirely new and

8. JOSEF JOHANN GRAF FRIES (1765–1788). Oil on canvas. Signed and dated by Angelika Kauffmann, 1787. Museum der Stadt Wien. $49\frac{5}{8} \times 40\frac{1}{8}$ in. (126 × 102 cm).

6

10. THESEUS AND THE MINOTAUR. Engraving after an antique marble group in Villa Albani, Rome. Included in F. de Clarac, *Musée de sculpture antique et moderne*, Planches v, Paris 1839–41, pl. 811 A.

11. THE TRIUMPH OF THESEUS. Engraving after an antique painting at Herculaneum. Inscribed: 'Fran. Lauega Ispan. delin. Portici, Roccus Pozzi Rom. sculp. Portici' Included in *Le Pitture antiche d'Ercolano . . . 1*, Naples 1757, Plate v.

12. HERCULES. Engraving after an antique marble statue in Palazzo Altemps, Rome, Included in F. de Clarac, *Musée de sculpture antique et moderne*, Planches v, Paris 1839–41, plate 802 F.

original" way of representing Theseus; "the fight and the victory appeared until now the only events worthy of sculptors". And in a phrase which, perhaps intentionally, recalls Winckelmann, he commented that Canova "ne rendette nobile lo stesso riposo".[35] The most obvious, if also the most cynical, reason that may be advanced for Canova's selection of the Theseus subject is that a reference occurs to it in Ovid's *Metamorphoses* within a couple of pages of the story of Daedalus and Icarus, to which his previous mythological work had been devoted. And, as his letter to Falier reveals, he had consulted Ovid rather than the much longer and fuller account of the Theseus legend in Plutarch.[36] Although he had put his foot on the road to self-improvement by acquiring translations of works by Cicero and Seneca even before he left Venice,[37] he was far from being even moderately well-educated and his handwriting was still barely literate. It would therefore be rash to attribute his choice of subject to any very deep intellectual process—though he might well have been given advice by his more erudite friends. One may, however, suggest very tentatively that he saw in Theseus's victorious struggle with the Minotaur a symbol of his own combat with the naturalistic rococo style. And the monster is certainly treated more

naturalistically than the young hero. He may also have been drawn to the subject partly because it was uncommon in the visual arts both ancient and modern. There were in fact few renderings of any incident from the story of Theseus and the Minotaur that Canova would certainly have known. The combat was illustrated on a few Greek vases[38] and a gem in the Mariette collection—of which he may well have seen an engraving.[39] The same scene was represented in a small marble group in Villa Albani (fig. 10) which Winckelmann had identified as Hercules and Achelous.[40] If a *bozzetto* in the Tadolini collection can be accepted as Canova's first idea for the group it would seem that he began by following these antique renderings very closely.[41] Hamilton may, indeed, have dissuaded him from representing the combat because his first sketch was too close to an antique prototype.

Another antique rendering of the theme which could have been known to Canova was the painting at Herculaneum of the triumph of Theseus (fig. 11).[42] It is, however, worth noting that this shows Theseus with a club and not with the sword Canova had originally intended to place in his hand. It would seem unlikely, therefore, that he had it in mind when creating his *Theseus and the Minotaur*. But he must surely have

7

13. THE LUDOVISI ARES, Drawing by Canova of 1780, after a marble statue in Museo Nazionale delle Terme, Rome. Museo Civico, Bassano. (37·4 × 22·1 cm.)

14. THE BELVEDERE TORSO, Drawing by Canova of 1779 after the marble statue in the Vatican Museum, Museo Civico, Bassano. (32·2 × 23·8 cm.)

derived the archaeologically "correct" formula for representing the bull-headed monster from one or more of these sources.[43]

Canova's Theseus is seated in an attitude reminiscent of antique representations of Hercules Invictus.[44] He may have derived something from another antique gem in the Mariette collection[45] or, more probably, from a statue in Palazzo Altemps, Rome (fig. 12)[46] There were other seated figures which could have helped him to determine the pose—the famous Ludovisi Ares and the Belvedere Torso, both of which he had drawn (figs. 13, 14), and a bronze statue of a seated Hermes from Herculaneum.[47] The head of Canova's Theseus, with its closely curling hair, and the drapery over the thigh

are reminiscent of the Ludovisi Ares. But although Canova may have had these antiques in mind when he began to model his Theseus, it would be a mistake to suggest that he settled down to produce a kind of identikit Graeco-Roman statue of a seated male figure.[48]

Unfortunately none of Canova's drawings or bozzetti for the *Theseus and the Minotaur* appear to have survived and we can therefore only surmise the various stages in the creative process.[49] A drawing at Bassano has been exhibited as a sketch but was clearly executed after the group, or the final *modello* for it, had been completed and it does not seem to be by Canova's hand.[50] A so-called *modellino* at Possagno (figs. 15–16) also shows the group

15 & 16. THESEUS AND THE MINOTAUR. 'Modellino' in gesso for Canova's group. Gipsoteca di Possagno. Height 28¾ in. (73 cm).

in its definitive form and must therefore have been modelled after Canova wrote to Falier on December 29, 1781, if not after the marble had been finished.[51]

Canova's early biographers record two revealing anecdotes about the reception of the completed group. Cicognara says that Zulian showed a cast of the head of Theseus to a group of artists without telling them what it had been taken from. They all fell neatly into the trap and declared that it was certainly of Greek workmanship, though none could name the original piece.[52] In a somewhat similar story, D'Este recounts that, in order to tease a French sculptor called "Suasy", he showed him casts of an arm and hand of the Minotaur and part of the foot of Theseus, with the same effect.[53] The other story, also told at the expense of the French,[54] occurs in both the anonymous biography of about 1804 and D'Este's *Memorie*. While finishing the Theseus, Canova had a visit from the Director of the French Academy accompanied by a *pensionnaire*. After inspecting first the *Daedalus and Icarus*, then the *Theseus and the*

Minotaur, the Director asked Canova why he had changed his style and advised him to keep to the naturalistic manner of the earlier work—even though he appears to have thought that the Daedalus was copied from the cast of a living man.[55] The story has the ring of truth. The Director of the French Academy in 1782 was Louis-Jean-François Lagrenée, who was aged about 60 and the practitioner of a delicate late rococo style. He would hardly have responded favourably to the monumental severity of Canova's first successful essay in the neo-classical idiom. Indeed, the work must have come as something of a shock to several of the more old-fashioned artists in Rome. Cicognara says that it was generally realised that the group "appriva all' arte un nuovo cammino" and that "si vide sconfitta l'invidia, e gli artisti canuti resero il primo omaggio di ammirazione sincera allo scultore di Possagno".[56] But D'Este seems to have been nearer the mark when he commented that Canova's first success in Rome procured him also his first enemies.[57]

9

To understand the stir caused by the *Theseus* it is necessary to know something of the artistic situation in Rome in the early 1780's. The two leaders of the anti-rococo movement, Piranesi and Mengs, had died in 1778 and 1779. Although the city was thronged with rich foreigners, few wished to patronise any contemporary Italian artists apart from Pompeo Batoni. The Accademia di S. Luca had become a stronghold of reaction, freely admitting foreign artists and the occasional big-wig, but excluding young Italians with forward-looking ideas, alienating most of the more interesting of its members and electing a succession of singularly un-distinguished *principi*.[58] A few weeks after his first arrival in Rome in 1779 Canova wrote to a friend in Venice: "qui si ritrovano pocchi valentuomini tanto in scoltura quanto in Piture fuori che il Sr. Battoni".[59] Many other visitors to Rome made similar comments. Gustav III of Sweden writing to Lergis Carl on December 9, 1783, remarked: "Cette Italie, le berceau des arts et des sciences semble prêt à rentrer dans la barbarie d'où elle a tiré le reste de l'Europe. Les arts ne sont pas plus ce qu'ils ettoit et dans toute l'Italie il ne trouve plus qu'un seul peintre fameux Pompeo Batoni. Elle ne peut pas même nous présenter un sculpteur degne de paraitre aux yeux de Sergel".[60] But on January 1, 1788 we find the new director of the French Academy in Rome, Ménageot, in a letter to a comte d'Angiviller, repeating these sentiments with a significant change: "Vous ne pouvez pas imaginer, Monsieur le comte, dans quel état est à présent l'école de peinture romaine; il n'y a absolument personne qu'on puisse citer, si n'est un sculteur vénetien nommé Canova, qui se distingue par un véritable talent; mais tout le reste est pitoyable, on ne retrouve pas l'ombre de l'ancienne écolle romaine, et l'on ne conçoit pas comment, au milieu de tant de belles chauses, l'art peut être tombé dans un goût aussi pauvre, aussi maniéré, en un mot aussi éloigné des grands maîtres et de la nature."[61] The last sentence with its references to the marvels of Rome and a modern style that was impoverished, mannered, far from the great masters and from nature, could hardly be more characteristic of neo-classical art criticism or more clearly summarise what Canova was struggling to overcome.

The situation was not quite as dire as these critics suggested. There were in fact three fairly distinct groups of artists in Rome at that moment. First of all there was the old guard represented by members of the Accademia di S. Luca and the exclusively Italian Virtuosi del Pantheon, who were living on the distinguished reputation of the Roman school and working either in a style handed down from the classicists of the Seicento or, more rarely, a sweet rococo manner derived from mid-eighteenth century France. The second group consisted of the *pensionnaires* of the Académie de France, many of whom were in the forefront of the new artistic movement (Jacques-Louis David was there from 1775–80 and 1784–5) but who kept themselves very much to themselves in Palazzo Mancini. Even those Frenchmen who were not officially attached to the Académie appear to have mingled little with their Roman contemporaries— Prud'hon writing from Rome in 1785 remarked that he had not bothered to learn Italian as he was living entirely among the French.[62] There was, however, a third international group, dominated by the British with Gavin Hamilton as *doyen* and including the Irish sculptor Christopher Hewetson besides artist-anti-quaries like Thomas Jenkins and James Byres. As Canova's diary reveals, it was with this group that he allied himself. (It should be remembered that to Romans the Venetian Canova was almost as much a "foreigner" as the English, Germans or French). This group appears to have been close to most of the more interesting Italian artists in the city—Quarenghi the architect, Volpato the engraver, Cades the painter and also Pompeo Batoni.

Canova's diary suggests that he summed up the situation in 1779 both accurately and quickly. So far as sculpture was concerned he noted that more copies and restorations of antiques were being executed than original works. He was impressed by a pair of angels carved by Agostino Penna, whom he called the best sculptor in Rome, but much less so by his exuberant monument in S. Maria del Popolo.[63] He was also impressed by the statue of Piranesi which was being carved by Giuseppe Angelini, who had recently returned from working under Nollekens in England and whom Canova saw frequently during these first months in Rome.[64] But the most prosperous sculptors were those engaged in copying after the antique. In Cavaceppi's studio Canova noted copies so well carved "che sembrava impossibile poter lavorare il marmo così bene"; but, he added, "queste copie mi piaque poco".[65] At Albacini's he discovered that an assistant had been working on the copy of a single Roman bust for fourteen months and still needed another five months to finish it.[66] He made no comment, but other remarks on copies suggest that he must have been shocked at this expense of time on what he regarded as servile work.

There was, of course, a sound financial reason for the practice of copying antiquities in preference to executing original works. The most generous patrons of the arts in Rome were foreigners who turned a blind eye to nearly all post-classical works of sculpture and wanted to buy only antiquities or copies of antiquities. Prices received by Vincenzo Pacetti, a Roman sculptor a little more than ten years older than Canova, reveal the situation. In 1774 Pacetti was paid 550 scudi for a monument with a life-size figure of Fame and a putto, for the Cathedral of St. John, Valletta. For carving a bust of Pius VI he was paid 150 scudi in 1781, and for the monument to Mengs in SS. Michele e Magno in Borgo, Rome, he received 230 scudi in 1784–5. But for carving a copy of the little "Apotheosis of Homer" in Palazzo Colonna he was paid 400 scudi in 1787 and for the copy of an Amazon for the King of Poland he received 900 scudi also in 1787. In 1774 he charged Gavin Hamilton 300 scudi for "restoring" a single statue of a Roman Emperor. And he almost certainly made even more money from the traffic in antiquities which he restored himself.[67]

Excavations could yield very handsome profits—and the number of damaged statues which were dug up naturally provided plenty of work for sculptors. In 1783 Giovanni Volpato, the engraver, remarked in a letter to Giuseppe Remondini that he had begun excavating seriously; his capital outlay was more than 1000 scudi but he foresaw that he would make much more than 1000 scudi profit. Next year he sold the King of Sweden a group of Apollo and the nine Muses for 3000 zecchini (6000 scudi).[68]

The thousand zecchini (2000 scudi) that Josef von Fries gave Canova for the *Theseus and the Minotaur*, was a high price for any modern work of sculpture, and a quite exceptionally high one for the production of a young and relatively unknown artist.[69] It was in fact ten times as much as Canova had been paid by Pisani for his *Daedalus and Icarus*. And it compares favourably with the prices given for antiquities that were supposed to be of high quality. Even at this early stage in his career Canova had begun to achieve "antique status" in commercial terms. Within a few years critics were to compare his works with the most celebrated antiques and to discuss whether he ought to be called the "modern Phidias" or the "modern Praxiteles".

The reasons for the great and immediate success enjoyed by the *Theseus and the Minotaur* are not far to seek. Few, if any, earlier eighteenth-century statues had so perfectly expressed the "noble simplicity and calm greatness" which Winckelmann had singled out as the distinguishing characteristic of the best antiques.[70] And this had, of course, been achieved by imitation rather than copying. To quote Winckelmann again: "For us the only way to become great and, if possible, inimitable is the imitation of the ancients. The opposite of independent thought is for me the copy not the imitation." But what, it may reasonably be asked, did the young and barely educated Canova know of these theories?

As we have already seen, even before he left Venice Canova had been opposed to the suggestion that he should begin his career in Rome by making copies of antique statues. Although, as a student, he had modelled miniature copies of two antiques—the Belvedere "Antinous" and the Uffizi Wrestlers,[71] he felt that the work of a copyist was beneath his artistic dignity. In Rome, however, possibly as a result of conversations with Gavin Hamilton, he came to realise that to copy nature (in the modern sense of the term) was no less demeaning. Neo-classical theorists argued that ideal beauty could be achieved in a work of art only by a rigorous process of selection from nature, guided by the example of the antique. They encouraged artists to prepare themselves by the closely interrelated activities of drawing from the nude model in the life class and drawing from the antique. During his first visit to Rome Canova spent a great part of his time in both these exercises. The antiques to which he devoted most attention were the statues of "Castor and Pollux" on Monte Cavallo, then supposed to be by Phidias. At Bassano there are no fewer than twenty-five drawings of these statues,[72] which he later called "canoni dell' arte'.[73] The influence of these figures on his *Theseus and the Minotaur* is more profound than that of any of the other antique sources I have already cited. Canova would have noted in them a way of simplifying muscles and regulating proportions on which a young English sculptor, John Deare, was to comment only a few years later. "The muscles swell very much but they run quick or sharp against each other with great attention to contrast such as small nipples and navel," Deare wrote beside one of his sketches; "the sides full of muscles, opposed to the large masses of the breast, small knees, long threads of drapery opposed to the mass of the body or limbs".[74] It was for such lessons in the process of selecting from nature that neo-classical artists resorted to the antique.

But Canova was not interested only in such formal problems. He was an eager student of all techniques of carving. His diary reveals this again and again—in the Cappella San Severino in Naples, no less than in Cavaceppi's and Albacini's studios. In a revealing passage, the Venetian architect Gianantonio Selva records that when he and Canova visited the Vatican for the first time in 1779, Canova ran from statue to statue savouring qualities he discovered in the marbles "più che nelle copie in gesso che a mio piacere avea sempre presentati in Venezia".[75] Throughout his career he gave the greatest attention to subtleties of carving, distinguishing between textures of flesh and cloth, hair and fur, and producing contrasts of extra-ordinary refinement. Unfortunately the *Theseus and the Minotaur* has suffered from weathering, but it is still possible to see something of the virtuoso accomplishment in carving which must surely have contributed largely to its success. The drapery over the right and under the left thigh is rendered with an astonishing naturalism, which may be paralleled in antique sculpture and provides a striking contrast with the work of even the best mid-eighteenth-century Roman sculptors like Bracci and della Valle, who used their great folds of heavy blanket-like drapery expressively or merely decoratively.[76]

The subject of the group is also of great importance. Canova succeeded in creating an ideal image of the youthful hero, not flushed with triumph but pensive and perhaps pondering the outcome of his feat. Like so many neo-classical works of art, it also had a patriotic message. Whereas rococo artists had generally presented Theseus as the lover and deserter of Ariadne, Canova showed him as the saviour of his people. He had, indeed, appeared in this role in a Pompeiian painting where he is depicted with the Athenian children who kiss his hands. But, as Isabella Teotochi Albrizzi pointed out in her book on Canova, Theseus had overcome not a personal enemy—"dell' inimico della Patria ci trionfa, la quale rende ormai libera con questa generosa uccisione da un orrido, e vergognoso tributo". Canova's Theseus, she found, "bella di bellezza ideale", adding: "Ogni uom, che l'ammira, vorebbe rassomigliargli; ed ogni donna si sente in petto il cuore d'Arianna".[77] It is a personal opinion, but one which serves as a reminder that the coldness some modern critics have found in Canova's works was not apparent to his contemporaries.

If we now return to the *Daedalus and Icarus* (fig. 5) we can appreciate the nature of the stylistic change which separates it from the *Theseus and the Minotaur*.[78] The subject of the Daedalus group is classical. Canova followed the text of Ovid very closely. He beautifully caught the mood of the passage which begins with a description of how Icarus "laughingly captured the feathers which blew away in the wind, or softened the yellow wax with his thumb, and by his pranks hindered the marvellous work on which his father was engaged". And he faithfully illustrates the lines: "While he was giving Icarus these instructions how to fly, Daedalus was at the same time fastening the novel wings to his son's shoulders. As he worked and talked the old man's cheeks were wet with tears, and his fatherly affection made his hands tremble. He kissed his son whom he was never to kiss again. . .".[79] Yet the subject is anecdotal rather than serious in a neo-classical sense. It could be rendered tragically, but Canova's group is no more than playfully sentimental. This is emphasised by the *mouvementé* composition based on spirally curving lines. The treatment of the two bodies is remarkably naturalistic, with the tired creased flesh on the chest and belly of Daedalus well contrasted with the firm young flesh of Icarus. It is easy to see why Lagrenée should have supposed that Canova had worked from the cast of a living model. This is sculpture aspiring to the condition of waxworks—only colour is needed to make it deceptively life-like. On the other hand, the drapery which falls from Daedalus's right hip is functionally meaningless, indeed rather disturbing unless seen merely as a device to strengthen the tapering base of the group. Yet this work is a *tour de force* of technical virtuosity which it would be hard to parallel in Italy or even France at this period. It still exerts a strong emotional and aesthetic appeal—and had he executed nothing else Canova would occupy a place of some importance in the history of Venetian sculpture. His next two works were much less successful. Indeed the Poleni statue is an artistic failure, as Canova himself realised—no more than a pastiche of the antique. The small statue of Apollo crowning himself (fig. 6) is also a derivative work, owing the posture to Mengs and the treatment of the torso to the antique.[81] Both statues are products of the "antique revival" rather than of Neo-classicism. The *Theseus and the Minotaur* may thus be regarded as Canova's first neo-classical work. It answers the current demand for works of art that were serious in both subject and execution, of universal significance and appeal, noble in character, grand in conception, simple in composition and outline, true to the materials in which they were executed and also true to nature—in the late eighteenth-century meaning of the phrase. But, as we have seen, it was still dependent on antique prototypes and shows little advance on the early type of Neo-classicism practised by Mengs or Gavin Hamilton.

It was not until he executed the monument to Clement XIV, which he began as soon as the *Theseus and the Minotaur* was finished, and which exactly corresponds in date with David's *Oath of the Horatii*, that Canova's style fully matured and the neo-classical revolution in sculpture was effected. As Antonio D'Este remarked: "Se il gruppo di Teseo sul Minotauro segno l'era del risorgimento della statuaria, questo deposito taglio il nodo Gordiano".[82]

Notes

Sources cited frequently in the notes:

Bassano: Manuscript collection of the Biblioteca Civica, Bassano del Grappa. The reference numbers are those given by A. Sorbelli: *Inventari dei manoscritti delle biblioteche d'Italia*, LVIII, *Bassano del Grappa*, Florence, 1934.
Bassi Gipsoteca: E. Bassi: *La Gipsoteca di Possagno*, Venice, 1957.
Bassi Museo: E. Bassi: *Il Museo Civico di Bassano: i disegni di Antonio Canova*, Venice, 1959.
Cicognara: L. Cicognara: *Biografia di Antonio Canova*, Venice, 1823.
D'Este: A. D'Este: *Memorie di Antonio Canova*, Florence, 1864.
Malamani: V. Malamani: *Canova*, Milan, 1911.
Missirini: M. Missirini: *Della vita di Antonio Canova*, Milan, 1824.
Quaderni: A. Canova: *I quaderni di viaggio*, ed. E. Bassi, Venice-Rome, 1959.

1. Lord Herbert: *Pembroke Papers* 1780–94, London, 1950, pp. 281, 283.
2. Accession number A5–1962. Bought by the Victoria and Albert Museum with the assistance of the National Art-Collections Fund. The work is of white marble, 145·4 cm high, 158·7 cm long, 91·4 cm wide (maximum).
3. *Extracts of the Journals and Correspondence of Miss Berry*, ed. T. Lewis, London, 1865, I, p. 103. An enthusiastic account of the group was published in *Giornale delle Belle Arti*, no. 5. Rome, 1784.
4. *Bassano* 6022, anonymous biography written c. 1804. There has been some confusion about the dating of these early statues. A note in Canova's own hand, written c. 1787, *Bassano* 6091, states that the *Eurydice* was 'lavorato alli Predazzi' when he was no more than 17 years old, i.e. in 1773–74, while the *Orpheus* was 'fatta a Venezia . . . e questa è stata esposta in Sensa' in 1776. But Canova's memory may have been at fault and it seems more probable that he carved the *Eurydice* in 1775. The public interest shown in these very early works may be demonstrated by the inclusion of a brief and somewhat confused entry for Canova in the last edition of the *Abecedario pittorico*, Florence, 1776, p. 1367. The two statues are now in Museo Correr, Venice.
5. In a notebook, *Bassano* 6097, Canova recorded 'adi 29 Maggio 1777 io principio la statua del orfeo in marmo'. The statue is now in the Hermitage Museum, Leningrad.
6. For the Aesculapius statue now in the Museo Civico, Padua, see *Bassano* 6091. In the same document Canova lists the *Daedalus and Icarus* as his fifth work, immediately after the Aesculapius. His notebook, *Bassano* 6097, reveals that he received from Pisani 150 *ducatti* to buy marble for the group on October 7, 1777; 50 zecchini on February 13 1778; and a further 40 zecchini on April 3, 1779, when the work was presumably finished.
7. *Quaderni*, p. 27. Some additional scraps of information relating to the 'Quaderni' were published by me in *Arte Veneta*, 1960, p. 254.
8. *Quaderni* p. 38–39. On November 19 Canova recorded that he had heard that the gesso was still at Trieste. On the same day he wrote a letter addressed to 'Stim. Dr. Marco' (Mario?) asking for help in getting the cast to Rome (Biblioteca Labronica, Leghorn, MS. II 343). The anonymous biographer, *Bassano* 6022, suggests that Falier had introduced Canova to Zulian before the latter was appointed ambassador in Rome and that Zulian had asked Canova to execute copies after the antique for him while still in Venice.
9. *Quaderni* p. 137.
10. *Bassano* 30, B. 15. 1.
11. *Bassano* 6022.
12. *Missirini*, vol. I, pp. 46–48. Missirini may well have had access to Canova's papers while writing his biography.
13. *Bassano* 6091.
14. *Bassano*. R.8.
15. *Bassano* 6022.
16. *Quaderni* fig. 10.
17. *Missirini*, p. 53.
18. The anonymous biographer, *Bassano* 6022, says that Canova executed *bozzetti* of both subjects and showed them to Hamilton who 'prevelse la seconda azione dicendogli che la gioventù deve applicarsi allo studio della semplicità, e tanto più allora che predelegerarsi lo stil di maniera'.
19. The letter is printed in *Cicognara* p. 79–80.
20. T. Roberti's biography (written under Canova's guidance), *Bassano* 30. B. 15. 1.

21. *Bassano* 6022. The same source states that Canova's Venetian works were executed with 'assai pochi punti dell' abbozzo in marmo' and that it was not until he settled in Rome that he acquired a more advanced technique of 'l'arte di cavar da punti'. It is tempting to suggest that he learned the more elaborate technique of pointing from the sculptors engaged in copying antique marbles.

22. The anonymous biographer, *Bassano* 6022, states that the pension was of 300 ducats for three years. This is repeated by Missirini who says that the decree granting the pension was dated December 2, 1781 and signed by Giuseppe Gradenigo. *Malamani* p. 22, however, reduces the sum to 25 'ducati d'argento' and *Bassi Gipsoteca* p. 36., repeats this sum but reduces the time to two years: neither of these authorities quotes a source.

23. *Cicognara* p. 58 states that it passed from Rezzonico into the collection of Marshall Daru. The statue, sold at Galerie Charpentier, April 27, 1951, lot 73, is inscribed: *Ant. Canova, venet. Facieb. 1781*: for this reference I am indebted to G. Hubert: *La sculpture dans l'Italie Napoléonienne*, Paris, 1964, p. 69.

24. *Cicognara*, pp. 80–82.

25. *Bassano* 6090.

26. *D'Este* p. 29–30. *Malamani* p. 26 generously translated D'Este's Italian back into Venetian—'Lo ghavé fato vo no mi— donca feghene vu quel che volé'.

27. *Bassano* 6091.

28. *Bassano* 30. B. 15. 1.

29. N. Palmerini: *Catalogo delle opere d'intaglio di Raffaello Morghen*, Florence, 1810, p. 22 records that Morghen engraved the plate in 1787 'in tempo di villeggiatura nella campagna di Albano'.

30. G. A. Guattani: *Memorie per le belle arti*, IV, Rome, 1788, p. 43.

31. I am most grateful to Mr. Terence Hodgkinson for information about Josef von Fries and his family, which he generously placed at my disposal and also for drawing my attention to Angelika Kauffmann's portrait reproduced here. For more information about Fries's patronage see Hermann Burg: *Der Bildhauer Franz Anton Zauner und seine Zeit*, Vienna, 1915, *passim*.

32. The painting was also engraved for Fries by Raphael Morghen. It is now at Ascot Wing, Berkshire. The attribution to Andrea del Sarto was rejected by S. Freedberg: *Andrea del Sarto* Cambridge, Mass, 1963, II, p. 91–92, but accepted by J. Shearman: *Andrea del Sarto*, Oxford, 1965, II, p. 247.

33. The print was published by Alessandro Mollo and is mentioned by H. Burg *op. cit.* Although Canova's friends normally kept him informed of the movement of his works, I have found no reference to Lord Londonderry's purchase of the group in the archive at Bassano. This suggests that Lord Londonderry may have bought it towards the end of his mission, shortly before or after Canova's death. Canova was acquainted with Lord Castlereagh to whom he gave a bust of Helen, after 1815: this bust belongs to the present Lord Londonderry. While in Vienna, Lord Londonderry also bought the Andrea del Sarto *Madonna* from the Fries family and, from Caroline Murat, Correggio's *Mercury Instructing Cupid* and *Ecce Homo* now in the National Gallery, London (Nos. 10 and 15).

34. A frescoed ceiling by Francesco de Mura in Palazzo Reale, Turin is devoted to the Theseus legend but strangely omits the combat with the Minotaur, see *Paragone*, 1962, no. 155, p. 39. A pensionnaire at the French academy in Rome, F.-M. Suzanne modelled a statue of Theseus which was completed before May 1780 and received in Paris by September 2 of that year when it was judged to be in the 'goût de nature et de vérité' cf. A. de Montaiglon and J. Guiffrey: *Correspondance des directeurs de l'Académie de France à Rome*, Paris, 1905, XIV, p. 45. I have not been able to trace this work or any reproduction of it.

35. F. Tadini: *Le sculture e le pitture di Antonio Canova pubblicate fino a quest' anno 1795*, Venice, 1796, p. 38–39.

36. The 'standard' Italian translation of the Metamorphoses appears to have been that by G. A. dell'Anguillara first published in Venice in 1563 and frequently reprinted. But either Canova's memory was at fault or he had made use of a less exact translation for there is no description of Theseus wounding and cutting off the head of the Minotaur in Ovid's very brief version of the story. *Metamorphoses* VIII, 172–76.

37. Entry in one of Canova's notebooks, *Bassano* 6097.

38. Notably a kylix in the British Museum and another in the Louvre.

39. P. J. Mariette: *Traité des pierres gravées*, Paris, 1750 reproduced in S. Reinach: *Pierres gravées*, Paris 1895, pl. 90, no. 76.

40. J. J. Winckelmann: *Monumenti inediti*, Rome, 1767, p. 134 states that the group had previously been identified as *Theseus and the Minotaur*. S. Morcelli, S. Fea and E. Q. Visconti: *Villa Albani*, Imola, 1870 p. 38, restore the identification as *Theseus and the Minotaur*.

41. This *bozzetto* belonged to Canova's pupil A. Tadolini and is now in the possession of his descendant. It was published by S. Tadolini in *Bollettino d'Arte*, 1925–26, p. 185. The style of modelling is, however, closer to that of the *bozzetti* executed around 1800 than the few that survive from the 1780s. The attribution is traditional and cannot be accepted without reserve.

42. First if rather badly reproduced in Cochin and Bellicard: *Observations sur les antiquités d'Herculaneum*, Paris, 1754, pl. 15; see also R. Zeitler: *Klassizismus und Utopia*, Uppsala, 1954, p.78.

43. It is perhaps significant that the Minotaur's body is distinctly *peloso* only on the Greek vases cited in n. 38. He may perhaps have been influenced also by a 'bust' of the Minotaur in the Vatican Museum, *sala degli animali*, no. 232.

44. C. Vermeule: *European Art and the Classical Past*, Cambridge, Mass., 1964, p. 135 cites in this context the little Hercules Invictus high up on the north side of the arch of Constantine.

45. P. J. Mariette: *op. cit.*, I, p. 35, repr. S. Reinach: *op cit.*, pl. 128.

46. This statue is still in the cortile of Palazzo Altemps where Canova made *schizzi* on April 20, 1780 (*Quaderni* p. 101 and 122) but the only such drawings that are now known are of other statues. Cf. *Bassi Museo* p. 121. There was a similar statue in Bartolomeo Cavaceppi's collection (F. de Clarac: *Musée de sculpture antique et moderne*, V, Paris, 1851, p. 20) which Canova also visited (*Quaderni*, pp. 33, 140).

47. For the Ludovisi Ares and the Belvedere Torso *Quaderni*, fig. 11, 1; he mentioned the bronze statue 'di maravigliosa Bellezza' February 5, 1780, *Quaderni*, p. 79.

48. R. Zeitler *op. cit.* p. 79 points out that the Minotaur, and especially the relationship of his left arm to his body, is in a pose reminiscent of Hector in Gavin Hamilton's painting: *Achilles Dragging the Dead Hector Round the Walls of Troy.*

49. *Bassi Gipsoteca* p. 51 refers to 'numerosi disegni, rimasti al Museo Civico di Bassano, interessanti anche per le varianti successive analizzate dello scultore . . .' but the same writer's excellent catalogue of the drawings at Bassano mentions none of them!

50. Reproduced in *Mostra Canoviana: Catalogo* ed. L. Coletti, Treviso, 1957, unnumbered plate; R. Zeitler, *op. cit.* p. 77 convincingly identified this sketch as Bonaventura Salesa's preliminary drawing for Morghen's engraving.

51. The gesso belongs to the Accademia delle Belli Arti, Venice and is on loan to the Gipsoteca in Possagno; another cast is in the Galleria Querini Stampalia, Venice, *Bassi Gipsoteca* p. 51.

52. *Cigognara* pp. 11–12.

53. *D'Este* pp. 56–57. 'Suasy' is something of a mystery. He may have been L.-P. De Seine or J.-P. Le Sueur or, more probably, Antoine Chaudet who arrived at the French Academy in Rome in 1784.

54. This may be a legacy of the German neo-classical attitude to French art, or even a distant reflection of Winckelmann's almost pathological Francophobia.

55. *Bassano* 6022 where the Director is named *Lagrené* and the student *De chêne* (for L.-P. De Seine). *D'Este* p. 28 provides a much longer account of the conversation (but he was always bad at foreign names and calls the Director *La Grêve*).

56. *Cicognara*, p. 12.

57. *D'Este*, p. 26.

58. According to a letter by G. B. Nocchi of 1773 Batoni was already alienated from the Accademia di S. Luca by that date (Biblioteca Governativa, Lucca, 2790). Mengs, who was *principe* in 1771, had been preceded by Mauro Fontana, Francesco Preziado and Andrea Bergondi; he was followed by Carlo Marchionni, Ferdinando Raggi, Anton von Maron, Agostino Penna, Antonio Asprucci and Vincenzo Pacetti. Canova was to be excluded from membership until 1800.

59. Biblioteca Labronica, Leghorn. II/343.

60. C. D. Moseline: 'Den Lengustavcaska Tideas Rumsinrednigar Pä Stockholms Slott' in *Nationalmusei Årsbok*, Stockholm, 1940. I am indebted to Mr. Anthony M. Clark for this reference.

61. A. de Montaiglon and J. Guiffrey *op. cit.* xv, p. 209.

62. *Gazette des Beaux Arts*, 1896, II, p. 510.

63. *Quaderni*, p. 39–40.

64. The statue is in S. Maria del Priorato, Rome. Angelini never fulfilled his early promise and when he died in 1811 Vincenzo Pacetti commented in his diary 'è stato anni 19 con una fissazione tale che quasi dava in pazzia' (the diary is in Istituto del Risorgimento Italiano, Rome).

65. *Quaderni*, p. 33.

66. *Quaderni*, p. 139.

67. *Giornale di Vincenzo Pacetti*, Biblioteca Alessandrina, Rome, Ms. 321. It is difficult to assess the profits made by Pacetti

from dealing in antiquities as he seldom mentioned the prices he paid for individual pieces. Some sale prices were very modest, e.g. a Muse sold to Thomas Jenkins in 1778 for 260 scudi.

68. *Bassano*, Cart. Remondini, 6917, 6922, 6929.

69. Other prices are no less revealing. Pompeo Batoni, the most famous Italian painter of the day, seems to have received a maximum of 3000 scudi for a single altarpiece—for Lisbon, in 1781 and charged only 200 scudi for a full-length portrait. (A. M. Clark in *Mostra di Pompeo Batoni* ed. I. Belli-Barsali, Lucca, 1967, p. 49). Prices paid to sculptors in England were sometimes very high: John Bacon received £3,421 (13,684 scudi) for his statue of Lord Chatham for the Guildhall in 1782 (R. Gunnis: *Dictionary of British Sculptors*, 1953, p. 26). But in 1787 the Earl of Bristol and Bishop of Derry paid Flaxman for his large two-figure group of *The Fury of Athamas* £600 (2,400 scudi) which included the cost of the marble (R. Gunnis *op. cit.* p. 148).

70. J. J. Winckelmann: *Gedanken über die Nachahmung der griechischen Werke*, Dresden and Leipzig, 1756, p. 21.

71. Both terracottas are now in the Accademia, Venice.

72. *Bassi Museo* pp. 33–37.

73. *D'Este* p. 18.

74. Victoria and Albert Museum. E. 189–1966.

75. *Bassano* 4930. The casts of antique statues in Venice were those in Palazzo Farsetti.

76. For Canova's attention to drapery see *D'Este*, pp. 45–46.

77. I. Teotocchi Albrizzi: *Opere di Scultura e di plastica di Antonio Canova*, Pisa, 1821, I, p. 61. Between 1782 and 1821 the concept of patriotism changed radically. Contessa Albrizzi may well have had the 'vergognosa' subjection of Venice to Austria in mind when she wrote these lines, for Canova had already begun to emerge in his 'Risorgimento' role as the one heir to Italy's lost greatness (cf. Byron, *Childe Harold IV*, LV, 'Such as the great of yore, Canova is today'). In 1783, however, a work of art's patriotic subject matter would have had no nationalistic overtones, and it would be pointless to seek them in the *Theseus and the Minotaur*.

78. Quatremère de Quincy: *Canova et ses ouvrages*, Paris, 1834, p. 34 states that when he first met Canova and saw both the Daedalus and Theseus groups, 'L'une, lui dis-je, banale et vulgaire, se borne à calquer en quelque sorte l'individu, elle n'adresse par à une réalité, si l'on peut dire, matérielle, qu'un sens borné, et mérite à peine le nom d'art'.

79. Ovid: *Metamorphoses VIII*, 183–235.

80. It is perhaps significant that Canova preserved no record of the Poleni statue. He did, however, keep a gesso of the *Daedalus and Icarus* which is now at Possagno (*Bassi Possagno* pp. 47–49 where it is described as the *modello originale* though it is more likely to be a cast).

81. See my article in *The Connoisseur*, December, 1959, p. 226.

82. *D'Este*, p. 304. But C. L. Fernow, Canova's severest contemporary critic, regarded the group as 'der erste und letzt Versuch des Künstlers im Stile der Alten'; cf. *Über den Bildhauer Canova und dessen Werke*, Zürich 1806, p. 79.

A Masterpiece by Girolamo dai Libri

MIRELLA LEVI D'ANCONA

WHILE leafing through the cuttings from illuminated manuscripts in the Department of Prints and Drawings of the Victoria and Albert Museum, I came across the beautiful illumination illustrated opposite (No. E. 1168–1921). It is attributed to the school of Northern Italy and has been dated late 15th century.[1] The illumination is especially striking for the large human figure terminating in the body of a dragon which forms the letter B. Monumental in design, it is striking in colour: the body of the man is part blue and part a deep-green monochrome, which contrasts with the tooled gold background, meant to imitate brickwork. Within the field of the initial, David depicted as a bald-headed old man, is seated in Oriental fashion, on a Persian rug, playing a stringed instrument that resembles a guitar. He is garbed in light pink and blue, with dark-red sleeves highlighted with gold, and is shown as a king wearing his crown. Behind him are standing four courtiers, dressed in Turkish fashion, with turbans. The figure on the left is especially striking, with his yellow costume, green shoes and lavender sash. The light and bright colours of his clothes, as well as those of David, contrast with the purple column and with the brilliant blue and dark green of the letter B. David is not only placed in the centre of the composition, but is also set off by the greatest concentration of light. The background is delicately toned down, with pale-blue sky and blue-green grass.

When I first saw the illumination, I was struck by its beauty and immediately realized that it must be the work of a great artist. The gaily coloured rug with its detailed design, and the graphic way in which each hair is recorded in the fur of the little dog playing with the monkey in the foreground, at first called to mind Girolamo da Cremona.

On the other hand, the light colours, and especially the delicate landscape, firmly placed the illumination in the school of Verona. My first reaction was then to attribute it to the most outstanding illuminator of the Veronese school in the second half of the fifteenth century, Girolamo dai Libri. The London illumination is unquestionably the work of a great master, and Girolamo dai Libri is one of the best known illuminators of Northern Italy, celebrated by Vasari not only on his own merits, but also for having been the master of Giulio Clovio.[2]

To check if the work was really by Girolamo dai Libri, as I was inclined to believe, I turned for comparison to some illuminations attributed to him:

1. A *Nativity* on fol. 5 of the Antiphonal B.I.3(A.2) in the Pinacoteca Tosio Martinengo in Brescia (fig. 9), which comes from the Church of S. Francesco in Brescia.[3]
2. An *Adoration of the Magi* on fol. 5 (fig. 10) in the Book of Hours of Daniele Banda in Montecassino (the so-called "Filelfo Hours").[4]
3. An illumination with *Apollo and the Muses* on fol. iv. of Ms. 277–A Ext. in the Library at Wolfenbüttel.[5]
4. A *Resurrection of Christ* (fig. 8) in the Castelvecchio Museum in Verona, no. 311.[6]
5. A miniature with the *Elevation of the Host* (fig. 11), also in the Castelvecchio Museum in Verona, no. 313.[7]
6. The Prayer Book of Eleanor Gonzaga, Duchess of Urbino; in the Bodleian Library in Oxford, Ms. Douce 29.[8]
7. The Astle-Asdaile Missal in the Pierpont Morgan Library in New York, M. 306.[9]
8. An initial M signed "Hieronymus f." formerly at Quaritch and now in the Victoria and Albert Museum in London.[10]
9. Five Antiphonals in the Cathedral of Spilimbergo, near Udine,[11]

and many other illuminations attributed to Girolamo dai Libri.

However I soon realized that to proceed among the many attributions made to the artist resembled walking through quicksands. Nowhere could I find firm ground on which to lay foundations for an attribution. The *Adoration of the Magi* in the Filelfo Hours (fig. 10) turned out to be signed by "Ercules" on the lance in the centre of the composition and to be dated 1469—before Girolamo's birth. It is not an "Adoration of the Magi" but a scene of the donor, Daniele Banda, paying homage to the Virgin Mary.[12] The Gonzaga Hours in Oxford have more recently been attributed to Giulio Clovio, but are probably not even by him.[13] The Wolfenbüttel illumination, after having been attributed to Liberale da Verona, is now believed to be the work of the Lombard illuminator Giovan Pietro Birago.[14] The Astle-Asdaile Missal in the Morgan Library is signed by Francesco Bettini from Verona, who must have been helped by another artist, whom I believe to be a Frenchman.[15] The initial in the Victoria and Albert Museum signed "Hieronymus f." turned out to

I. INITIAL B WITH DAVID, from a Psalter illuminated by Girolamo dai Libri, 1502. Victoria and Albert Museum, MS. E.1168–1921.

1. THE DEPOSITION, by Girolamo dai Libri, 1490. Malcesine, S. Stefano.

children, two of whom became illuminators like their father and grandfather: Francesco and Callisto.

Vasari tells us that Girolamo dai Libri painted, when he was only sixteen, a *Deposition of Christ* for the altar of the Lisca family in the Church of S. Maria in Organo in Verona (fig. 1) and that his father, Francesco dai Libri, was very proud of Girolamo's achievement.[20] If the story is true and Girolamo was really sixteen when

2. ALTARPIECE OF ST. ANNE, by Girolamo dai Libri, about 1519. Verona, S. Polo.

be an early work (signed) by Girolamo da Cremona.[16] The Spilimbergo Antiphonals are documented works by Giovanni de Cramariis from Udine.[17]

Obviously, if I wanted to attribute the illumination with David in the Victoria and Albert Museum to Girolamo dai Libri, I could not use as comparison works which turned out to be by such a variety of artists, dating from different periods and coming from different regions of Italy and France! I had first to find out if there are any documented or signed works by Girolamo dai Libri, and then, on the basis of these, to establish whether or not the London illumination could be his. Girolamo dai Libri, son of Francesco (called the Elder by Vasari[18]) was born in Verona in 1474.[19] Between 1501 and 1514 he married Cecilia, the sister of a rich glass manufacturer from Vicenza, and had by her five

3. THE VIRGIN AND CHILD WITH SS. BARTHOLOMEW AND ZENO, by Girolamo dai Libri, 1497. Berlin, Staatliche Museen.

in the church of S. Anastasia in Verona. On that altar was placed an altarpiece by Girolamo dai Libri[24] depicting the Virgin and Child between the Saints Thomas and Augustine, the latter giving a book to a

he painted the *Deposition*, the painting should date 1490. It would be the earliest documented work we have by Girolamo dai Libri.

Soon afterwards (about 1495) Girolamo is supposed to have painted the altarpiece with St. Anne, the Virgin Mary and the Christ Child between Saints Joachim and Joseph for the altar of the Baughi family, dedicated to the Virgin Mary, in the Church of S. Paolo in Campo Marzo in Verona (S. Polo).[21] The painting is still in that church and has the busts of the two praying donors in the foreground (fig. 2).

At about the same time Francesco and Girolamo dai Libri received payments for illuminations made for the church of S. Maria in Organo in Verona.[22]

In 1497 Girolamo painted the altarpiece for the chapel erected by Zenone Bonalini and Bartolino da Pressana in the church of S. Maria in Organo in Verona (fig. 3). The chapel later came under the patronage of the Counts Dal Pozzo, who in 1721 substituted a *Pietà* by Daniele Peracca for Girolamo's painting. Girolamo's painting passed in 1821 from the Solly collection to the Berlin Museum (No. 30).[23]

Between 1488 and 1502 the Centrego family from Verona erected an altar on the south wall of the transept

4. THE CENTREGO ALTARPIECE, by Girolamo dai Libri, 1498–1502. Verona, S. Anastasia.

5. THE NATIVITY WITH SS. JOHN BAPTIST AND JEROME AND TWO RABBITS, by Girolamo dai Libri, about 1516. Verona, Museo di Castelvecchio.

kneeling Augustinian monk. The busts of the donors, Cosimo Centrego and his wife Cipolla, appear below (fig. 4).

On October 7, 1502, Girolamo received payment from S. Maria in Organo for having illuminated a miniature in a Psalter.[25]

On November 12, 1515, Francesco Morone and Girolamo dai Libri started painting the organ shutters in the church of S. Maria in Organo. They promised to finish half of the work before April 13, 1516, and the other half before June 8 of the same year.[26] They also painted the walls and the ceiling above the organ. The organ was later removed from the church and its shutters ended up in the parish church of Marcellise.[27] In 1516 Girolamo had moved from the parish of S. Paolo to that of S. Sebastiano.[28] At about that time he painted the *Nativity with two rabbits* (fig. 5) for the chapel of the Maffei family in the church of S. Maria in Organo. The patronage of that chapel changed to that of the Odoli family, and then to that of the Zanoli family. Between 1718 and 1720 the painting by Girolamo dai Libri was removed from that chapel and placed in the dormitory of S. Maria in Organo (which

was an Olivetan monastery at the time), until in 1812 the painting was placed in the Verona Museum (No. 290).[29]

In 1518 Girolamo dai Libri, Paolo Morando (called Cavazzola), and Francesco Torbido collaborated on the altarpiece of S. Maria della Scala in Verona. Cavazzola painted a *St. Roch*, which he dated 1518; Torbido a *St. Sebastian*; and Girolamo dai Libri painted a *St. Anne with the Virgin Mary, the Christ Child and three musician angels at their feet* (fig. 6). He signed the painting on a canntellino at the feet of St. Anne. HIERONYMUS A LIBRIS F; it is now in the National Gallery in London.[30]

On April 23, 1519, Girolamo dai Libri was paid 36 lire for illuminating 215 large letters in a choir book of S. Maria in Organo, and on March 31, 1520, he was paid for 256 illuminations in another choir book of the same church.[31]

In 1526 Girolamo painted the altarpiece for the fourth chapel to the left in the church of S. Giorgio in Braida in Verona. He signed and dated the painting as follows: "MDXXVI Mens. Mar. xxviiii—Hieronymus a Libris pinxit".[32]

According to Vasari, Girolamo also illuminated several choir books for the Church of S. Giorgio in Braida.[33] It was the year 1526, and Girolamo at the time lived for a while in the parish of S. Giovanni in Valle in Verona.[34]

After painting several other works, Girolamo painted in 1530 the altarpiece for the main altar of the Toccoli chapel in the church of S. Maria della Vittoria Nuova in Verona (fig. 7), which in 1812 entered the Verona Museum (No. 339)[35] and is commonly called the "Madonna dell'ombrellino" on account of the coloured umbrella held by a putto over the Virgin's throne. The painting depicts the Virgin and Child enthroned between Saints Joseph and the Archangel Raphael with Tobias. It is signed and dated on the steps of the throne.

The chronology of Girolamo's last works is so uncertain that I will omit mentioning them. He died on July 2, 1555.[36]

Even without any documentation, the two signed works by Girolamo dai Libri in the London National Gallery (fig. 6) and in the Verona Museum (fig. 7) would allow us to attribute to him the other paintings here reproduced. The painting in Berlin (fig. 3) very much resembles the London one (fig. 6), both in composition (with three musician angels as repoussoir figures) and in facial types. The altarpiece in S. Anastasia (fig. 4)

6. ALTARPIECE OF ST. ANNE, by Girolamo dai Libri, signed, datable 1518. London, National Gallery.

7. THE TOCCOLI ALTARPIECE, by Girolamo dai Libri, signed and dated 1530. Verona, Museo di Castelvecchio.

closely resembles the one in the Verona Museum (fig. 7). The painting in S. Polo (fig. 2) resembles both the London one (fig. 6) and the one in the Verona Museum (fig. 7). The *Nativity with two rabbits* (fig. 5) is compositionally different from the other paintings here reproduced. However, St. Joseph in that painting closely resembles the same Saint in the S. Polo painting (fig. 2) and the face of the kneeling St. John the Baptist (fig. 5) resembles the faces of the Virgin and St. Anne in the London painting (fig. 6) and the face of the Archangel Raphael in the Verona Museum (fig. 7). Even in his earliest work Girolamo has an easily identifiable style; the face of one of the weeping Maries (fig 1.) next to St. Benedict is not too different from the face of St. Anne in the London painting (fig. 6), and the face of the mourning John (fig. 1) resembles that of the Archangel Raphael in the Verona Museum (fig. 7).

If we now turn to the illumination with David in the Victoria and Albert Museum (colour pl.), we have no difficulty in recognizing in it Girolamo's hand, in spite of the differences in technique and format between illumination and easel painting. The turbaned courtiers behind David in the London illumination (colour pl.) resemble the two turbaned figures in the Malcesine *Deposition* (fig. 1) The little dog playing with the monkey (colour pl.) resembles the dog in the Verona Museum painting (fig. 7). The head of David (colour pl.) resembles that of St. Anne in London (fig. 6) and that of St. Joseph in the picture at S. Polo (fig. 2). The head of the first courtier to the left (in yellow garb) in the London illumination resembles that of St. Joseph in the *Nativity with two rabbits* (fig. 5). The handling of folds in the sitting figure of David resembles that in the crouching turbaned figure at the right of the Malcesine *Deposition* (fig. 1). The rocky peaks softly covered with grass and bushes are the hallmark of Girolamo: a glance at the Malcesine *Deposition* (fig. 1) and the London painting (fig. 6) will suffice.

9. THE NATIVITY, attributed to Girolamo dai Libri and dated 1490, from an Antiphonal (B.I.3, [A.2,] fol. 5.) Brescia, Pinacoteca Tosio Martinengo.

8. THE RESURRECTION. Illuminated initial attributed to Girolamo dai Libri. Verona, Museo di Castelvecchio, no. 311.

10. HOMAGE TO THE VIRGIN MARY. Illumination in the Book of Hours of Danicle Banda, fol. 5. Montecassino, Abbey.

11. THE ELEVATION OF THE HOST. Illuminated initial attributed to Girolamo dai Libri. Verona, Museo di Castelvecchio, no. 313.

All these similarities clearly point to Girolamo dai Libri as the author of the London illumination. If we try to date the illumination on the basis of its style, we will find a greater similarity with Girolamo's first works. The composition is less congested than in the Malcesine *Deposition* (fig. 1) and the Berlin painting (fig. 3), but it is with these paintings, and especially the first one, that we note the greatest resemblance. In his early works Girolamo has a tendency to block the background with hills; while later he opens up the distant landscape.

This opening of the background starts with the beautiful view of a winding river in the *Nativity with two rabbits* (fig. 5). Therefore we may date, stylistically, the London illumination between 1495 and 1515.

The London illumination shows a large letter B which encloses the scene with David playing a stringed instrument (colour pl.). Doubtless it illustrates the beginning of Psalm 1: "Beatus Vir qui non abiit in consilio impiorum". An illustration of this Psalm, almost always with a musician David, usually heads the Psalter in the fifteenth century. Considering the large size of the London illumination, we can safely assume that it comes from a choir book, probably from a Psalter-Hymnal or a Psalter-Antiphonal.[37] Now there is a payment made in 1502 to Girolamo dai Libri for the beginning of a Psalter illuminated for the church of S. Maria in Organo in Verona.[38] I think that this payment may be linked with the London illumination, which I have attributed to Girolamo dai Libri and dated between 1495 and 1515. Thus we have now a documented work by the artist on which to base all further attributions of illuminations.

I do not think that this is the place to re-examine all the attributions of illuminations suggested for Girolamo dai Libri. I will simply state that the large illumination with the *Resurrection of Christ*, attributed to Girolamo by Berenson (fig. 8), seems not only to be his, but also to come in all likelihood either from the same manuscript as the London illumination (fig. 1) or from a companion manuscript, as it shares with it the peculiar tooling of the gold background to imitate brickwork. Here, too, the landscape is blocked by a hill in the background. Unlike the London illumination, which has been trimmed down to the picture, the *Resurrection* in Verona shows some lines of text and music, so we can establish that it comes from a Psalter Antiphonal and that it illustrated Psalm CI "Domine exaudi", the first words of which are visible in the photograph, above the illumination (fig. 8).

If the illumination with the *Elevation of the Host* (fig. 11), also in the Verona Museum and also attributed to

Girolamo dai Libri by Berenson,[39] is by him, it must be an early work, made when Girolamo collaborated with his father on the choir books of S. Maria in Organo.[40] The rigid posture of the priest, the disproportion between the upper and lower parts of his body, the poor handling of the drapery in the acolyte, the hesitant treatment of perspective and the congested space are all telling details which betray an inexperienced artist.

The Brescia *Nativity* (fig. 9), which dates before 1490, when the manuscript in which it is contained was given to the church of S. Francesco in Brescia, has been attributed to Girolamo dai Libri by Calabi.[41] It seems to be his, and to show the artist at his earliest stage, even before the Malcesine *Deposition*. Vasari tells us, and documents from S. Maria in Organo dated 1493 corroborate the information, that Girolamo collaborated with his father Francesco dai Libri on his earliest illuminations. The style of the Brescia *Nativity* shows a very strong influence from Francesco dai Libri. It is interesting to note that it shows a great resemblance with yet another work which has been attributed—wrongly—to Girolamo: the illumination with Daniele Banda paying homage to the Virgin Mary, on fol. 5 of the Filelfo Hours (fig. 10). These Hours have been attributed to Girolamo by Berenson,[42] but they date over twenty years before the Brescia *Nativity* (fig. 9) and five years before Girolamo's birth.[43] Moreover they are signed, as already stated, by another artist, "Ercules". A study of the Filelfo Hours and of the Paduan artists who came in contact with "Ercules", including Francesco dai Libri, will be made elsewhere. Although it would be of interest because it would better explain the origins of Girolamo's style, it would entail the discussion of too much material, part of which is as yet unexplored.

To conclude, the London *David* (colour pl.), the most striking and beautiful illumination I know by Girolamo dai Libri, seems to be a documented work by him, part of the Psalter for which the artist received payment in 1502.[44]

Notes

1. In the *Catalogue of Miniatures, Leaves and Cuttings from illuminated manuscripts*, London, Victoria and Albert Museum, 1923 p. 90, the illumination is dated 16th century and simply called Italian.

David is said to be playing on his harp. The illumination comes from the David M. Currie Bequest, 1921, and measures 11 × 10¾ in.

2. G. Vasari, *Le Vite*, v, Florence, 1880, pp. 330 and 333, Life of Girolamo dai Libri. J. Bradley, *The Life and Works of Giulio Clovio*, London, 1891, p. 75, discusses the possible relationship between the two artists, deriving from Clovio's apprenticeship with Girolamo dai Libri. Bradley's work will be referred to hereafter as Bradley, *Clovio*.

3. The Brescia manuscript has been attributed to Girolamo dai Libri by E. Calabi, 'I Corali miniati del Convento di S. Francesco a Brescia', *Critica d'arte*, III, April 2, 1938, pp. 62–65 and fig. 14. The Brescia choir books were given in 1490 to the Monastery of S. Francesco in Brescia by Francesco Sanson, General Minister of the Franciscan Order.

4. The attribution of the Filelfo Hours to Girolamo dai Libri was suggested by B. Berenson, *Italian Pictures of the Renaissance*, London, 1932, p. 258 and the same work in Italian translation, *Pitture Italiane del Rinascimento*, Milan, 1936, p. 222. Berenson was unaware of the fact that the *Nativity* in the Filelfo Hours is signed by another artist, 'Ercules', and that the manuscript is dated 1469, that is five years before Girolamo's birth. The signature by 'Ercules' and the date 1469 have been pointed out by Professor Luigi Michelini Tocci of the Vatican Library in a lecture held at the Sodalizio fra studiosi d'arte in Rome, 1968. His study will be published shortly, in the '*Colloqui*' *del Sodalizio*.

5. The manuscript in Wolfenbüttel was attributed to Girolamo dai Libri by Berenson, *Italian Pictures*, cit., p. 259, in spite of the fact that it had been attributed to Liberale da Verona by P. D'Ancona, 'Di alcuni codici miniati conservati nelle biblioteche tedesche e austriache', *L'Arte*, 1907, pp. 30–31, and reproductions. The work is now believed to be by the Lombard illuminator Giovan Pietro Birago, a Milanese priest who lived in the late 15th century.

6. The illuminations coming from the Buri collection in the Verona Museum were attributed to Girolamo dai Libri and Liberale da Verona by G. Trecca, *Catalogo della Pinacoteca Communale di Verona*, Verona, 1910, pp. 50–52. This author, however, does not attempt to distinguish between attributions to these two artists. The *Resurrection* described there as No. 311 was attributed to Girolamo dai Libri by Berenson, *Italian Pictures*, p. 259.

7. The *Elevation of the Host*, also attributed to either Girolamo dai Libri or Liberale da Verona by Trecca, *op. cit.*, p. 51, was specifically attributed to Girolamo by Berenson, *op. cit.*, p. 259. However L. di Canossa, 'La famiglia dai Libri', *Atti dell' Accademia d'agricoltura, scienze, lettere, arti e commercio di Verona*, Serie IV, vol. XII, 1911, p. 29, says that for the illuminations in the Verona Museum art historians have been able to make only an approximate attribution to Girolamo, his illuminations being mixed with others by Liberale da Verona and other artists. These illuminations have come to the Verona Museum from the Buri collection in Verona and are believed to have been cut out of the choir books of the churches of S. Maria in Organo, S. Giorgio in Braida and S. Nazaro e Celso in Verona. Some still bear the picture of an organ, the emblem of S. Maria in Organo.

8. The Prayer Book of Eleanor Gonzaga, Duchess of Urbino, in the Bodleian Library in Oxford, Ms. Douce 29, was attributed to Girolamo dai Libri until Bradley, *Clovio*, pp. 316–323 attributed it to Giulio Clovio. I do not think it is by him either.

9. The Morgan Library Missal was attributed to Francesco dai Libri and his son Girolamo by Bradley, *Clovio*, p. 82 and by L. Dorez, 'Pontifical peint pour le Cardinal Giuliano della Rovere par Francesco dai Libri de Verone', *Monuments et Mémoires publiés par l'Académie des Inscriptions et Belles Lettres*, XVII, Paris, 1909 pp. 99–124. See also: *Italian Manuscripts in the Pierpont Morgan Library*; Catalogue compiled by M. Harrsen and George K. Boyce, New York, 1953, n. 60 pp. 33–34, where the manuscript is attributed to Francesco Bettini from Verona and a French artist. A bibliography with a list of the most recent attributions will also be found there.

10. The illumination in the Victoria and Albert Museum in London, Ms. 1184, formerly at Quaritch (and before that in the J. T. Payne collection), was attributed to Girolamo dai Libri by Bradley, *Clovio*, pp. 74–75, with a facsimile of Girolamo's signature between pages 64 and 65. It was still attributed to Girolamo dai Libri in the Victoria and Albert Museum *Catalogue of Illuminated Manuscripts, Part II, Miniatures, Leaves and Cuttings*, London, 1908, p. 94. More recently I have published the illumination as a signed work by Girolamo da Cremona and dated it 1451 on the basis of a dated illumination in the Wildenstein Collection which possibly comes from the same manuscript. A more recent bibliography of the attributions will also be found there (M. Levi D'Ancona, 'Postille a Girolamo da Cremona', *Studi di Bibliografia e di Storia in Onore di Tammaro de Marinis*, Verona, 1964, III, pp. 45–104).

11. The five Antiphonals in the Cathedral of Spilimbergo were attributed to Girolamo dai Libri by B. Magni, *Storia dell'arte italiana dalle origini al secolo XX*, Rome, II, 1905, p. 255. They have recently been published by Mons. Lorenzo Tesolin, *Gli Antifonari di Spilimbergo*, Udine 1966, who has found out that the series is composed of five Graduals and one Antiphonal, for which there are documents of payment between the years 1494 and 1498 made to the illuminator Giovanni de Cramariis from Udine. See also the bibliography given there (including the attributions to Girolamo dai Libri) and the documentation on the real illuminator, Giovanni de Cramariis.

12. See note 4.

13. See note 8.

14. See note 5.

15. See note 9.

16. See note 10.

17. See note 11.

18. Vasari, *op cit.*, v, p. 326.

19. Girolamo's birth date can be established from his father's declaration in the census of 1492, in which Girolamo is said to be eighteen years old: Archivio Municipale di Verona, Antichi Archivi Veronesi—Anagrafi for the Parish of S. Paolo in 1492, declaration of Francesco dai Libri. The document is quoted in C. Bernasconi, *Studi sopra la storia della pittura italiana dei secoli XIV e XV e della scuola pittorica veronese dai medj tempi fino a tutto il secolo XVIII*, Verona, 1864, p. 230. note. Bernasconi also quotes a declaration made by Girolamo dai Libri in 1529 (Anagrafi, S. Paolo) in which the artist says he is 54 years old (therefore born in 1475). The documents are also given in L. di Canossa, *op. cit.*, pp. 7–8, 38. The declaration of 1529 had already been given by Bradley, *Clovio*, p. 74. Vasari had given Girolamo's birth as 1472 (Vasari, *Vite*, v, p. 327).

20. Vasari, *ibid.*, p. 327. The painting is now in the Parish church of S. Stefano in Malcesine. See also G. Gerola, *Le antiche pale di S. Maria in Organo di Verona*, Bergamo, 1913, p. 34.

21. Vasari, *Vite*, v, p. 328; B. Dal Pozzo, *Le Vite de'pittori, degli scultori et architetti veronesi*, Verona, 1718, pp. 43, 257. According to Dal Pozzo, this painting was on the main altar of that church. Vasari does not state precisely how soon after the Malcesine *Deposition* (1490) Girolamo painted the altarpiece of S. Paolo in Campo Marzo (S. Polo). However, he mentions it immediately after the *Deposition*, and this might lead us to date the painting about 1495. R. Wittkower, 'Die Schüler des Domenico Morone: Francesco Morone, Gerolamo dai Libri, Paolo Morando gen. Cavazzola', *Jahrbuch für Kunstwissenschaft*, 1927, p. 208 n. 10, mentions that it has been attributed sometimes to Domenico Brusasorci, and also to Francesco Morone. However, he states that it is definitely by Girolamo dai Libri and dates the painting around 1519, on stylistic grounds. Certainly the handling of the anatomy in this painting (fig. 2) is much more masterly than in the 1490 *Deposition* (fig. 1) and in the Berlin painting of 1497 (fig. 3) (see especially the handling of hands). Its composition is also more advanced, with its figures moving freely in the vast landscape instead of being cramped in the foreground as they are in the Malcesine *Deposition* (fig. 1) and in the Berlin painting (fig. 3). In the latter see especially the group of angels piled one on top of another and the two lateral Saints, added as an after-thought. Obviously the artist still had to master the technique of painting and especially that of perspective in his first two works; while in the S. Paolo painting (fig. 2) he already shows mastery of them.

22. Monastero di S. Maria in Organo, *Registri uscita*, July 27, 1495, payment made to 'Hieronymo fiolo de mo francesco miniador' and another payment made on August 16 of the same year. The documents are given in L. di Canossa, *op. cit.*, pp. 11, 39 Appendice C n. 2.

23. Gerola, *op cit.*, pp. 32, 33, and L. di Canossa, *op. cit.*, pp. 9–10. According to Milanesi (in Vasari, *Vite*, v, p. 329 n. 3) there was an inscription on the painting, stating that 'Franciscus filius Dominici de Moronis pinxit MDIII'. I do not know if the inscription is still on the painting. Both the signature of Francesco Morone and the date were fakes.

24. This painting was on the altar facing the Sacristy at the time of Dal Pozzo, *op. cit.*, p. 217, who attributed it to Francesco Morone. For the attribution to Girolamo dai Libri see Wittkower, *op. cit.*, p. 207, n.4. A comparison with the paintings now in Malcesine (fig. 1), in Berlin (fig. 3) and in the church of S. Polo in Verona (fig. 2), will tell us that the painting is by Girolamo dai Libri and dates after the Berlin painting. There-fore we can safely date it around 1498–1502, and possibly nearer the latter date. The motif of the two donors placed as repoussoir figures in the front of the painting (fig. 4) is repeated in the S. Polo painting (fig. 2).

25. Verona, S. Maria in Organo, Registro uscita fol. 190v. The artist received L.12 s.10 d.3 for his work, which is the customary payment for a large figured initial (a full-page illumination in a choir book was usually paid L. 30 or 31). The document of payment is published in di Canossa, *op. cit.*, p. 39 Appendice C n. 3 and also p. 11 n. 5. I shall return to this payment because I believe it refers to the illumination now in the Victoria and Albert Museum.

26. Gerola, *op. cit.*, pp. 23–28, and especially p. 25 n. 6 for the documents of S. Maria in Organo; Wittkower, *op. cit.*, p. 208 n.8.

27. L. di Canossa, *op. cit.*, pp. 12–13; B. Magni, *op. cit.*, II, p. 256.

28. L. di Canossa, *op. cit.*, p. 13.

29. Gerola, *op. cit.*, pp. 5–7; Wittkower, *op. cit.*, p. 207 n. 2; L. di Canossa, *op. cit.*, p. 4.

30. G. Frizzoni, *Arte italiana nel Rinascimento*, Milan, 1891, p. 307; Wittkower, *op. cit.*, p. 208 n. 9; L. di Canossa, *op. cit.*, p. 15.

31. L. di Canossa, *op. cit.*, pp. 15–16, 40 Appendice D n. 1; Gerola, *op. cit.*, p. 25 n. 4.

32. Alinari photograph 13458 and 13459; Wittkower, *op. cit.*, p. 209, n. 13 and fig. 14.

33. Vasari, *op. cit.*, v, p. 330; L. di Canossa, *op. cit.*, pp. 17, 30. According to the latter, a choir book from the church of S. Giorgio passed from the Museo Moscardo to the collection of Count Miniscalchi Erizzo in Verona. Di Canossa attributes its illuminations to Girolamo dai Libri.

34. L. di Canossa, *op. cit.*, p. 17.

35. Wittkower, *op. cit.*, p. 210, n. 16 and fig. 15; L. di Canossa, *op. cit.*, pp. 18–19, 22.

36. Vasari, *Vite*, v, p. 331; Dal Pozzo, *op. cit.*, p. 44.

37. Abbé V. Leroquais, *Les Psautiers manuscrits latins des bibliothèques publiques de France*, Macon, 1940–41, I, pp. LVII–LVIII, LXIX, XCII–XCVII.

38. See note 25.

39. See note 7.

40. See note 22.

41. See note 3.

42. See note 4.

43. The Filelfo Hours date 1469 while Girolamo dai Libri was only born in 1474.

44. Part of the material discussed in this article is the result of research conducted with the help of three most generous grants from the American Council of Learned Societies in 1964, 1965 and 1966.

A Design for a Candlestick by George Michael Moser, R.A.

SHIRLEY BURY AND DESMOND FITZ-GERALD

THE Department of Prints and Drawings purchased in 1968 a design for a candlestick (fig. 1) by George Michael Moser (1706–1783). It may be dated to about 1745, and it would be hard to find another English design of the period that shows a more delicate touch in the handling or a greater mastery of the rococo style and its resources. If we compare the drawing with the engraved *oeuvre*[1] of Juste-Aurèle Meissonnier, one of the most brilliant exponents of the manner, we find no exact parallel in theme, but ample evidence in the treatment of *rocaille* ornament to show that Moser had studied the book more profitably than most of his English contemporaries.

Meissonnier was not Moser's only source of inspiration in this drawing. The roots growing out of the girl's toes and the laurel leaves sprouting from her hair and her fingers are an obvious allusion to Bernini's famous Apollo and Daphne of 1622–4.[2] The difference between the two figures illustrates the distance between baroque and rococo, as well as the distinction between imaginative sculpture of a scale approximating to life-size and decorative art which is necessarily rendered in miniature. The pose is roughly the same in both figures, with the arms raised above the head, and the head turned to look back. But whereas Bernini's Daphne is flying through space, intent on escape, Moser's Daphne has her legs crossed, and her body is twisted in a typical rococo spiral extending from her toes to the tip of her fingers. There must presumably have been a companion piece in the shape of Apollo.

We do not know whether a faithful rendering of the design was ever made, nor do we know what material the artist had in mind. But what we know of the artist himself would suggest that he played an important part in the development of English rococo design. He was not an Englishman by birth,[3] but like many influential artists in this country he came to England at an early age, lived all his life here and became an Englishman. He was one of the founders of the Royal Academy and was appointed its first keeper, a post which he held until his death in 1783. Sir Joshua Reynolds, who knew him well, wrote his obituary. "He was a native of Switzerland," Reynolds tells us, "but came to England very young, to follow the profession of a chaser in gold, in which art he has always been considered as holding the first rank. But his skill was not confined to this alone; he possessed a universal knowledge in all the

1. George Michael Moser's drawing for a candlestick was inspired by Meissonnier's *œuvre* and Bernini's Daphne from his Apollo and Daphne group in the Galleria Borghese, Rome. Victoria and Albert Museum (E. 4885–1968).

branches of painting and sculpture, which perfectly qualified him for the place that he held in the Academy, the business of which principally consists in superintending and instructing the Students . . . He may truly be said in every sense to have been the FATHER of the present race of Artists; for long before the Royal Academy was established, he presided over the little Societies which met first in Salisbury Court, and afterwards in St. Martin's Lane, where they drew from living models."[4]

It has lately been suggested by Mark Girouard in a

2. Candlesticks by Frederick Kandler dated 1752 and copied from others by Paul de Lamerie. (Reproduced by courtesy of the Ashmolean Museum.)

3. A pair of candlesticks in a private collection by Paul de Lamerie and made in 1750. Both these and those in the Ashmolean show considerable similarities to the Moser design.

series of articles in *Country Life* that these "little Societies" mentioned by Reynolds were the true nursery of English rococo design.[5] Besides Moser, they were frequented by Gravelot, Roubiliac, Hayman, Hogarth and other artists of kindred spirit who introduced a little sparkle and gaiety into the decorative arts in England, which until then had been under the solemn sway of Burlington and Kent and their Palladian followers. A notable contribution to the rococo manner was made by this band of artists in the embellishment of the pleasure gardens at Vauxhall in the late thirties and during the forties. There is evidence that some members of the group were in direct contact with several prominent silversmiths. The latter included Paul de Lamerie, one of the best-known of Huguenot craftsmen,[6] who from 1738 lived and had his workshop at Gerrard Street, Soho, within easy reach of St. Martin's Lane. In his case, the connection is established through William Hogarth, who is reliably credited with having engraved the salver made by de Lamerie in 1728–9 from the Exchequer Seal of Sir Robert Walpole and now in the museum collections.[7]

There is, however, little or nothing in the way of records to prove the existence of an association between de Lamerie and Moser. We know that Moser designed silversmiths' work as well as chasing it, but he never entered a mark of his own at Goldsmiths' Hall and his plate was therefore marked by the firms who commissioned it. The museum has some of his designs for watch-cases[8] and an actual example executed in gold, signed by him but not, of course, hall-marked.[9] There are also in existence several splendid boxes bearing his signature, one of which is in the Wrightsman Collection, New York.[10] But none of these help to resolve the problem of Moser's silverwork.

If we attack the question from the other end, working **28** back from the craftsman to the designer, it becomes

apparent that de Lamerie was indeed influenced by Moser and his friends. We may take it even further, and suggest that he knew of Moser's drawing, or of another like it, and perhaps used it as the basis of a number of candlesticks and candelabra dating from the second half of the forties. P. A. S. Phillips, de Lamerie's biographer, illustrates a pair of candelabra hallmarked for 1747 on a theme closely related to the drawing under consideration.[11] The pair have rococo bases strikingly similar to that in the Moser design, but the human figures forming the central columns are aged Bacchic terms, the legs of each replaced by balusters entwined by vines. These were de Lamerie's version of a traditional form of caryatid candlestick. In the following year he produced a more thorough-going rococo variant of this theme. Two candlesticks in the Ashmolean Museum, both dated 1748, have stems composed respectively of a young male and female term.[12] The direct reference to Apollo and Daphne has disappeared, but it is surely significant that the figures are young, and that the movement of the trunks is not halted by a stiff upright, as in the candelabra illustrated by Phillips, but is continued by a swirling complex of scrolls. The design of the de Lamerie candlesticks of 1748 was copied in 1752 by Frederick Kandler in a candelabrum and candlestick (fig. 2) which are also in the collections of the Ashmolean Museum.[13] It will be seen from these that a garland falling from the junction of the head and the base of the nozzle makes a somewhat awkward substitute for the second upraised arm of the Moser drawing, though it redeems itself by taking the place of the drapery across the body.

De Lamerie later dropped the upper end of the garland and began the swag over one shoulder, carrying it across the front of the body and turning it back again in a curious version of the rococo S-bend, as may be seen in two candlesticks illustrated in fig. 3, which form part of an exceptionally impressive service of rococo plate executed for an eminently Tory and rococo-minded noble household in 1750. Again, male and female figures appear: we need not, for the purposes of this notice, concern ourselves with the fact that the candlestick to the left of the illustration is a later replacement made by William Pitts, probably for Rundell's, the Royal Goldsmiths of the Regency, who sponsored the revival of the rococo style in the early years of the nineteenth century. Examples of the originals by de Lamerie surviving in the service show that Pitts was a most faithful copyist.

In many respects, it must be admitted that all the silver discussed falls short of Moser's conception. If we examine such motifs as the garland, even in its revised version of 1750, it lacks the graceful counterpoint of arm and drapery which adds movement to the drawing.

Movement is lost, too, by the direct attachment of heads to candle-holders, which if Moser's drawing had been followed would have been supported by a spiralling column of hair as well as by hands. The trunks of the bodies are made to appear too rigid in consequence. But other elements display considerable skill in the translation of the draughtsman's suggestions into plate. The fine scroll bases with their floral ornament may be cited, and the leafy edges of the nozzles, while by no means exact renderings of the original, are certainly in its spirit.

It would be pleasant to end by deducing from the foregoing that Moser himself was responsible for chasing some of these candlesticks. Unfortunately we cannot go as far as this, but we may suggest that the drawing does throw new light on the artist's professional contacts.

Notes

1. Juste H. Aurèle Meissonnier, *Oeuvre . . .*, c. 1734. The Department of Prints and Drawings has recently acquired a later edition, dating c. 1745.

2. R. Wittkower, *Gian Lorenzo Bernini*, 1955, pl. 14 (*ill*). The sculpture is in the Galleria Borghese, Rome.

3. *Dictionary of National Biography*, XIII, 1909, p. 1074.

4. Malone (ed.), *The Works of Sir J. Reynolds*, I, 1798, pp. XLVI, XVLII.

5. M. Girouard, 'English Art and the Rococo', in *Country Life*, CXXXIX, 1966, pp. 58–61, 188–90, 224–27.

6. De Lamerie was born April 9 1688 and baptised a week later at the Walloon Church of s'Hertogenbosch. He was apprenticed to Pierre Platel in London in 1703, and made free in 1712. He died in 1751.

7. Charles Oman, 'English Engravers on Plate', III, in *Apollo*, CLXV, 1957, pp. 286–89.

8. D. 141–147–1890.

9. M. 63–1954.

10. The cover of this box is embossed with a representation of Mucius Scaevola.

11. P. A. S. Phillips, *Paul de Lamerie*, new ed., 1968, pl. CLIII.

12. C. J. Conway Gift, 1959.

13. These also form part of the C. J. Conway Gift.

A Windsor Tapestry Portrait

WENDY HEFFORD

THE Museum has recently acquired its first tapestry woven at the Royal Windsor Manufactory.[1] It is, appropriately enough, a portrait of Queen Victoria (fig. 1). She stands against a sombre background, directly confronting the spectator, her hands clasped before her holding a scroll. The Garter motto surrounding the Royal Arms is barely visible behind her, cut by the frame at the right. The Queen is dressed in black, which, with the dull background, heightens the delicate, glowing colours of face and hands and emphasises the skilful highlighting of silk and jewelry.

The painter who copied the portrait for the weavers, the original artist, and the director and manager of the Windsor works are named on the tapestry: *P. Levin nach Angely* 1877/WINDSOR H. HENRY M. BRIGNOLAS.

Heinrich von Angeli had a high reputation as painter of royalty. In October 1873 the German Crown Princess wrote to her mother, Queen Victoria: "I am being painted by M. Angeli from Vienna, who is the first portrait painter in Germany nowadays, the only one who can replace Winterhalter except Richter".[2] The Queen, who had herself felt the loss of Winterhalter, was able by March 1875 to record in her Windsor Journal: "After luncheon, saw, in the corridor, the celebrated artist Angeli of Vienna, who has come over on purpose to paint my portrait . . .".[3] One portrait of 1875 was the original of the tapestry.[4]

Before the tapestry was begun, early in 1877, a working copy of the portrait was made by Phoebus Levin, a German painter working in London c. 1855–1878. It was presumably he who added the crown, altered details in the dress and substituted the scroll for a handkerchief in the original; but he reproduced exactly pose, features and expression. In the weaving of the tapestry these were so perfectly recreated that E. M. Ward, R.A., and Lord Leveson Gower, seeing it on the loom, agreed that it was "faithful to the original, and with perhaps a little more life".[5]

That Henry and Brignolas should be named on the tapestry suggests it may have been the first work to be completed on the Windsor looms, a supposition strengthened by what is known of their early history. The manufactory was founded in 1876 through the initiative of H. C. J. Henry, interior designer[6] and artistic advisor to the furnishing firm of Gillow & Co. Henry persuaded Brignolas to leave employment at Aubusson, bringing with him six weavers to man four looms in temporary accommodation at Windsor. Their first commission came from Messrs. Gillow & Co. A set of tapestries with scenes from *The Merry Wives of Windsor* after cartoons by T. W. Hay was ordered, to decorate the Jacobean dining room in the Pavilion of the Prince of Wales at the Paris Exhibition of 1878; and the portrait of the Queen was to be set into the panelling of the room above the fireplace, somewhat incongruously presiding over the revels of the Merry Wives. The portrait was described as "nearly finished" in August 1877 by a report which mentioned only the cartoons of the *Merry Wives*: the small, single panel was probably completed before any of the larger hangings.

The tapestries were much appreciated at the Paris Exhibition, the *Merry Wives*[7] winning a gold medal. What is more, they were sold: the entire dining room was purchased by Sir Albert Sassoon and installed in his house at 25 Kensington Gore.[8] Other sets of tapestries had been commissioned, and these and repairs of old tapestries were on hand at Windsor. The Queen was a leading patron, purchasing tapestry furniture-covers and, later, hangings depicting the royal residences, and ordering the repair of tapestries from Holyrood. The venture seemed to be a commercial success. Expansion of the factory necessitated a move to Manor Lodge in July 1877 until a permanent building could be erected on nearby Crown land. By 1882 the workers were installed in a Queen Anne style house designed by Walter Lyon, and the manufactory was officially designated "Royal".[9] Prince Leopold, who had encouraged Henry to set up the workshop, was President of an impressive Committee to guarantee its future.[10] Good publicity was ensured by frequent public display at local, national and international exhibitions, helped by enthusiastic praise in the Press for the successful tapestry revival.

But in that year, 1882, William Morris condemned the Windsor works for adopting the style of the Gobelins manufactory in Paris, and prophesied: "if it does not change its system utterly (it) is doomed to artistic failure, whatever its commercial success may be".[11] In France during the nineteenth century tapestry weaving had declined into a rather soulless repetition of former works and exact copying of paintings not necessarily suitable for tapestry. Warp threads were more closely spaced, weft threads more finely spun, and shades of colour multiplied to incredible numbers in attempts to

1. TAPESTRY PORTRAIT OF QUEEN VICTORIA, after Heinrich von Angeli, woven at Windsor, 1877.
Height 3 ft. ½ in. (92·7 cm). Width 2 ft. 10½ in. (87·7 cm). Victoria and Albert Museum (T. 94–1968).

reproduce in tapestry the fluidity of painting. Morris condemned this as "a more idiotic waste of human labour and skill it is impossible to achieve".[12]

Windsor, with its French weavers, had deliberately set out to emulate the Gobelins. Wool was dyed on the premises in 5,000 shades as early as 1877. The warp threads in the portrait of Queen Victoria are nine to the centimetre, and the larger hangings were hardly less fine. The result with the latter was not only the artistic failure predicted by Morris, but also financial disaster. The detailed work took so long that the finished product was prohibitively expensive. Walter Henry Harris estimated that: "To drape a tolerable sized room with Old Windsor tapestry cost something like 1,000 guineas".[13] Once the Crown and the Committee of Guarantors were provided with tapestries the market was practically exhausted. In 1895 the Art Journal sadly reported the closure of the factory and sale of stock: the looms were sold to Aubusson and the cartoons "many by eminent artists, realised absurdly low prices".[14]

From the number of tapestries woven in the course of this shortlived enterprise, we have in the portrait of Queen Victoria perhaps the only work which was neither handicapped by the lack of understanding of these "eminent artists" for tapestry design, nor impaired by excessive fineness of weave. In a portrait, where the main aim is to achieve a likeness, the painterly qualities of the woven copy are laudable, a technical triumph of a different kind from the creation of a tapestry wall hanging. We are fortunate to have acquired at once an interesting example of Windsor tapestry and an excellent portrait of the Queen who was patron to both manufactory and Museum.

Notes

1. T. 94–1968.
2. and 3. *Letters of Queen Victoria*. Second series, 1862–1885. Edited by G. E. Buckle. 1926.
4. Formerly at Windsor, this portrait is now in the State Apartments of Kensington Palace, in the King's Privy Chamber.
5. *The Furniture Gazette*, August 18, 1877, p. 131.
6. He designed the interiors of the Midland Railway Hotel, St. Pancras, and of the Carlton Club.
7. *The Furniture Gazette*, August 18, 1877, p. 131. As the last part to be woven would have been almost plain, the portrait was probably finished shortly after this report and some time before the next, in *The Furniture Gazette*, January 26, 1878, mentioned that it had been completed.
8. A graphic description is given in Stanley Jackson: *The Sassoons*, 1968, p. 61.
9. *Illustrated London News*, April 29, 1882, p. 414.
10. When Prince Leopold died in 1884, his brother the Prince of Wales became President.
11. and 12. *The Lesser Arts of Life*, a lecture by William Morris published in *Lectures on Art* by Poole, Richmond, Poynter, Michelthwaite and Morris, 1882.
13. Walter Henry Harris: *Royal Windsor Tapestries*, privately printed. Connected with tapestries sent to Chicago in 1893, this was written c. 1893–95.
14. *The Art Journal*, 1895, p. 224.

Two Mughal Lion Hunts

ROBERT SKELTON

In 1965, the Museum was fortunate in acquiring a small but distinguished group of Indian paintings from the collection of the late Captain E. G. Spencer-Churchill, M.C. Two of these, related in subject matter, were the generous gift of the National Art Collections Fund. They both show incidents from the royal sport of lion hunting as it flourished in Northern India under the Mughal dynasty at the beginning of the seventeenth century. In one of these pictures (I.S. 96–1965) the corpse of a huge lioness is being carried from the field by bearers (colour plate II). The other (I.S. 97–1965) shows a sleek and powerful creature attacking a mounted elephant, whose riders are poised for the kill (fig. 1).

In Western Asia, and indeed in India itself, the lion hunt was always esteemed a kingly pursuit and often celebrated in official art. The late Assyrian reliefs from Kuyunjik record this ruthless sport with heartless sensitivity. At Persepolis under the Achaemenid dynasty of Iran the royal confrontation takes on the appearance of a dignified ritual act. On Sassanian silver plates, such august Iranian monarchs as Shāhpūr II are shown discharging arrows into their fearsome adversaries from fleet stallions. In India, Shāhpūr's near contemporary, Chandragupta II (c. A.D. 375–415), is shown unmounted as he bends his bow no less impressively within the smaller compass of a splendid coin-type.

The hunting feats of Bahrām Gūr, who came to the Iranian throne a few years after Chandragupta's death, were particularly celebrated. He not only appears mightily smiting his savage prey on contemporary silver but his name became a byeword for such prowess in Persian verse and was even familiar in Victorian drawing rooms through the mediation of Edward FitzGerald. The repetition of Bahrām's exploits by poets other than Khayyām, notably Firdawsī and Nizāmī, make him a familiar figure in Persian illustrated manuscripts. In these, the lion-slayer motif continued in Near Eastern art until it became a model for Indian representations of the subject under the Mughal Emperors, whose painting studio was founded by Persian masters in the sixteenth century. Thus a picture, now in Russia,[1] of the Mughal Emperor Jahāngīr shooting an arrow at a lion from his prancing horse, calls to mind such Persian prototypes as "Bahrām Gūr killing a wild ass" from Shāh Ṭahmāsp's great

manuscript of Nizāmī's poems, where the poses of horse and rider are identical;[2] "Bahrām killing a lion", from the same manuscript;[3] or "killing a dragon" in another famous Nizāmī manuscript that was later owned and autographed by Jahāngīr.[4]

In his personal memoirs, this Mughal Emperor frequently records his exploits in hunting the King of Beasts and we gain some insight into the restricted status of this particular game from the journal of Sir Thomas Roe, the ambassador of King James I, who accompanied the court when it stayed in the fortress city of Mandu in the year 1617. Sir Thomas was allotted quarters in one of the deserted buildings of this former capital of the Khaljī rulers of Malwa and relates that on May 25: *a lion and a woolfe used my house and nightly put us in alarume, fetching away sheepe and goats out of my court and leaping a high wall with them. I sent to aske leave to kill it, for no man may meddle with lions but the King, and it was granted: I ranne out into the court upon the noyse, and the beast, missing its prey, seized on a little Island dogge before me, that I had long kept, but the woolfe one of my servants killed, and I sent it the King.*[5]

A more explicit account of the royal prerogative in relation to this sport is given in the somewhat later memoirs of another European writer, François Bernier, who visited India during the reign of Jahāngīr's grandson, Aurangzeb. He writes that, *of all the diversions of the field, the hunting of the lion is not only the most perilous, but is peculiarly royal; for except by special permission, the Kings and Princes are the only persons who engage in the sport.*[6] Then, after describing the mode of hunting in some detail he mentions an occasion when the lion escaped from the area enclosed by nets and the whole army was detained at great inconvenience in difficult country for several days until the same beast was found and again surrounded so that the Emperor could carry out the kill. He explains *the weighty reason of this long detention in such abominable quarters* with some scorn. *You must know, then, that it is considered a favourable omen when the King kills a lion, so is the escape of that animal portentous of infinite evil to the state. Accordingly, the termination of the hunt is attended with much grave ceremony. The King being seated in the general assembly of the Omrahs, the dead lion is brought before him, and when the carcass has been accurately measured and minutely examined, it is recorded in the royal archives that such a King on such a day slew a lion of*

1. A Mughal prince spearing a lioness. Mughal, c. 1604–5. Victoria and Albert Museum. 6¼ × 7½ in. (16 × 19·2 cm). (I. S. 97–1965).

such a size and of such a skin, whose teeth were of such a length, and whose claws were of such dimensions, and so on down to the minutest details.[7]

Thus Bernier not only confirms the statement made by Sir Thomas Roe, but also provides evidence that the superstitious basis for the restriction was still recognised at the Mughal court of his day just as in Europe the old relationship between lions and royal persons was remembered in John Fletcher's:

Fetch the Numidian lion I brought over;
If she be sprung from royal blood, the lion

He'll do her reverence, else . . .
He'll tear her all to pieces.[8]

Both Bernier and Fletcher make it clear that this special relationship between kings and lions extends to issue of the blood royal as well as to actual monarchs. In the case of each of the two paintings considered here it will be argued that the human protagonists in the combat were princes rather than the reigning emperor himself. In one of these paintings (fig. 1) we are greatly assisted by the fact that we see the destined victor in the act of spearing his victim from the back of an elephant. The

II. A dead lioness being carried from the field. Mughal, c. 1602–4. Victoria and Albert Museum. $5\frac{7}{8} \times 6\frac{7}{8}$ in. (15×17.5 cm).
(I. S. 96–1965).

2 & 3. The battle of Ahmedabad, by Sūr Dās. From the Chester Beatty *Akbar nāma*, ff. 187v. and 188r. Mughal, 1604–5.

evidence of both Roe and Bernier assures us that he is likely to be a member of the royal house and since the painting can be shown to date from the first years of the seventeenth century, the task of his identification is simplified.

If one first seeks confirmation of the date one cannot fail to be impressed by the close resemblance which the picture bears in style to illustrations in a royal manuscript of the *Akbar nāma*, now divided between the Chester Beatty Library and the British Museum (figs. 2–4).[9] This work is an official history of the reign of Jahāngīr's father, Akbar (1556–1605), for whom the Mughal school of painting came into being. From the many illustrated manuscripts surviving from Akbar's reign we can trace the evolution of the school through several stylistic

phases. A brief consideration of these will show why this lion hunt can only be placed at the end of Akbar's reign together with the Chester Beatty manuscript.

In early works of the Mughal school, such as the undated *Ṭūṭī nāma* manuscript in Cleveland[10] and the more ambitious *Dāstān-i Amīr Hamza*, or *Hamza nāma* manuscript[11] one can observe the progress made by the Persian masters and their Indian assistants in forging an integrated style through all the stages from the uneasy adjustment of disparate elements to the achievement of a thoroughly unified and mature vehicle of expression. As S. C. Welch has aptly observed *The Hamza-nāma is a vision of the world through the eyes of a lion* for the pages, at their best, *startle us with Dionysiac turbulence, broad handling, and strident, expressive colour.*[12]

37

4. Akbar on the elephant, Lakhna, by Farrukh (Chcla) with the portrait of Akbar by Manohar and other portraits by Anant. From the Chester Beatty *Akbar nāma*, f. 32v. Mughal, 1604–5.

5. Akbar's party hunting tigers, outline by Basāwān, colouring by Sarwan. From the Victoria and Albert Museum *Akbar nāma* (I.S. 2–1896 18/117). Mughal, c. 1590.

With the completion of this great work over a period of fifteen years by 1582 the staff of the studio attached to the royal library went on to produce the superb copies of the Hindu epics, now in Jaipur,[13] and this achievement was followed by a series of three dynastic histories in uniform style and format in which the energy and grandeur of the epic illustrations is scarcely diminished. The first of these was the *Tārīkh-i Khānadān-Tīmūriya* in the Khudā Bakhsh Library at Patna, which can be dated on internal evidence to the years A.D. 1584/5.[14] It appears to have been followed after an interval of about five years by the Victoria and Albert Museum's famous manuscript of the *Akbar-nāma* (fig. 5) and after another half-decade the series was completed with a copy of the *Chingīz nāma*, now in Tehran, which is dated in the colophon to the year 1004 A.H. = A.D. 1596.[15] In all of these works we see the mature style broadly and energetically handled in a manner that is perfectly suited to the dramatic events portrayed. However, in the *Chingīz nāma* of 1596 one can perhaps detect a slackening of the vigour, which characterizes the group as a whole.

It was at this point that the royal studio appears to have adopted a new policy. Between the years 1595 and 1598 a group of sumptuous poetical manuscripts was produced at Lahore in which the bold masculine style, so well suited to the character of the epics and historical works, gave way to one of growing refinement and

38

concern for perfection of finish. A feature of this phase was the increased tendency for the individual artist to be fully responsible for a miniature instead of sharing its production with others.[16] Only the leading artists were employed on this series of *de luxe* manuscripts and their association with the project appears to have led the style generally towards a new delicacy and fineness of technique, well suited to the mood of the Persian classical romances, which formed the main texts illustrated at this time.[17]

If we compare the Chester Beatty *Akbar nāma* (figs. 2–4) with its more vigorous predecessor in the Victoria and Albert Museum (fig. 5) its debt to these developments of the fifteen-nineties is quite clear. It is in an altogether more restrained style than that of the earlier copy of the work. More attention is paid to finely stippled modelling, transpositions of colour are less abrupt and the smoothly sensitive drawing is subject to less assertive rhythms. These features have long been recognised and the resultant dating of the book to the very end of the reign is now confirmed by the recent re-appearance of the missing first volume, of which one miniature (f. 145v.) is dated 21 Sha'bān, A.H. 1012, i.e. January 25, A.D. 1604.

When a typical illustration from this manuscript (fig. 4) is compared with the Spencer-Churchill lion hunt, the similarities are so close that, but for a difference in format, one could easily take the latter for a detached miniature from the manuscript. There are the same muted tones, careful modelling and smooth line in each case. On this account there is every justification for regarding the two as virtually contemporary. Thus with the date of the painting established, i.e. c. 1604–5, it is possible to take the further step of identifying the chief personage represented in it.

The fact that this person is almost certainly a member of the royal house has already been argued but the likelihood of this being the Emperor himself may at once be discounted. Despite a general resemblance between his features and those of Akbar (cf. fig. 4) the moustache is decidedly longer than is found in any of the many contemporary likenesses of the Emperor. All that the general resemblance suggests is that the man is a close relative rather than Akbar himself.

The most obvious alternative is inevitably Akbar's eldest son, Salīm, who came to the throne as the Emperor Jahāngīr so soon after the miniature was painted. Jahāngīr's memoirs so frequently confess his enthusiasm for lion hunting that he seems the perfect

6. Portrait of Prince Dāniyāl, by Manohar. Mughal, c. 1605–10. By courtesy of the Metropolitan Museum of Art, New York.

candidate but contemporary likenesses do not permit this identification. Compared with the prince in the picture, Salīm affected a slightly smaller moustache, grew his sideburns less heavily and with a curl instead of trimming them at the bottom. Salīm also possessed a less prominent jowl.

It is clear, therefore, that to solve this problem we must seek the likeness of another member of the royal family, whose features are less well known. The answer is to be found in a hitherto unpublished portrait of Salīm's younger brother Dāniyāl (fig. 6), which once formed part of a royal album sold at Sotheby's in 1929.[18] In this picture, now in the Metropolitan Museum of Art,[19] we find exactly the heavy jowl, prominent sideburns and drooping moustache of the prince in the hunting scene. There can be no question about the identification of the Metropolitan Museum's portrait, since Jahāngīr has written very firmly on the picture in his own hand "Portrait of my late brother, Dāniyāl: it is like him". As a junior son of Akbar, Dāniyāl does not occupy very much space in contemporary annals and it is again to his elder brother that we are indebted for a brief biographical note. *Dāniyāl was of pleasing figure, of*

39

exceedingly agreeable manners and appearance; he was very fond of elephants and horses. It was impossible for him to hear of anyone as having a good horse or elephant and not take it from him. He was fond of Hindi songs, and would occasionally compose verses with correct idiom in the language of the people of India,[20] which were not bad.[21]
Jahāngīr also relates that towards the end of Akbar's reign, his brother was sent to conquer the Deccan, where he died in the middle of his 33rd year from excessive drinking. It appears that he was fond of guns and hunting with the gun. He named one favourite weapon *yaka ū janāza*, i.e. "the same as the bier" and composed a couplet to be engraved on it, celebrating its lethal qualities. When his father sent orders for him to be denied alcohol he had one of his servants fill the gun with double-distilled spirits and bring it to him in secret. As soon as he drank this he fell victim to the omen which he had himself composed.[22] This was assumed to have resulted from the alcohol combining with gunpowder and rust in the weapon's barrel. The death took place at Burhanpur on March 11, 1605.

Work on the Chester Beatty *Akbar nāma* was almost certainly still in progress during this year and in view of the close relationship of the hunting miniature with this manuscript it seems likely that the picture was painted only shortly before or after Dāniyāl met his death. This is also consistent with his age in this picture (approximately 30 years), which is not far short of that at which he died.

Several points remain uncertain. Does the picture commemorate an actual incident? For whom was it painted? Who was the artist? Of these, only the last can be answered with any certainty but it gives an indication of the place where the picture was painted and thus, indirectly, of the possible patron. We do not know whether Dāniyāl had his own studio of painters at Burhanpur during his stay in the Deccan between 1599 and 1605, as his brother Salīm had at Allahabad during roughly the same period, but our evidence points to the fact that the picture was, in any case, painted at the Mughal court itself.

The first pointer towards this conclusion is found in a manuscript of the translation from a Hindu work called the *Yog Bāshisht* in the Chester Beatty Library. This manuscript was completed in 1602, and since several of its folios bear the names of royal artists, it can be concluded that it was prepared in Akbar's studio at Agra.[23] A careful examination of one miniature (fig. 7),

showing the battle between two Hindu kings, reveals another version of the compositional group of the elephant, riders and victim, that forms the principal element in the hunting scene. There is also a running figure wearing bells, although he approaches from a different direction. In several respects, the *Yog Bāshisht* illustration differs from the other version. It is, after all, a battle scene and the victim is thus a man, whose riderless horse gallops from the scene. The position of the victim, the elephant's trunk, and its rear legs are all slightly altered. Nevertheless, the essentials are the same, and the two riders are using the same weapons in each case.

If we ask which is the earlier of these two versions we are bound to admit that they are virtually contemporary, though the stylistic relationship with the Chester Beatty *Akbar nāma* suggests that the lion hunt is just slightly later. Of the two compositions, however, it is the more successful and lucid. The *Yog Bāshisht* illustration is the one which has the appearance of being an adaptation. It, therefore, seems probable that an earlier version existed and was known to both of the painters of these miniatures. This earlier version has not come to light, but a slightly later version of the composition is found in another picture of a lion hunt from the Clive collection, recently sold at auction in London. This shows the Emperor Jahāngīr hunting lions, and there is evidence that it was painted at the Mughal court only a few years after the two versions already discussed.[24] The whereabouts of the Clive miniature is no longer known, but its composition can be studied in a later copy forming part of a Shāh Jahān period album in the Bodleian Library (fig. 8).[25]

In this picture of Jahāngīr's lion hunt it will be seen that the riderless horse appears, as in the *Yog Bāshisht* battle scene, and is in this case explained by its fallen rider, savaged by the lion, which is in turn being attacked by the elephant and hunters. The positions of the Emperor's arms and of the elephant's trunk, on the other hand, are nearer to those of the Spencer-Churchill picture than to the battle scene. Moreover, the two versions of the Jahāngīrī picture differ from both of these earlier paintings, which show the man mounted on the rear of the elephant shooting an arrow. Thus the Jahāngīrī version of the design contains some elements which appear in each, but not both, of its predecessors, while they have at least one common feature which is altered in the later version. The most natural conclusion to draw from these facts is

7. King Vidūratha engaged in battle with the king of Sindhu. From the *Yog Bāshisht*, f. 50v. Mughal, completed December 1602. By courtesy of the Chester Beatty Library (MS. 5).

8. The Mughal Emperor Jahāngīr hunting lions, after an original by Farrukh Chela. Mughal, mid-seventeenth century. By courtesy of the Bodleian Library (MS. Douce Or. a.1, f. 33r.).

that all three versions go back to an earlier original, probably a lion or tiger hunt, containing all the features common to two or more of the versions known to us. Of these three derived compositions both the earliest (fig. 7) and the latest (fig. 8) appear to have been made in the royal studio. Consequently there is good reason for thinking that the Spencer-Churchill version was made there also.

An even more conclusive reason for believing that the picture was done at Agra is provided by the identity of the artist; and the evidence for this again lies in the Chester Beatty *Akbar nāma*. For, whatever difficulties normally beset us when we attempt to attribute unsigned Mughal miniatures, this manuscript docs provide a very sound basis for doing so, especially in a case like this where the unsigned miniature is really comparable with work in the manuscript. Beneath each of its miniatures a library clerk has inscribed the name of the artist and the individual traits of the different

hands here are sufficiently marked for the reliability of its inscriptions to be unquestionable.

There is one artist alone in the manuscript, whose work is identical with that of our miniature. This is Sūr Dās Gujarātī, who was responsible for folios 34v., 40r., 47v., and 106r. of the British Museum's portion of the manuscript, and folios 53v., 54r., 84r., 157v., 158r., 162v., 163r., 187v., and 188r. of the larger portion in the Chester Beatty Library. In common with the hunting scene, many of these miniatures are executed in *nīm qalam*—a technique in which the pigment is built up into an opaque coating over parts of the picture only and much of the surface is left uncoloured or only lightly tinted or stippled. Sūr Dās was not the only painter who employed this technique in the Chester Beatty manuscript, but in details of landscape, particularly of the smooth rocks of the horizon and small trees on the skyline, his work closely resembles the picture under discussion (figs. 2 and 3). The **41**

9. Detail of fig. 1.

10. Detail from a miniature by Sūr Dās depicting the nobles of Gujarat submitting to Akbar. From the Chester Beatty *Akbar nāma*, f. 158r. Mughal, 1604–5.

11. Detail of a miniature by Makund depicting Akbar's assault on the fortress of Hajipur. From the Chester Beatty *Akbar nāma*, f. 202v. Mughal, 1604–5.

relationship with the hunting scene is no less evident in the skill with which Sūr Dās depicts elephants.

Of course, these points alone are insufficient for an attribution to be made, but there is a particular mannerism occurring in this artist's contributions to the manuscript, which is seen in identical form in the hunting picture. Around the outlines of the human and animal figures the artist has indicated the presence of grass with light calligraphic strokes as though it is growing from the figures themselves. The device was common in earlier Mughal paintings but by the time of this manuscript's production it had largely gone out of fashion and Sūr Dās was among the few to use it. Among these, only the painter La'l comes near to treating this device in the same way as Sūr Dās and even then he is unable to resist carrying it over almost every available patch of soil.[26] La'l is not, however, a candidate for the authorship of the lion hunt. At this stage in his career his work lacks the incisive drawing and clarity of design that claims the Spencer-Churchill picture for Sūr Dās. The qualities which mark him out as the painter of this picture are seen very clearly if we compare the curious figure of a Hindu retainer wearing a girdle and garters fringed with bells (fig. 9) with a similar figure of his from the *Akbar nāma* manuscript (fig. 10).[27] The relationship between these two details is further underlined when they are contrasted with a similar bell-clad figure from the hand of Makund, who also practised the *nīm qalam* technique (fig.11)[28]. In view of the fact that Sūr Dās was evidently very active on the *Akbar nāma* project at the time when the hunting picture was painted, there seems little question

that the picture could only have been made at Agra, where the court was then in residence. Dāniyāl had been stationed in the Deccan since 1599, so if the picture commemorates an actual incident—as was often the case with other Mughal hunting scenes featuring members of the royal house—it seems possible that an account of the killing reached the court by way of the *Akhbārāt*, or regular news letters, which passed between the Mughal viceroys and the imperial establishment.[29] It could, of course, be argued that, since the Indian lion is confined to the Gir forest in Gujarat, the incident is either imaginary or refers to an occasion before 1599, when Dāniyāl left for the Deccan. Both of these alternatives are indeed possible but the argument does not seem any more applicable than that of A. S. Altekar, who advanced the theory that Chandragupta II's "lion-slayer" coin type, mentioned earlier, was struck to commemorate the conquest of Gujarat.[30] We have ample evidence that in early Mughal times the lion roamed a much wider area of India than it does now. Furthermore, the province of Khandesh in which Dāniyāl was stationed is contiguous to Malwa, where, as we have seen, Sir Thomas Roe encountered a lion about ten years afterwards.

The fact that Dāniyāl is here shown using a spear, when his love of hunting with a gun was considered worthy of remark in what amounts to his obituary in Jahāngīr's Memoirs, does suggest that we are dealing with an actual event. For an imaginary celebration of his known love of hunting would recognise also his fondness for the gun as a weapon. Without further evidence, however, the issue must remain unresolved.

It is also uncertain whether the picture was prepared to gratify the ailing Emperor's interest in his absent son's activities, or was to have been sent to Dāniyāl himself, either as a gift, or to his own order. Perhaps it was commissioned by the wily old Khān-i Khānān, to whom the prince's welfare was entrusted, in order to reassure Akbar that Dāniyāl was not, after all, the enfeebled dipsomaniac that rumours were suggesting. If so, the plan misfired, for the aged Emperor lived just long enough to grieve over his son's demise. Whether or not the Khān-i Khānān had been falsely setting Akbar's mind at rest and thus felt himself embarrassingly compromised, the vengeance which he brought down upon Dāniyāl's unhappy associates in the affair of the smuggled spirits can well be understood.[31]

If the picture was not made for Akbar but was simply ordered for Dāniyāl in Burhanpur it certainly must have been returned to Agra almost immediately with the prince's effects; for it was a rule in the Mughal kingdom that a deceased officer's property lapsed to the crown. It was not until later that offices and possessions were retained on an hereditary basis. In either case, a series of librarians' notes on the reverse together with imperial seal impressions and an inscription in Rājasthānī Hindī indicate that it remained in the imperial library for many years before it found its way into the collection of the Mahārānās of Udaipur along with a number of other Mughal pictures bearing similar annotations. The circumstances of its acquisition by Captain Spencer-Churchill are not known. However, the companion painting bears similar inscriptions on its reverse and can likewise be shown to have belonged at earlier times to both the imperial Mughal and Udaipur collections.[32] Thus the two pictures have been as closely linked in their fortunes as in their subject matter. Indeed, when we come to examine the hunting picture from Captain Spencer-Churchill's collection, we find that although its place of origin was different, the association of these two with each other has lasted almost from the time when they were painted.

On the face of it, this picture of the dead lioness (Colour plate) poses a greater problem than its companion, for it shows us only the majestic victim and her humble transporters. The royal hunter does not appear. Nevertheless a series of circumstances affecting the Mughal royal family at this time enable us to reconstruct its origin and whereabouts during

the year or two before the two pictures came together and again it is pictorial style which provides the vital clues.

It has already been seen that during the fifteen-nineties while the Mughal capital was at Lahore the Mughal style of painting appears to have changed its direction. The effects of this change have been noted in the Chester Beatty *Akbar nāma* and in the hunting scene here associated with it. It is clear, however, that impressive as it is, the picture of the dead lioness cannot be connected with this trend towards refined perfection of technique. Nor in its dreamy pathos does it belong to that earlier phase of Mughal painting in which the figures bustle energetically within crowded compositions. There is a weariness in these bearers, as they convey their ponderous burden to the measuring implements of her ceremonial post mortem, that would not be countenanced in the more optimistic historical style (fig. 5), where the figures bristle with vitality and render exaggerated gestures. The answer is that the patron of this picture, although a man who seriously cared about painting enough to have commissioned a masterpiece, was not at that moment in a position to command those more senior talents under whom the new direction was being taken. This patron was Salīm, the future Emperor, Jahāngīr. His fondness for painting, boasted in his memoirs, or reported by Roe, has been remarked upon so often that there is no need for these well-worn sources to be quoted again. Instead, attention can be drawn to a little-known passage in a letter written by the Jesuit father, Jerome Xavier, in which he refers to an encounter with the prince at Lahore in 1598.[33] *One day as I visited him I found him with two painters, who were tracing out by the application of colour some small pictures, one of which represented the Angels appearing to shepherds and the other the Descent from the Cross; and when he asked what these meant and of whom they were likenesses, I renewed the discourses I had previously entered on before him regarding the sacred passion of our Lord Christ.*

There is, in the large Clive album in the Victoria and Albert Museum, a picture of the Descent from the Cross (fig. 12, I.S. 133 (79)–1964), which is clearly copied from a sixteenth-century Flemish print, based in its turn on a missing composition of Raphael preserved through an engraving of Marcantonio Raimondi.[34] This extremely fine Indian version is in exactly the style that has already been mentioned in connection with the series of poetical manuscripts executed at Lahore during

12. The Descent from the Cross. Mughal, 1598. Victoria and Albert Museum (I.S. 133–1964, f. 79).

the late fifteen-nineties[35] and there is good reason, there-fore, to consider that this Descent is one of the very two pictures that Father Xavier saw being painted under Salīm's supervision at Lahore in 1598.

If Salīm was enjoying the services of his father's best artists at this time, and even without the evidence of this picture there is no reason to think otherwise, the situation very soon changed. For some years the prince had been showing some signs of disobedience and by the middle of the year 1598 there was a serious rift between him and his father. Also, towards the end of the same year, the court terminated its stay of more than twelve years at Lahore and moved back to Agra. Salīm was ordered to proceed on an expedition against the ruler of Mewar, but after a short stay at Ajmer he revolted, tried without success to capture Agra, and then went on to Allahabad, where he set up court as an independent king. From then on until November 1604, Salīm spent most of his time at Allahabad in defiance of his father. There was another abortive attempt on Agra in 1602 and an attempted reconciliation in 1603, but in the main the situation was a stalemate. Akbar could have taken steps to quell the revolt but left matters as they were.

In Allahabad, Salīm was his own master, surrounded himself with favourites and settled down in the fort. He could not, however, indulge his fancy for paintings to the same advantage as before. The best imperial artists were in Agra, where they were soon to illustrate the Chester Beatty manuscript and, of course, the other of our hunting scenes. Nevertheless Salīm did manage to take some painters into his employment at Allahabad during these few years; for this fact is demonstrated by two manuscripts that were written and illustrated there. One of these, a copy of the *Dīvān* of the poet Ḥasan Dihlavī, was finished in the summer of 1602 by the scribe Mīr 'Abd Allāh and illustrated with fourteen unsigned miniatures. It is now in the Walters Art Gallery, Baltimore.[36] The other book is a Persian translation of a Hindu work entitled *Rāj Kunwar*, now in the Chester Beatty Library.[37] This was written at Allahabad by the scribe, Burhān, in 1603–4 and illustrated with fifty-one miniatures similar in style to those of the Walters Gallery manuscript and likewise unsigned (figs. 13 and 14).

In the miniatures of these two manuscripts there is an over-all stylistic unity, which is itself a distinguishing feature of the group. Compared with the resources of the imperial establishment, Salīm's studio appears to have been small and closely knit. The selected talent which had been asserting their individuality during the last few years at Lahore were still in evidence at Agra. Consequently, the illustrations executed there show a greater range of imagination and technique than those of the Allahabad manuscripts. Compositions are generally more complex, with an ambitious develop-ment of spatial relationships. Drawing tends to be more sophisticated and illusionistic effects are sought through subtle adjustments of tone produced by minutely working over the surface with the brush. In the Allahabad miniatures, on the other hand, the composi-tions are relatively simple, with fewer figures occupying a larger part of the stage (compare figs. 13 and 14 with figs. 2, 3 and 4). Similarly, the brushwork is broader, with washes of colour in preference to the minute stipple that so often finds a place in the imperial productions.[38]

Once these distinctions are recognised, it is an easy matter to associate the picture of the dead lioness with Allahabad rather than Agra.[39] It has all the features recognised in the work of Salīm's studio, even to the point of slightly exaggerating them. Thus the figures occupy a very large part of the landscape, which is simple in conception. These figures of bearers tend to be flattened on to the page surface like those of the men,

3. Rāj Kunwar proceeding in the guise of a yogī. From the *Rāj Kunwar*. Mughal (Allahabad), 1603–4. By courtesy of the Chester Beatty Library.

14. Rāj Kunwar resting below a tree. From the *Rāj Kunwar*. Mughal (Allahabad), 1603–4. By courtesy of the Chester Beatty Library.

who watch the passing yogī in the *Rāj Kunwar* manuscript (fig. 13)[40] and there are similarities with the Allahabad miniatures in the free drawing of plants, whose leaves tend not to be outlined.

If we accept these stylistic indications that the Spencer-Churchill painting should be associated with Prince Salīm's studio, it is inevitable that we should search the Memoirs, written by him later as the Emperor Jahāngīr, for some reference to an incident during his life as a prince with which the picture can be associated. The Memoirs commence, of course, with Jahāngīr's accession and most of the anecdotes of his hunting exploits refer to incidents which took place after that date. Quite late in his reign, however, something happened which reminded him of an occurrence that took place in his earlier years and he relates that *It happened to me once when I was prince that I had gone out in the Punjab to hunt lions.*[41] *A powerful lion appeared out of the wood. I fired at him from the elephant, and the lion in great fury rose and came on the elephant's back, and I had not time to put down my gun and seize my sword. Inverting the gun, I knelt, and with both*

hands struck him with the stock over the head and face so that he fell on to the ground and died.[42] On the face of it, there is no connection between this incident and our miniature, since it mentions a male animal and Jahāngīr is always specific about the sex of his victims. In fact, he made it a rule that he would not shoot female lions[43] but, as he freely confesses, this was not always kept.[44] In the Chester Beatty collection (manuscript 50, No. 1) there is a painting, which depicts this precise incident of Jahāngīr defending himself with the stock of his gun (fig. 15). It also shows, in the foreground, the inert body of another beast being carried off the field. What is significant, is the fact that the composition of the foreground group is clearly another version, in reverse, of the principal elements of the Spencer-Churchill painting.

When we compare these two versions in detail, it is clear that the Chester Beatty picture uses a different version of the design that is consistent with the modified use of a tracing. Thus among the differences from the other version one may note that the rear legs of the

15. Prince Salīm hunting lions in the Punjab. After a late sixteenth century original by Miskīn. Mughal, c. mid-seventeenth century. By courtesy of the Chester Beatty Library.

another version of this subject, formerly in the Eckstein collection, which again shows the complete composition.[45] This Eckstein picture bears a reliable attribution to Miskīn, which Mr. Basil Gray accepts, dating the picture to about 1610 and connecting it with an incident which occurred in that year.[46] This date has, however, been contested by Mr. S. C. Welch,[47] who was unaware of the actual incident depicted but pointed out inconsistencies in Gray's identification and plausibly advanced the view that the miniature should be associated in date with a manuscript of the *Anwār-i Suhaylī*, now in Benares, which was completed in 1596 in Lahore. Welch's view is borne out, now that the incident has been shown to have taken place while Jahāngīr was a prince. Also, since the Emperor specifically states that it happened in the Punjab, there is good reason to believe that the event was illustrated by Miskīn soon after its occurrence, when, as we have seen, Salīm appears to have been patronising such leading court painters there.

Thus, although Salīm does not appear in the Spencer-Churchill version, the composition of the picture has been firmly connected with another in which he appears. This earlier picture was evidently taken by the prince to Allahabad when he set up court there and was thus known to the anonymous painter, who has re-used part of the composition. The beast being transported in the Eckstein picture appears to have a mane. It is not possible, therefore, to connect the lioness of the Allahabad version with the incident related in Jahāngīr's Memoirs. As we have seen, he usually avoided shooting female lions but, in this case, the proportions of the beast are so spectacular that it is no wonder that, having broken his rule, Salīm should have had the killing commemorated. Indeed, as the prince was anxiously biding his time at Allahabad in fear of his father's retribution, the commissioning of this painted testimony to his success over such a giant adversary may have proved a much needed boost to his faltering morale.

beast are not fastened over the pole and the leg of the party's leader has wrongly been shown partly behind and partly in front of his companion's staff.

In style, this picture is obviously later than the reign of Jahāngīr and is probably not earlier than the middle of the seventeenth century. However, it does not merely combine elements from earlier pictures, for there is

Acknowledgements

I am indebted to Dr. R. J. Hayes of the Chester Beatty Library, Dublin, and to Mr. N. C. Sainsbury of the Bodleian Library, Oxford, for assisting me with photographs and permission to reproduce material from these institutions. The late Dr. Ganesh Gaur, Mr. Simon Digby and Kumar Sangram Singh were kind enough to offer suggestions concerning the reading of an intractable inscription. I am also most indebted to Dr. W. G. Archer for reading the manuscript and drawing my attention to a serious error in the original argument.

Notes

1. S. I. Tyulayev, *Indian Art in Soviet Collections*, 1955, plate unnumbered.

2. L. Binyon, *The Poems of Nizami*, 1928, pl. XVI.

3. *ibid.*, pl. XV. It is significant in this context that one of the founders of the Mughal school worked on this manuscript before leaving Persia.

4. I. Stchoukine, *Les peintres des manuscrits tîmûrides*, 1954, pl. LXXXIII.

5. *The Embassy of Sir Thomas Roe to India, 1615–19*, edited by W. Foster, 1926, p. 365.

6. François Bernier, *Travels in the Mogul Empire*, edited by A. Constable, 1891, p. 378.

7. *ibid.*, p. 379.

8. *The Mad Lover*, IV,V.

9. For the portion comprising the second and third volumes of the work see T. W. Arnold and J. V. S. Wilkinson, *The Library of A. Chester Beatty. A Catalogue of the Indian Miniatures*, 1936, I, pp. 4–12 & II, pls. 6–37. For the first volume see *The British Museum Report of the Trustees 1966*, 1967, pl. 69 and pls. LII and LIII, also R. Pinder-Wilson, 'History and Romance in Mughal India', *Oriental Art*, XIII, No. 1, 1967, pp.63–4.

10. S. Lee and P. Chandra, 'A Newly Discovered *Tuti-nama* and the Continuity of the Indian Tradition of Manuscript Painting', *The Burlington Magazine*, CV, No. 729, 1963, pp. 547–554.

11. H. Glück, *Die Indischen Miniaturen des Haemsae-Romanes*, 1925.

12. S. C. Welch, *The Art of Mughal India*, 1963, p. 24.

13. Only the *Razm nāma* has been published, see T. H. Hendley, *Memorials of the Jeypore Exhibition*, IV, 1883.

14. P. Brown, *Indian Painting under the Mughals*, Oxford, 1924, pl. XXXIV. I hope to demonstrate the date in a forthcoming article.

15. A. Godard & B. Gray, *Iran* (U.N.E.S.C.O. World Art Series), 1956, pls. XXIX to XXXIV, also J. Marek and H. Knížková, *The Jenghiz Khan Miniatures from the Court of Akbar the Great*, 1963.

16. This practice was not, of course, unknown in the historical MSS. and it is also found in high-class poetical MSS. of an earlier date, such as the pocket-sized copy of Anwarī's *Dīvān* written at Lahore in 1588 (S. C. Welch, *op. cit.*, p. 162 and pls. 4A–4D). However, the work on the series of MSS. referred to here entailed a concentration of the leading talents in a direction that appears to have affected the course of the school as a whole.

17. For a discussion of this group of MSS. see S. C. Welch, 'The Emperor Akbar's *Khamsa* of Nizami', *The Journal of the Walters Art Gallery*, Baltimore, 1959, pp. 87–96.

18. The curious history of this album following its sale is related by B. Hollander, who describes how the authenticity of the paintings was vindicated in a court of law (*The International Law of Art*, 1959, pp. 112–13 and 170–1). As an ironic postscript to the story one must add that certain of the pictures are indeed late copies (c. 1800) but the Dāniyāl portrait forms part of the album's nucleus of genuine pictures.

19. Accession No. 55.121.10.32.

20. It must be remembered that the court language was Persian.

21. *The Tūzuk-i-Jahāngīrī or Memoirs of Jahāngīr*, tr. by A. Rogers, ed. by H. Beveridge, I, 1909, p.36.

22. *ibid.* pp. 34–35.

23. Arnold and Wilkinson, *op. cit.*, I, pp, 21–25 & II, pls. 48–49.

24. Messrs. Christie, Manson & Woods, *Catalogue of Important Manuscripts and Drawings Oriental Miniatures and Manuscripts*, December 18, 1968, lot 76, frontispiece. This miniature has an attribution on the reverse to Farrukh Chela and an inscription identifying the figure behind Jahāngīr as Suhrāb Khān and a mounted figure as Prince Parvīz. Suhrāb Khān was drowned in 1620 at the age of 26 and had been ordered to ride on the *front* of Jahāngīr's private elephant on the expedition to Gujarat (Oct. 1617–Sept. 1618). Parvīz was not with his father at this time. The incident has not been identified but since Farrukh Chela worked for Akbar it is possible that the figure mounted behind Jahāngīr has been incorrectly identified and that the picture was painted early in Jahāngīr's reign. Parvīz is shown as a young man, a fact which lends support to this view.

25. MS. Douce, Or. a.1, f. 33r. The Bodleian miniature differs from its Jahāngīrī original in a few inessential details, such as the attitude of the young man seated behind the Emperor, and the removal of figures from the tree, etc. The Douce album contains yet another version of this subject in which Akbar is the chief protagonist and the elements of the landscape are much altered (f. 32v.).

26. Arnold and Wilkinson, *op. cit.*, II, pls. 7 and 14.

27. f. 158r.

28. Chester Beatty *Akbar nāma*, f. 202v.

29. The Emperor and his son did meet briefly at Burhanpur in February 1601 but otherwise they were not together during this period.

30. R. C. Majumdar and A. S. Altekar, *The Vākātaka-Gupta Age*, 1967, p. 170.

31. They were beaten to death.

32. Each of these paintings bears a number of Mughal imperial seal impressions with notes in Persian recording the occasions when the pictures were inspected. In addition, each has a Rājasthānī inscription. The Rājasthānī inscription on I.S. 96–1965 (the dead lioness) is an inspection note dated 1111 A.H. = 1699/1700. An identical note appears on a picture from the Udaipur collection (now in the National Museum of India, No. 50. 14/9), which also bears a number of Mughal seals and inspection notes. On the other painting (I.S. 97–1965), of Dāniyāl spearing a lioness, is a Rājasthānī inscription which mentions the administration of Shāhzāda Mu'azzam and a certain Maqsūd Beg. This seems to be an interpretation of a Persian inspection note, which mentions Maqsūd Beg, dated in the 48th year (of Aurangzeb), i.e. 1703/4 A.D.

33. E. D. Maclagan, 'Jesuit Missions to the Emperor Akbar', *Journal of the Asiatic Society of Bengal*, LXV, Pt. I, 1896, p. 74.

34. A. Bartsch, *Le peintre-graveur*, 1811, XIV, 1813, p. 37 (II.32).

35. Compare, for example, an illustration attributed to Manohar from the *Khamsa* of Amīr Khusraw copied at the court in 1597/8: E. J. Grube, *The Classical style in Islamic Painting*, Venice, 1968, pl. 94.

36. R. Ettinghausen, *Paintings of the Sultans and Emperors of India*, New Delhi, 1961, pl. 8.

37. MS. 37. One illustration is reproduced in the Library's brochure, *The Chester Beatty Library, Dublin*, 1958, pl. 7.

38. Apart from the Chester Beatty *Akbar nāma*, the qualities of the Agra studio's output are well exemplified by a manuscript of Jāmī's *Nafaḥāt al Uns* in the British Museum, which was copied at Agra in 1603 (MS. Or. 1362), see D. Barrett and B. Gray, *Painting of India*, Skira, 1963, pp. 96–97 and E. Wellesz, *Akbar's religious thought reflected in Mughal painting*, 1952, pl. 35.

39. In doing so, of course, one must bear in mind that we are dealing with separate studios rather than different schools and there were almost certainly artists at Agra whose work stood closer to the Allahabad miniatures than that found in the two MSS. cited above (footnote 38). A case in point is the manuscript of the *Yog Bāshisht* in the Chester Beatty Library (MS. 5), written in 1602, almost certainly at Agra, since it has several miniatures ascribed to court artists (Arnold and Wilkinson, *op. cit.*, I, pp. 21–25 and II, pls. 48–49). It is not easy to separate some of the Yog Bāshisht miniatures from those of Salīm's studio but even here the distinctions noted above generally hold good. The painters who worked for Salīm possibly had their apprenticeship working on such MSS. as the dispersed *Razm nāma*, dated 1007 A.H.=A.D. 1598, of which the major portions are in the Baroda Museum and the British Museum. Although produced by the Lahore studio, this manuscript was less ambitious than the poetical series referred to above and provided work for a number of lesser talents. Compare, for example, fig.

14 of the present article with Wellesz, *op. cit.*, pl. 31. If Salīm's artists were recruited among those who had worked on the 1598 MS., there were certainly others associated with that project who went to Agra. It was the temporary isolation of Salīm's studio under a concerned patron, which accounts for any differences between the two groups.

40. Contrast, for example, the bearers in a miniature by Dhanrāj in the Chester Beatty *Akbar nāma* (Arnold and Wilkinson, *op. cit.*, II, pl. 13).

41. The word used in the Persian text is *shīr*, which has the meanings of either 'lion' or 'tiger'. Rogers has consistently translated this as 'tiger', although in many cases, such as this, it can be shown that Jahāngīr was referring to lions. I have amended the passage accordingly.

42. *Tūzuk-i-Jahāngīrī*, translation, II, p. 270.

43. *ibid.*, I, p. 287.

44. *ibid.*, I, pp. 166, 276, 287.

45. Sir Leigh Ashton (ed.), *The Art of India and Pakistan*, 1950, pl. 234. The present ownership of this picture is not known.

46. *ibid.*, p. 157, No. 708.

47. S. C. Welch, 'Mughal and Deccani Paintings from a private collection', *Ars Orientalis*, V, 1963, p. 224.

Notes on Two Paintings

C. M. KAUFFMANN

A Sicilian Painted Crucifix of the 15th Century

THE painted Crucifix reproduced in fig. 1 has recently been cleaned by Mr. H. Rogers of the Conservation Department, and is now on view in Room 11. The surface has been badly rubbed on the left side of the body, especially on the loin-cloth, and also on the face, but otherwise the condition was found to be better than its appearance had led one to expect. The open-work frame appears to be a later addition.

Bought by the Museum in 1895, this Crucifix is traditionally said to have formed the rood of the parish church of Hever, Kent, but there is now no firm evidence to support this provenance.[1] It was exhibited at the *English Medieval Paintings* . . . exhibition of the Society of Antiquaries in 1896, when a critic described it in glowing terms as "one of the most beautiful objects in the Library . . . painted rood from a church in Surrey [sic], in remarkably good condition . . . This is the finest rood of English medieval work we have ever seen".[2]

This patriotic sentiment was not accepted in the more sober columns of the *Proceedings of the Society of Antiquaries* (2nd ser., XVI, 1895-7, p. 205) in which the cross was described as a "painted rood of the 15th century from Hever, Kent . . . The painting of this is now considered Italian".

From that time it was catalogued and exhibited as Italian 14th Century, but recently Mr. Everett Fahy suggested that it was Sicilian, late 15th Century, somewhat in the manner of Antonello da Messina. This illuminating suggestion was fully endorsed by Professor V. Scuderi of Palermo.[3] Indeed, Professor Scuderi suggested that it might be an early work of Antonio de Saliba (?1467 after 1535), who was recorded in 1480 as a collaborator of Iacobello, the son of Antonello da Messina. Antonio de Saliba tended to paint the Virgin and Child in a landscape in the manner of Antonello, but he did, on occasion, return to a more archaic form in the rendering of Christ's body. Professor Scuderi's attribution remains tentative, but his comparison of the Crucifix with Antonio de Saliba's *Deposition* in Rabato, Malta, is striking, not only for the body of Christ, but also for the figure of St. John.[4]

The large painted wooden crucifix appears to have been primarily an Italian phenomenon. Carved wooden crucifixes and crosses in a variety of other materials have a long history, but the monumental painted wooden crucifix emerged—as far as can be seen from the very fragmentary evidence—in Italy in the 12th century. They were popular in Italy, particularly in Tuscany and Umbria, in the 13th and 14th centuries; there is an early Umbrian example of c. 1200, showing Christ alive on the Cross, in the Museum (No. 850–

1. PAINTED CRUCIFIX, attributed to Antonio de Saliba (?1467–after 1535), Sicilian School, late 15th century. Tempera on poplar, $85\frac{1}{2} \times 60\frac{3}{4}$ in. (217 × 154 cm.) Victoria and Albert Museum, 323–1895.

1900, Room 24).[5] Such crosses were placed in various parts of the church, in particular above the altar, in the apse, on the triumphal arch or at the choir screen.[6] In many of them the head and halo of Christ is raised from the background by some two inches, which suggests that they were placed at a considerable height. In Tuscany the popularity of these crosses declined in the 15th century, but in Sicily the tradition continued throughout the century. There is a splendid one in the Cathedral at Piazza Armerina by an unknown artist who takes his name from this work, and there are others in the Museum at Palermo.[7]

The iconography of the Museum's crucifix, as of the other Sicilian examples of the 15th century, is thoroughly traditional. Indeed, though painted not long before 1500, the type is unchanged from that of c. 1300. For it was at that time that the strongly curving body of Christ, typical of 13th century crosses, was replaced by a calmer pose, in which the body lies straight against the Cross, bent only slightly at the knee, with a single nail piercing both feet. An early example of this type is the crucifix by Deodato Orlandi in S. Miniato al Tedesco, Florence, dated 1301,[8] and it remained the usual form from that time. The earliest crosses have scenes of the Passion in the terminals, but from about 1230 these are replaced by half-length figures of the Virgin and St. John.

The upper terminal contains the "Pelican in her piety", pecking her breast and causing the blood to flow in order to feed her famished young. This legend is found in early medieval Bestiaries where it is paralleled by the sacrifice of Christ's blood to save the parched soul of mankind. Originally derived from a passage in the Psalms (Psalm 102.6), this comparison was well-known to medieval commentators and consequently the pelican is quite often depicted from the 13th century as a symbol of the Crucifixion.[9] It appears frequently at the top of painted crosses in the 14th century,[10] and occurs on most of the 15th century Sicilian examples, including those in the churches at Piazza Armerina and Agira.[11] Finally, the crown of thorns is also a 14th century feature which appears on most of the 15th century Sicilian crosses.[12] The influence of Antonello da Messina may be detected in the facial types of the Virgin and St. John, but in general the artist adhered strictly to the traditional forms of the painted crucifix.

Notes

1. I should like to acknowledge the help of the Rev. J. B. Collins, Vicar of Hever.
2. *The Artist*, XVIII, July–December 1896, p. 358f. (repro.).
3. Letter in Department of Paintings files.
4. S. Bottari, *La Pittura del Quattrocento in Sicilia*, 1954, fig. 163.
5. This has been reproduced several times before it was cleaned: R. van Marle, *The Development of the Italian Schools of Painting*, I 1923, p. 201 fig. 93; E. Sandberg-Vavalà, *La Croce Dipinta Italiana*, 1929, p. 636f, fig. 415; E. B. Garrison, *Italian Romanesque Panel Painting*, 1949, p. 187, no. 475.
6. Sandberg-Vavalà, *op. cit.*, p. 73.
7. Bottari, *op. cit.*, figs. 91ff, 35, 146.
8. Sandberg-Vavalà, *op. cit.*, p. 893, fig. 557.
9. L. Réau, *Iconographie de l'Art Chrétien*, I, 1955, p. 94ff.
10. See, for example, Sandberg-Vavalà, *op. cit.*, figs. 562, 563, 569; P. Beye, 'Ein unbekanntes Florentiner Kruzifix aus der Zeit um 1330/40', *Pantheon*, 25, 1967, p. 5ff, figs. 2, 3, colour plate.
11. Bottari, *op. cit.*, figs. 91, 98.
12. *Loc. cit.*, figs. 35, 92, 98, 139, 189.

A "Saturday Painting" by Johann Melchior Roos

IN the bequest of John Parsons, acquired by the museum a hundred years ago, there is a painting of *Brigands attacking Wagoners*, formerly attributed to Johann Heinrich Roos (1631–85) of Frankfurt (fig. 1). On the back is a label inscribed by Parsons "Bot. of Gale in Holborn about 3 or 4 year since, he did not know who painted it. I find the name on the right foreground 'J. Roos', July 1868 JMP".
After Parsons' discovery the painting was catalogued and labelled J. H. Roos.[1] However, this attribution was not accepted by Herman Jedding in his recent monograph on the artist. Jedding seems to have been unaware of the signature, and attributed the picture to Matth. Scheits (c. 1625/30–c. 1700) of Hamburg.[2] The signature is doubtless genuine, yet one can understand Jedding's doubts concerning the attribution to Johann Heinrich Roos. For the composition of Parsons' picture is characterised by violent action and almost excess of movement which distinguishes it sharply from the unruffled calm and static poses of J. H. Roos's work.
This apparent contradiction is solved by the discovery of a pen drawing with the identical composition,

1. Johann Melchior Roos (1663–1731): BRIGANDS ATTACKING WAGONERS. Oil on oak panel, 13¾ × 18 in. (35 × 4·57 cm.) Victoria and Albert Museum, 541–1870.

2. Johann Melchior Roos (1663–1731): BRIGANDS ATTACKING
WAGONERS. Pen and ink, and wash. Signed, and dated at the
Hague, 1685. Glade Gallery, New Orleans.

though set in an open landscape, (Glade Gallery, New
Orleans, fig. 2) which is signed and dated *JM Roos
1685 a la Hay*. This is Johann Melchior Roos (1663–
1731), the son and pupil of Johann Heinrich. The
Museum's picture would seem to be based on this
drawing and it also should be attributed to Johann
Melchior.

There is another version in oil, identical but slightly
reduced at the left and lower edges (panel, 33·5 × 43 cm;
present whereabouts unknown, photograph in Witt
Library, Courtauld Institute). This was formerly
called Wouvermans, but might more accurately be
described as by or after Johann Melchior Roos.

Like his father, Johann Melchior was primarily a
painter of animals, but he also painted portraits and
figure subjects. Born in Heidelberg in 1663, his family
settled in Frankfurt when he was four years old. He was,
for some years, a pupil of his father and subsequently,
in 1684–5, a member of the Drawing Academy at the
Hague. It was at this time that the drawing of the
Brigands' attack (fig. 2) originated. In 1686–1690 he was
in Italy where he came under the influence of his
brother Philipp Peter (1657–1706), better known as
"Rosa da Tivoli", follower of Salvator Rosa and
Gaspard Dughet. After brief periods in Nürnberg and
Heidelberg, Johann Melchior settled in Frankfurt in
1695. He was fortunate enough to be commissioned by
Count Lothar Franz von Schönborn to paint animal
pieces for his newly built palace at Pommersfelden, but
his notorious laziness made him a source of bitter

disappointment to his patron. In a letter to his cousin,
dated March 1711, the Count grumbles about the
painter: ". . . you do not really know this slovenly
fellow Roos, for he has no equal in the whole world. He
has been working for a year and a half on one painting
and even this I shall not receive by October . . . "[3].
Count Schönborn was not alone in seeing Johann
Melchior as a "dissolute dog" ("einen liederlichen
Hundt"). In Frankfurt he was widely known as
"Samstags-Roos", for it was said that he only painted
on Saturdays when his wife needed money to do the
shopping. Perhaps this accounts for the rarity of his
paintings.

His landscapes are, like those of his father and elder
brother, Italianate, or at any rate reminiscent of the
nothern artists who worked in Italy in the 17th
century. The drawing of the *Brigands' attack*, however,
was produced at the Drawing Academy at the Hague
and looks as though it was inspired by a Dutch composition. Wouvermans, in particular, painted similar
scenes—there is one in the Liechtenstein Gallery,
Vaduz—though nothing identical by him has come to
light. Indeed, the general similarity of the composition
to those of Wouvermans is sufficiently marked that it
need come as no surprise to note that the second
version in oil, mentioned above, was wrongly attributed
to Wouvermans and the photographs filed as such in the
Witt Library.

In adapting the composition of the drawing for the oil
painting, the artist has made the action take place
against a background of classical ruins reminiscent of
the Colosseum. This makes it seem likely that the
painting was carried out after his visit to Italy in
1686–90, a few years later than the drawing upon
which it is based. The fact that it is on oak panel
suggests that it was painted north of the Alps rather
than in Italy.

Notes

1. South Kensington Museum, *A Catalogue of the National Gallery of
British Art . . . with a supplement containing works by modern foreign
artists and old masters*, 1893, p. 184.

2. Hermann Jedding, *Der Tiermaler Joh. Heinr. Roos*, Strasbourg
1955, p. 292, no. 54.

3. Jedding, *op. cit.*, p. 184f. Jedding contains the most recent
account of Johann Melchior's life.

Some Unrecognised Venetian Woven Fabrics

DONALD KING

THE Victoria and Albert Museum possesses several interesting patterned silk textiles of the thirteenth and early fourteenth centuries, of a type which has been found in various parts of western Europe, and which is characterised by the use of a main warp of coarse linen; because of the mixture of materials, textiles of this class are commonly described as half-silks. Falke, finding many half-silks in Germany and supposing that the presence of linen indicated an origin in northern Europe, attributed them to Regensburg, on the grounds of their affinity with an altar-hanging probably woven for Regensburg cathedral.[1] The altar-hanging, however, is not, as he supposed, a half-silk, nor is it certain that it was woven in Regensburg, nor indeed is there any evidence that Regensburg, though it produced other types of textiles, ever wove patterned silks or half-silks.[2] Thus the attribution of half-silks to Regensburg, though it retains the affection of some scholars, has no factual basis.[3] A variant theory, advanced by Schmidt, while allowing that some half-silks were woven in Regensburg, claimed that others were woven in Cologne.[4] It is true that Cologne did employ the half-silk technique during the middle ages for many extant narrow textiles, under 20 cm. wide, with small patterns woven on simple looms, but there is no evidence that Cologne, any more than Regensburg, or indeed any other German city, possessed the technical knowledge to construct and operate the wide draw looms—capable of the automatic repetition of large patterns—on which most half-silks of the thirteenth and early fourteenth centuries were woven, in widths of about 120 cm. In recent times a number of half-silks, including one woven with the arms of Castile-Leon, have been found in Spain, notably at Burgos, and have been attributed to a Spanish origin—an attribution which, though not proven, is plausible, since Spain, unlike Germany, is known to have possessed the draw loom.[5] But a further proposal to attribute all early half-silks to Spain, or more precisely to Burgos—on the grounds of similarities between their patterns and those of stucco reliefs in the town—is purely speculative; there is no documentary evidence of the weaving of patterned silks or half-silks in Burgos.[6]

A new attribution will now be introduced, which, unlike its predecessors, is firmly based on the evidence of contemporary documents.

While most extant half-silks have patterns of animals, foliage and geometrical ornament, ten have figure subjects. Textiles with very similar figure subjects are described in several inventories and records. A half-silk preserved at the Wartburg shows the Nativity with angels and a shepherd (fig. 1); baudekyns[7] showing the Nativity were given to Durham cathedral in 1260 and 1285, and in 1295 St. Paul's cathedral in London possessed two cloths with this subject and a baudekyn with angels and shepherds. A half-silk in the Österreichisches Museum für angewandte Kunst, Vienna, shows the Adoration of the Kings; there is no precise parallel in the documents, though St. Paul's had several cloths and baudekyns with other Gospel scenes, notably the Crucifixion, Entombment and Resurrection. A half-silk formerly in the Musée des Tissus, Lyon, now missing, showed the Virgin and Child; in 1352 the church of Saint-Georges at Le Puy possessed three vestments of cloth of Venice with figures of the Virgin or the Virgin and Child. A half-silk in the Kunstgewerbemuseum, West Berlin, and the Museum des Kunsthandwerks, Leipzig, shows the Virgin and Child with angels; in 1311 the papal treasury at Perugia included a Venetian cloth with angels and full length figures of the Virgin "holding her son before her breast" as in the half-silk; angels also appeared in three other Venetian cloths at Perugia and in baudekyns at St. Paul's. A half-silk formerly in the Kreuzkirche, Rostock, now missing, showed the Virgin and Child with St. Nicholas; figures of St. Nicholas appeared in a dossal given by Pope Boniface VIII (1294-1303) to Anagni cathedral and in a Venetian cloth at Perugia. A half-silk in the church of Södra Råda in Sweden shows St. Peter with acolytes; baudekyns with figures of St. Peter were given to St. Paul's cathedral in 1271 and 1299, while other saints appeared in another baudekyn at St. Paul's and in a Venetian cloth at Perugia. A half-silk in the Kunstgewerbemuseum, West Berlin, shows Alexander raised into the air by griffins (fig. 3); the gifts of Pope Boniface to Anagni included a textile with the "story of Alexander raised into the air by griffins". A half-silk in the Gewebesammlung, Krefeld, shows, within circles, a king or queen between two unicorns; no precise parallel is recorded, but kings, queens or other figures accompanied by children, birds or lilies, often within circles, are recorded in a baudekyn at St. Paul's, a cloth

1. Half-silk, violet, yellow, white and gold; Wartburg, Eisenach. Baudekyns 'containing the story of the Nativity of the Lord' were recorded at Durham cathedral in 1260 and 1285, and St. Paul's, London, in 1295.

2. Half-silk; red, buff, white, violet and gold; 11 × 14 in. (28 × 36 cm). Victoria and Albert Museum, 8589–1863, acquired from the Bock collection, Aachen. 'Baudekyns' with men on horseback, in one case 'with birds on their hands', were recorded at St. Paul's, London, in 1295. Venetian cloths depicting kings were recorded at Rome in 1295, Perugia in 1311, and Le Puy in 1352.

of Venice in the Vatican, three Venetian cloths at Perugia and four cloths of Venice at Le Puy. A half-silk in the Victoria and Albert Museum shows a king on horseback carrying a hawk (fig. 2); St. Paul's cathedral possessed half a dozen baudekyns with men on horseback, in one case "with birds on their hands". A half-silk in Universitetets Oldsaksamling, Oslo, shows, beneath arches, a figure possibly representing Samson; Samson appeared in two baudekyns at St. Paul's (in one case beneath arches), two dossals at Anagni and a Venetian cloth in the Vatican.[8]

Though the clerks of Durham, London and Anagni proposed no attribution for textiles with figure subjects, their colleagues in Rome, Perugia and Le Puy ascribed them without exception to Venice. As far as is known to the present writer, not a single textile with a pattern of this type is ascribed in any contemporary document to any other weaving centre in Western Europe.[9] The silk-weavers of Venice, unlike their hypothetical competitors in Regensburg, Cologne or Burgos, are quite well documented. Venetian participation in the Fourth Crusade, culminating in the capture of Constantinople in 1203–4, gave the Republic a golden opportunity of developing her own industries at the expense of those of Byzantium. In 1247, a white silk cloth of Venice was purchased by the royal authorities in London. A Venetian decree of 1248 shows that the city then possessed a well-organised silk-weaving industry, producing cloths of gold, *purpurae* and cendals. The regulations of the Venetian silk-weavers, the *Capitulare Samitariorum* of 1265, show that they were then producing *catasamiti*, *diaspri*, *meçanelli*, *purpurae*, *samiti contrafacti* and *sarantasima*. Some of these were patterned cloths; *sarantasima*, for instance, are the *exarentasmata* which—according to Hugo Falcandus in 1189—"with their various patterns of circles, demand greater industry from the craftsmen and larger expenditure of materials". According to the 1265 regulations *sarantasima*, and possibly other silk cloths, were woven in Venice *de açis vel de seta*, with coarse linen (or hemp) or with silk. The alternative applied, not to the weft, for the regulations expressly forbade the use of weft threads of linen or cotton, but to the warp, for they decreed that warp threads must be 25% more numerous in cloths woven with silk than in those woven with coarse linen, a natural provision in view of the greater bulk of the linen thread. Thus *sarantasima de açis* were undoubtedly half-silks. Venetian silk textiles of various kinds appear in inventories compiled

3. Half-silk, yellow and red; Kunstgewerbemuseum, West Berlin. A textile with the 'story of Alexander raised into the air by griffins' was recorded at the Anagni cathedral, 1294–1303.

in London, Naples and Rome in 1295, in a Paris customs-list of 1296, and in a number of English, French and Italian documents of the early fourteenth century. In the two parallel accounts for the coronations of the French king and queen at Reims in 1317, cloth of Venice appears to be virtually synonymous with half-silk; where one account has *draps de Venise*, the other has *draps d'Ache* (= *de açis*, *di accia* in the Italian documents), both at 55s. per piece, much cheaper than *draps de Luques* and *draps de Turquie*, which were

4. Silk; pink, white, violet and gold; 5 × 4 in. (13 × 10 cm). Victoria and Albert Museum, T.60–1923. Probably part of a border, like that on the left of the Regensburg altar hanging (Figs. 5, 6.)

As the regulations of 1265 show that Venice wove all-silk as well as half-silk textiles, the contemporary all-silk textiles with figure subjects can likewise be attributed to Venice, especially since the five extant examples have virtually the same subjects, style, colouring and other details as the ten half-silks. Two lightweight silks, one at Le Mans Cathedral, the other divided between the Kunstgewerbemuseum, West Berlin, and the Gewebesammlung, Krefeld, both show the motif of kings on horseback, "with birds on their hands". Three medium-weight silks have religious subjects; one in the Historisches Museum, Bern, shows the motif of the Virgin and Child, with the Greek contraction MP ΘY which also appears on the half-silk in Vienna; one in the Victoria and Albert Museum, with an episcopal saint, is probably a fragment of a border (fig. 4), like the border of the third and by far the most important example, the altar frontal or dossal at Regensburg cathedral (figs. 5, 6).[11] Because this altar hanging includes the figure of a kneeling bishop, evidently the donor, identified by inscription as EPISCOPVS HEINRICVS, it is generally agreed that it was one of the many gifts of Bishop Heinrich von Rotteneck (1277–93) to his cathedral at Regensburg, and it has been assumed, as Regensburg had some reputation as a textile centre, that it was woven by local craftsmen. But there is no evidence that Regensburg weavers made anything other than plain, unpatterned textiles, and nothing whatever to suggest that they possessed the requisite skills to produce one of the greatest masterpieces of medieval pattern-weaving. On the other hand it was perfectly natural for a bishop of Regensburg to commission such a hanging from Venice, easily the nearest of the great silk-weaving centres of Europe, one with which Regensburg merchants are known to have conducted an active trade, and the only one which specialised in weaving figure subjects.[12] The main subject of the hanging is recorded in the inventories only in a gift of King Edward I to St. Paul's cathedral between 1272 and 1295, "two baudekyns with images of Christ crucified, Mary and John", which, though unattributed, were presumably Venetian; saints, angels and inscriptions like those of the hanging are recorded only in Venetian textiles. The stylistic resemblances between the hanging and the half-silks, which Falke took to be evidence that the latter were woven in Regensburg, are in fact evidence that the former was woven in Venice. It is true that all other extant Venetian textiles of this period

presumably all-silk stuffs. In the French royal accounts for the following year *draps à or sur chanvre, de Venise* is evidently another reference to Venetian half-silks.[10] The documents quoted and others like them show that Venice was one of the most important silk-weaving centres in Europe. They also provide unequivocal evidence that half-silks were woven in Venice in the thirteenth and early fourteenth century, evidence which exists for no other centre. Since, therefore, Venice is the only centre known to have woven figure subjects at this period, and also the only centre certainly known to have woven half-silks, the attribution to Venice of the ten extant half-silks with figure subjects seems established beyond reasonable doubt. The style of the designs is perfectly in keeping with this attribution.

5. Altar-hanging of silk; red, violet, white and gold; Regensburg cathedral. 'Baudekyns with images of Christ crucified, Mary and John' were recorded at St. Paul's, London, in 1295. Compare also an altar-hanging recorded at Perugia in 1311, 'consisting of a complete Venetian cloth, with a pattern of many figures of angels and of other saints'.

6. Drawing of the Regensburg altar-hanging, after *Zeitschrift für christliche Kunst*, 1, 1888. The kneeling donor, EPISCOPVS HEINRICVS, is Heinrich von Rotteneck, Bishop of Regensburg 1277–93.

have repeating patterns, unlike the very large non-repetitive pattern of the hanging; but this is a natural difference between ordinary commercial products for general sale and a specially commissioned work. Another similar work of the Venetian weavers is probably recorded in the Perugia inventory of 1311—"dossal or frontal for an altar, consisting of a complete Venetian cloth, with a pattern of many figures of angels and of other saints, and the said figures have inscriptions".[13] It has been argued that the Regensburg hanging includes at least one iconographical feature which is specifically German, namely the sword which pierces the breast of the fainting Virgin.[14] But in fact there is no reason to dispute the evident probability that the iconographical programme was laid down by the bishop or his advisers in Regensburg and communicated to the weaving-firm verbally, or perhaps even in a sketch design. The finished work, however, shows clearly enough that the final cartoon which the weavers used was not in a German Gothic but an Italo-Byzantine style, for which very close parallels—in

8. Venetian painting, late 13th century; Venice, Museo Marciano. The figures on the frame, a feature derived from Byzantine icons, recall the border of the Regensburg hanging.

7. Part of a painted chest-lid, Venetian, late 13th century; Venice, Museo Correr. The drawing and arrangement of the figures recall the Regensburg hanging. Bands of ornament on the same lid, not shown here, resemble ornaments on contemporary silks and half-silks.

composition, human types, drapery, musculature of Christ, and even such a detail as the red border with three small figures—can be found in Venetian paintings and mosaics (figs. 7,8,9).[15] The inscriptions point to the same conclusion; the Greek contraction $\overline{\text{IC}}$ $\overline{\text{XC}}$ on the label of the cross was usual in Venice, while the weaving of the bishop's name as ENRICVS, later emended to HEINRICVS by embroidering two additional letters, is pretty clear proof—if any further proof were needed—that the hanging was woven, not in Germany, but in Italy.

Besides the sixteen Venetian textiles with figure subjects recorded in the documents quoted above, the inventories of the Vatican (1295), Perugia (1311), Exeter cathedral (1327), Amiens cathedral (1347), Saint-Georges at Le Puy (1352) and St. Peter's, Rome (1361), describe nearly sixty Venetian textiles with patterns of animals and other ornament.[16] Doubtless

9. Venetian painting, first half of the 14th century; Venice, Museo Correr. The composition recalls that of the Regensburg hanging.

many Venetian half-silk and all-silk textiles with such patterns are still extant, but their identification presents problems, since, unlike the figure subjects, which only Venice is known to have woven, patterns of this type were produced in every major silk-weaving centre. It is true that only Venice is known to have woven half-silks. But half-silks were not a technical innovation which was likely to remain indefinitely the monopoly of a single centre; they were simply a particular grade of patterned silk, showy, but relatively inexpensive, and useful for vestments, hangings or other articles in which the stiff heavy texture resulting from the coarse linen thread was no great disadvantage. The evidence suggests that Venice was the principal purveyor of half-silks to Western Europe in the thirteenth and early fourteenth century, and hence that many, perhaps most, of the extant half-silks are Venetian, but it may well be that some were woven in other centres. Lucca, for example, was weaving half-silks in 1376 and may have done so earlier.[17] The half-silks found in Spain, including an example with the arms of Castile-Leon, may be Spanish, as has been suggested, though the possibility of an Italian origin can hardly be excluded—both Lucca and Venice wove textiles with foreign coats-of-arms.[18]

Although there is no simple criterion for identifying extant Venetian textiles with animals and other ornament, there is plenty of evidence on which attributions can be based. In style, colour and technical characteristics these textiles no doubt resemble the fifteen textiles with figure subjects already identified, and their geographical distribution will be similar, i.e. most will be found in the German-speaking and Scandinavian lands, which Venice was geographically better placed to supply than any of her competitors; German merchants had their own depot in Venice, the Fondaco dei Tedeschi, from 1228 onwards, while at the same time they dominated the Scandinavian trade. But examples will also be found in France and possibly, as the inventories suggest, in England and Italy. The inventories offer much detailed information on the patterns of the textiles and indicate, not surprisingly, that Venice followed Byzantine traditions of design more closely than other weaving centres.[19] In Venetian as in Byzantine textiles large motifs greatly outnumbered small motifs; in textiles from other centres the reverse was true. In more than a third of the Venetian patterns described—a much higher proportion than for any centre except Byzantium—the motifs were enclosed in circles; other Venetian patterns had no such compart-

10. Half-silk; violet and yellow; church of St. Servatius, Siegburg, Venetian cloths with griffins are recorded in 1295, 1311, 1352 and 1361.

other centre; extant textiles with lions which may be attributed to Venice include half-silks from Kloster Lüne, the Rhineland, the Roden collection, and Troyes cathedral (fig. 12), a medium-weight silk from Halberstadt cathedral (fig. 11), and a group of light-weight silks in various collections.[20] Griffins occurred in more than a sixth of the Venetian patterns described, a higher proportion than for any centre except Byzantium; extant examples include half-silks at Louannec, Siegburg (fig. 10) and Stockholm.[21] Animals mentioned less frequently are deer, dolphins, leopards, winged dragons and unspecified beasts; extant examples include a medium-weight silk with leopards at Bergen and a half-silk with winged dragons at Reims.[22] Eagles,

ments, or compartments of unspecified form, or archcs, or stripes (though stripes were commoner in Spanish and Tartar textiles). The commonest colours, in Venice as elsewhere, were gold, red and white; yellow is mentioned more frequently in Venetian than in any other textiles, and violet more frequently than in any except the Byzantine; blue and green were somewhat rarer. More than half the Venetian patterns—again a much higher proportion than for any centre except Byzantium—included ferocious animals. On the basis of these observations, an extant all-silk textile of the thirteenth or early fourteen century may be attributed to Venice with fair probability, and a half-silk with great probability, if it fulfils the following conditions: (a) if it is found within the known distribution-area of Venetian textiles, especially Germany, Scandinavia and France, (b) if it is stylistically and (c) technically similar to the textiles with figure subjects, (d) if its colouring resembles theirs, or that of Venetian textiles recorded in the inventories, (e) if it has large motifs, (f) or motifs in circles, (g) especially if they are ferocious creatures or other motifs recorded in the inventory descriptions. Lions are recorded in over a third of the **60** Venetian patterns, considerably more than for any

11. Silk; red and gold; 28 × 24 in. (71 × 61 cm). Victoria and Albert Museum, 1236–1864, formerly part of a hanging at Halberstadt cathedral. Venetian cloths with lions were recorded at Rome in 1295, Perugia in 1311, and Le Puy in 1352.

2. Half-silk; pink and gold; $6\frac{3}{4} \times 6$ in. (17×15 cm). Victoria and Albert Museum, 778–1893. Acquired in Paris, this piece is probably identical with one which is said by Viollet-le-Duc, *Dictionnaire raisonné du mobilier français*, IV, 112, to come from Troyes cathedral. Venetian cloths with lions in circles were recorded at Rome in 1295 and 1361, Perugia in 1311, and Le Puy in 1352.

13. Chasuble of half-silk; yellow and gold; Skara cathedral. Venetian cloths with eagles are recorded in 1295, 1311 and 1352.

14. Half-silk; red, voilet, white, green, yellow and gold, Regensburg cathedral. A Venetian cloth with a pattern of circles and stars was recorded at Le Puy in 1352. Venetian cloths with a chequered band, and with a colour-change on the median line of the motif, as here, were recorded at Perugia in 1311.

sometimes with two heads, were the favourite birds, recorded in more textiles from Venice than from other centres, but cocks, ducks, falcons, parrots, sparrow-hawks and unspecified types also occur; extant examples with eagles include half-silks at Skara (fig. 13) and Ambazac and a medium-weight silk at Halberstadt.[23] Other motifs were leaves, vines, stars, rosettes, trees, pines or pine-cones, lilies or fleurs-de-lis, and coats-of-arms, though several of these were less common in Venetian than in Lucchese, Spanish or Tartar textiles; an extant Venetian half-silk with stars

and rosettes is at Regensburg cathedral (fig. 14).[24] The list of attributions could be extended.[25] But the present study has now achieved its aim, by expunging some unfounded assumptions from the history of medieval silk-weaving, by establishing the importance of Venice as a silk-weaving centre in the thirteenth and early fourteenth centuries, and by identifying some characteristic examples of its production.[26] On the way, a number of interesting designs, both figurative and ornamental, have been added to the corpus of Venetian medieval art.

Notes

1. Otto von Falke, *Kunstgeschichte der Seidenweberei*, 1913, II, pp. 40–45. This elaborates an idea already advanced by Julius Lessing, *Die Gewebesammlung des Königlichen Kunstgewerbemuseums*, 1900–09, text to plates 94–104.

2. On medieval silk-production in Regensburg, see Hermann Heimpel, 'Seide aus Regensburg', in *Mitteilungen des Instituts für österreichische Geschichtsforschung*, LXII, 1954, pp. 270–298.

3. For a re-statement of the case for Regensburg see Christhelm Pielen, *Die Regensburger Halbseidenstoffe* (Dissertation, 1961); I am indebted to Dr. Elfriede Heinemeyer for furnishing me with a copy of this work.

4. J. Heinrich Schmidt, 'Deutsche Seidenstoffe des Mittelalters', in *Zeitschrift des deutschen Vereins für Kunstwissenschaft*, I, 1934, pp. 95–112. E. Rank, in *Die Seide*, 1927, had suggested that nearly all the half-silks should be attributed to Cologne.

5. Manuel Gómez-Moreno, *El Panteon Real de Las Huelgas de Burgos*, 1946, pp. 60–63; Florence Lewis May, *Silk Textiles of Spain*, 1957, pp. 60, 113–117.

6. Dorothy G. Shepherd, 'The Textiles from Las Huelgas de Burgos', in *Bulletin of the Needle and Bobbin Club*, XXXV, 1951, pp. 19–22. Dorothy G. Shepherd, 'La dalmatique d'Ambazac', in *Bulletin de Liaison du Centre International d'Etude des Textiles Anciens*, No. 11, January 1960, pp. 18–24.

7. Baudekyn was a type of textile commonly including gold thread.

8. Many of the extant half-silks with figure subjects are described and illustrated by Lessing, Falke and Pielen. On the Rostock piece see also *Die Kunst- und Geschichtsdenkmäler des Grossherzogtums Mecklenburg-Schwerin*, I, 1896, p. 232. On the Leipzig piece see *Festschrift für Johannes Jahn*, 1957, p. 216, Fig. 108. The Lyon piece is illustrated by M. Dupont-Auberville, *L'ornament des tissus*, 1877, and R. Cox, *L'art de décorer les tissus*, 1900, Pl. V, No. 23. On the Södra Råda piece see A. Branting and A. Lindblom, *Medeltida Vävnader och Broderier i Sverige*, II, 1929, p. 102, Fig. 155. On the Oslo piece, see Helen Engelstad, *Messeklaer og Alterskrud*, 1941, pp. 40, 122–3, Fig. 18.
For the texts relating to Durham and St. Paul's, see Otto Lehmann-Brockhaus, *Lateinische Schriftquellen zur Kunst in England*, 1955–60, sections 1464, 1476, 2911, 2930, 2932. For the Vatican, Emile Molinier, *Inventaire du Trésor du Saint-Siège sous Boniface VIII* (1295), 1888, Nos. 992, 1437. For Anagni, *Annales archéologiques*, XVIII, 1858, pp. 26–29. For Perugia, *Regesti Clementis Papæ V. Appendices*, 1892, pp. 417, 427, 428, 432, 434, 441. For Le Puy, *Revue des sociétés savantes des départements*, 5th series, VI, 1874, pp. 114–116.

9. That the ten extant half-silks with figure subjects were woven in western Europe is evident from their style and from the Latin inscriptions which appear on several; the Greek contraction MP ΘY on the Vienna piece suggests a centre—such as Venice—where such contractions were current. The only inscribed textile assigned in the inventories to a particular centre was a Venetian cloth at Perugia (*Regesti*, p. 428).

10. For the 1189 document see Francisque-Michel, *Recherches sur le commerce, la fabrication et l'usage des étoffes de soie*, I, 1852, pp. 81–2. For that of 1247, *Calendar of Liberate Rolls, Henry III*, 1245–51, p. 123. For that of 1248, Girolamo Zanetti, *Dell'origine di alcune arti principali appresso i Viniziani*, 1758, p. 97. For that of 1265, Giovanni Monticolo, *I capitolari delle arti veneziane*, II, 1905, pp. 27–38, 589–595. For those of 1295, Lehmann-Brockhaus, *op. cit.*, section 2950 (possibly another reference to a Venetian half-silk); Francisque-Michel, *op. cit.*, II, 1854, p. 471; Molinier, *op. cit.* For that of 1296, *Revue archéologique*, IX, 1852, p. 224. For those of 1317–18, L. Douët-D'Arcq, *Comptes de L'Argenterie des Rois de France au XIVe siècle*, 1851, pp. 54, 65, and *Nouveau Recueil de Comptes de l'Argenterie des Rois de France*, 1874, p. 13. The identity of *draps d'Ache* and *di accia* was first noted by the present writer in *Bulletin de Liaison du Centre International d'Etude des Textiles Anciens*, No. 27, 1968, p. 26.

11. The Le Mans piece is illustrated by A. Ledru, *La cathédrale Saint-Julien du Mans*, 1900, pl. III. On the Berlin-Krefeld piece see Lessing, *op. cit.*, pl. 81b, and Falke, *op. cit.*, p. 35, Fig. 285. On the Bern piece, J. Stammler, *Der Paramentenschatz im Historischen Museum zu Bern*, 1895, pp. 42–3; Falke, *op. cit.*, p. 42. On the London piece, the Museum's *Catalogue of Early Medieval Woven Fabrics*, 1925, No. 1062, pl. XXIV, and Falke, in *Pantheon*,

VIII, 1931, p. 371. On the Regensburg hanging, Jakob, in *Zeitschrift fur christliche Kunst*, I, 1888, pp. 425–434; Falke, *Kunstgeschichte der Seidenweberei*, II, pp. 40–41, 44, Fig. 303; E. Rank, in *Die Kunstseide*, XI, 1929, pp. 255–260; Sigrid Flamand Christensen in *Das Münster*, III, 1950, pp. 77–83. All these textiles, like the half-silks, are weft-faced compound twills; the lightweight pieces have a flimsy texture, without gold thread; the medium-weight examples include gold thread and the texture is denser (though not so stiff and heavy as that of the half-silks).

I am grateful to Dr. Elfriede Heineimeyer for bringing to my notice an unpublished silk depicting the Virgin and Child, in a German collection; it is probably Venetian, but rather later than the silks discussed here.

12. On trade from Venice to Regensburg, see Heimpel, *op. cit.*, and H. Simonsfeld, *Der Fondaco dei Tedeschi in Venedig*, 1887.

13. *Regesti Clementis Papæ V. Appendices*, 1892, p. 428. It may be noted in passing that the original dimensions of the Regensburg hanging are estimated to have been about 125 × 265 cm, quite close to the standard sizes of Venetian textiles as laid down in the regulations of 1265. There is, of course, no evidence that any German centre produced patterned silks in anything like this size.

14. Christensen, *op. cit.*, p. 81. This feature does, however, occur in Venetian painting, e.g. the polyptych of Paolo Veneziano in the Accademia, Venice, Rodolfo Pallucchini, *La pittura veneziana del Trecento*, 1964, Fig. 146.

15. I am indepted to Professor Pignatti for these illustrations. Cf. also Palluchini, *op. cit.*, Figs. 16, 192, 210, 243, etc.

16. For the Vatican, see Molinier, *op. cit.*, Nos. 824, 826, 934, 961, 975, 990, 1127, 1438, 1440. For Perugia, *Regesti Clementis Papæ V. Appendices*, 1892, pp. 418, 422, 428, 430–432, 435, 436, 438, 442. For Exeter, George Oliver, *Lives of the Bishops of Exeter*, 1861, pp. 313, 316. For Amiens, *Mémoires de la société des antiquaires de Picardie*, 1st Series, x, 1850, p. 271. For Le Puy, *Revue des sociétés savantes des départements*, 5th Series, VI, 1874, pp. 114–116. For St. Peter's, E. Müntz and A. L. Frothingham, *Il tesoro della basilica di S. Pietro in Vaticano*, 1883, pp. 25–29, 37.

17. A. Mancini, U. Dorini and E. Lazzareschi, *Lo Statuto della Corte dei Mercanti di Lucca del MCCCLXXVI*, 1927, p. 141. Cloths 'in the likeness of cloths of Venice' were being woven in Lucca in 1308; see *Archivio storico italiano*, 1st Series, x, 1847, 'Documenti', p. 65. In 1295 the well informed clerks of the Vatican were occasionally unable to distinguish Lucchese from Venetian cloths (Nos. 1016, 1438).

18. See *Regesti Clementis Papæ V. Appendices*, 1892, pp. 429, 441. Even if half-silks found in Spain are proved to be Spanish, there is no evidence that Spanish half-silks were extensively exported; the documents suggest that, in the later thirteenth and early fourteenth century, exports of silk textiles from Spain were slight compared with those from Venice and Lucca.

19. This and the following observations are based on an analysis of the descriptions, in the inventories already cited, of about thirty Byzantine and Spanish textiles, nearly sixty Venetian textiles, and about one hundred and twenty Lucchese and Tartar textiles; available descriptions of Genoese textiles are unfortunately too few for statistical comparison.

20. For the half-silks and the medium-weight silk see Falke, *op. cit.*, Figs. 310–312, 269. For the lightweight silks, Brussels, Musées Royaux du Cinquantenaire, *Catalogue d'étoffes*, 1927, No. 15; E. A. Stueckelberg, *Unveröffentlichte Walliser Gewebefunde*, 1923, 1924, Pl. 30, and in *Anzeiger für schweizerische Altertumskunde*, XXVI, 1924, p. 106; further examples in Liège and London. Cloths of Venice with lions, generally in circles, are recorded in Rome (1295, 1361), Perugia (1311) and Le Puy (1352); the combination of circles, lions and griffins, as in the Kloster Lüne example, is recorded only in Venetian and Byzantine textiles (Perugia, p. 442).

21. Falke, *op. cit.*, Figs. 259, 308; A. Branting and A. Lindblom, *Medeltida Vävnader och Broderier i Sverige*, II, 1929, Pl. 218. Cloths of Venice with griffins, sometimes in circles, are recorded in Rome (1295, 1361), Perugia and Le Puy.

22. For the Bergen example see Falke, *op. cit.*, Fig. 267, and Helen Engelstad, *Messeklaer og Alterskrud*, 1941, pp. 37, 121–2, Fig. 21; the only recorded textile with a pattern of circles and leopards, as here, is a cloth of Venice (Le Puy). For the piece on the binding of Reims MS. 230, see M. Sartor, *Les tapisseries, toiles peintes et broderies de Reims*, 1912, p. 17, Fig. 3; also Falke, *op. cit.*, p. 37, and H. Schmidt, in *Burlington Magazine*, LVII, 1930, pp. 184–194; the only recorded textile with winged dragons is a Venetian cloth (Perugia, p. 436).

23. Branting and Lindblom, *op. cit.*, Pl. 217; Dorothy G. Shepherd, 'La dalmatique d'Ambazac', in *Bulletin de Liaison du Centre International d'Etude des Textiles Anciens*, No. 11, January 1960, pp. 11–29; Falke, *op. cit.*, Figs. 296, 309. Cloths of Venice with eagles, sometimes with two heads, are recorded in Rome (1295), Perugia and Le Puy. The orphreys of the Skara chasuble, and those of the Stockholm chasuble with griffins, are probably the ornamental bands which, according to the inventories, were woven at the ends of textiles from most centres; the only record of such a band being cut off for use as an orphrey relates to a Venetian piece (Rome, 1295, no. 1334).

24. Falke, *op. cit.*, Fig. 315; Sigrid and Theodor Müller, 'Ein frühes gotisches Reliquiar im Regensburger Domschatz' in *Kunstgeschichtliche Studien für Hans Kauffman*, 1956, pp. 115–6, Fig. 4. Patterns of circles and stars, as here, are recorded only in cloths of Venice (at Le Puy) and Lucca; two features of this piece—the change of colour on the median line of the motif, and the chequered band at the end—are recorded only in Venetian cloths (Perugia, pp. 434, 442).

25. I am grateful to Fräulein Mechthild Lemberg for bringing to my notice two important unpublished Venetian half-silks with animal patterns, in a German collection.

26. Venice also produced fine gold embroideries in the early fourteenth century; for recent identifications of this work, see Grgo Gamulin, 'Alcune proposte per Maestro Paolo', in *Emporium*, CXL, 1964, pp. 147–155, and Donald King, 'A Venetian embroidered altar frontal', in *Victoria and Albert Museum Bulletin*, I, October 1965, pp. 14–25.

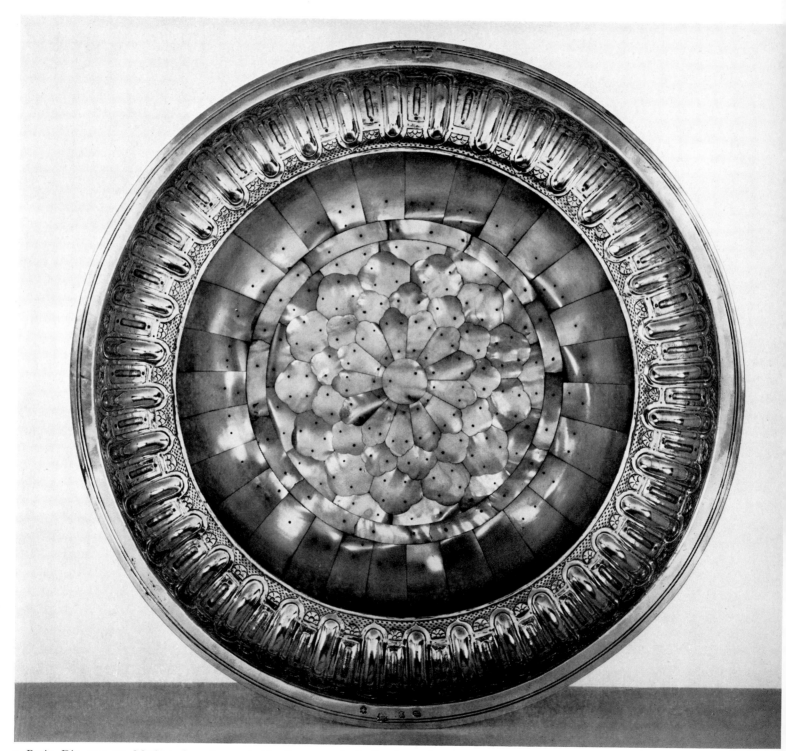

1. Basin. Dia. 33·5 cm. Mother-of-pearl mounted in silver, parcel-gilt. London, 1621. Maker's mark, a slipped trefoil in a shaped shield. Victoria and Albert Museum. *Bequeathed by Mrs. David Gubbay.* M. 17–1968.

Master Goldsmith

SHIRLEY BURY

The munificent bequest made by Mrs. David Gubbay to the Museum in 1968 includes a fine mother-of-pearl basin (fig. 1 and cover) mounted in silver, parcel-gilt. It no doubt once had a matching ewer. The piece bears the London hall-marked for 1621 and the maker's mark of a slipped trefoil in a shaped shield.[1] The goldsmith who used this mark has not been identified, but the new acquisition brings the number of his works in the museum to three. From their design and treatment we can infer something of the maker's activities. The other two pieces are unmarked except for the slipped trefoil. Like the basin, they consist of a decorative material set in silver. It is clear, therefore, that our goldsmith specialised in providing mountings for rare or prized materials. His workshop was perhaps connected with that of an earlier goldsmith working, apparently, from the mid fifteen-seventies, whose mark was three trefoils in a trefoil.[2] This earlier maker had a similar speciality; his workshop was responsible for several outstanding pieces incorporating exotic materials. Among the finest are the Gibbon Salt of 1576, made of rock-crystal mounted in silver-gilt, which belongs to the Goldsmiths' Company,[3] and a ewer and basin of agate, similarly mounted and hall-marked for 1579, in the possession of the Duke of Rutland.[4] We shall presently consider a piece bearing a third trefoil mark, which though entirely of silver bears some relation to the Museum group.

For present purposes, we may take the more important of the first two articles by our goldsmith. The Dyneley Casket (fig. 2) was purchased in March 1865 on the recommendation of J. C. Robinson[5] from a dealer who had successfully bid for it a few weeks earlier at the sale of antiquities from Bramhope Manor, the seat of Richard Dyneley.[6] The casket was described in the sale catalogue as "Circular Box and Cover of Alabaster, mounted with bands and rims of silver gilt . . . fitted with four small glass scent-bottles [the latter are a later addition]. *A curious example of English work of the time of Henry VIII.; and said to have been in the Dyneley family from that period.*"[7] The Museum accepted this dating until the early years of this century. The first revision, when the date of the casket was thought to be about 1610, was reflected in the second edition of Sir Charles Jackson's *English Goldsmiths and their Marks*, which appeared in 1921. Jackson illustrates a trefoil mark for 1610, citing the Dyneley Casket as his authority.[8] It has since transpired that the trefoil mark itself was wrongly represented by Jackson as having a short vertical stalk instead of the correct sharp-angled slip. The real mark

2. The Dyneley Casket. Height 18·4 cm. Alabaster mounted in silver-gilt. Maker's mark, a slipped trefoil in a shaped shield. About 1620. Victoria and Albert Museum, 24–1865.

appears in both the first and second editions of Jackson's work under the year 1623, a mounted ostrich egg cup then in the possession of Lord Swaythling being cited in this instance.[9] The Dyneley Casket, and a tankard of serpentine mounted in silver by the same maker which was acquired under the Bryan Bequest in 1912[10] have therefore been thought to date from about 1620.

There is no doubt that, for 1620, both the casket and the tankard are somewhat old-fashioned, even judged by the conservative standards of the early seventeenth century. The casket stands, for instance, on spherical ball and claw feet of a type frequently to be met with in Elizabethan plate. The Museum's Mostyn Salt of 1586 has feet of this kind.[11] The main decorative feature of the casket, which recurs on a band encircling the body of the tankard, is a repeating stamped pattern of Tudor roses and ovolos, a combination which again was popular in England during the sixteenth century. The ornament is used most generously on the Dyneley Casket, running round the rim and the base of the body and forming the central panel of the vertical straps. As far as can be judged, for the dimensions of the stamp are exactly the same, the same ornament was used on the elaborate finial of a large silver-gilt cup and **65**

3. Detail from a coco-nut cup with cover. Height 31·75 cm. The mounts are of silver. Amsterdam mark for 1590. Victoria and Albert Museum, *Bernal Collection*. 2117–1855.

cover at St. John's College, Cambridge.[12] Known as the Booth Cup, as it was probably given to the College by Robert Booth, Senior Bursar from 1558–9, it is fully hall-marked for 1616. The maker's mark is a trefoil in an irregular oval.[13] While we cannot of course assume a direct connection between the makers using the two marks on the grounds of a single stamp in common, as it may have been supplied by a specialist die-cutter, it may be worth noting that, from 1697–8, the opening date of the earliest surviving register of marks at Goldsmiths' Hall, we have evidence of goldsmiths entering several marks during their working life-time. In 1697 new marks were required by law, but during the eighteenth century and afterwards, when no legal compulsion is discernible, many goldsmiths entered a succession of marks with differing shields. It is therefore not inconceivable that the two seventeenth century single trefoil marks were registered by the same maker. It has long been recognized that the maker or makers using the single trefoil marks were likely to have been of foreign origin. E. Alfred Jones, in discussing the Booth Cup, suggested a German origin for its maker.[14] John Hayward has more recently returned to the subject of the Booth Cup in one of his articles in the *Connoisseur*, finding convincing internal evidence in its design to attribute it to a Dutch goldsmith working in London.[15] His argument is based partly on the bowl of the cup, which has a complex curve at its base unlike anything in English silver, although it can be paralleled in Dutch plate of some fifteen to twenty years earlier, and partly also on the splendid classical figures which decorate it. As he points out, Dutch silversmiths such as Adam and Paul van Vianen were outstanding practitioners of this type of ornament and had many able followers amongst their countrymen. Turning to the Gubbay dish, it is perhaps relevant that, making due allowance for a difference in scale, we can again find striking parallels between the treatment of the ovolo border and the decoration of a Dutch cup in the Museum collections bearing the Amsterdam mark for 1590.[16] The cup, of coco-nut mounted in silver, has a calyx (fig. 3) which exactly reproduces in miniature both the ovolo motifs and the stippled work spanning the grounds behind their upper segments. These motifs found their way into England well before the end of the century: the Great Seal Cup of Adam Loftus, now in the Ulster Museum, Belfast, was made in London in 1592–93 by the maker HL conjoined.[17]

66 We may perhaps end by postulating that our goldsmith

was a Dutchman, influenced like the rest of his country-men by German designers, who came to England during the second half of the sixteenth century[18] and stayed working here at least until the sixteen-twenties. If this were so, we can begin to understand the conser-vative nature of his design which, formed in his youth, changed only to the extent of incorporating a few motifs fashionable in his adopted country.

Notes

1. Sir Charles Jackson, *English Goldsmiths and their Marks*, 2nd. ed., 1921, p. 116.
2. *ibid.*, p. 103.
3. J. C. Carrington & G. R. Hughes, *The Plate of the Worshipful Company of Goldsmiths*, 1926, p. 37, pl. 17.
4. Sir Charles Jackson, *An Illustrated History of English Plate*, London, 1911, I, pp. 193, 194 (*ill.*).
5. J. C. Robinson's report to the Science and Art Department is dated February 17, 1865.
6. E. Walford, *The County Families of the United Kingdom*, 1875, p. 312. Richard Dyneley (1820–61) of Bramhope Manor, Otley, Yorkshire, was the son of Thomas Chamberlain of the same county. He succeeded to his uncle's estates in 1861, when he assumed the name of Dyneley by Royal licence.
7. *Catalogue of the Valuable Collection of Antiques . . . removed from Bramhope Manor*. Messrs. Christie, Manson & Woods, February 6–8, 1865. The casket was sold on February 7 (lot no. 293).
8. Jackson, *English Goldsmiths*, p. 112.
9. *ibid.*, p. 116. The cup is illustrated in the same author's *Illustrated History*, I, p. 212 (*ill.*).
10. C. C. Oman, *English Silversmiths' Work* (H.M. Stationery Office), 1965, pl. 44.
11. *ibid.*, pl. 27.
12. E. A. Jones, *The Old Plate of the Cambridge Colleges*, 1910, pl. LXXXIV.
13. Jackson, *English Goldsmiths*, p. 114.
14. E. A. Jones, *op. cit.*, p. XVII.
15. J. F. Hayward, 'The Mannerist Goldsmiths: 4. England, Part III', in the *Connoisseur*, CLXIV, 1967, p. 25.
16. *The Golden Age of Dutch Silver* (Victoria and Albert Museum, Small Picture Book No. 29), 1953, pl. 1.
17. *Museums Journal*, LX, March 1961, pp 320–21.
18. Hayward, *op. cit.*, p. 25.

Turner at East Cowes Castle

GRAHAM REYNOLDS

WHATEVER his contemporary reputation may have been as an architect, John Nash was certainly renowned in his own times for the lavish hospitality he dispensed at his neo-gothic home in the Isle of Wight, East Cowes Castle. He astonished local butchers by the amount of provisions he ordered for a prospective visit of his most important patron, the Prince Regent, in 1817.[1] Four years later Joseph Farington, in the month before he died, spent a fortnight at the Castle as the result of a pressing invitation from Mr. and Mrs. Nash. On this occasion he heard the story of Nash's life and was also regaled with such titbits of gossip as that, when Benjamin West had been a visitor, he "was not sufficiently abstemious, and in his diet and in drinking wine he perhaps indulged too much".[2]

It was no doubt as a result of a similarly friendly and pressing invitation that J. M. W. Turner found himself at East Cowes Castle in 1827. It is not known how he came to be asked, but it is certain that he stayed for longer than he had originally intended. This is shown by the existence of three letters which Turner wrote to his father during the stay.[3] In one of these he asks for "more light Trouzers" and other linen. He also asked his father to have two canvases measuring six feet by four feet prepared and sent to him at the Castle. While the exact extent of his visit is unknown, Turner is said to have arrived towards the end of July and certainly did not leave until after the second week in September. His host commissioned him to paint two pictures of the Regatta. Although the Royal Yacht Club[4] had been founded at Cowes in 1812, this was only the second year races were held. Turner evidently had a painting room in the Castle put at his disposal, and may have completed the pictures there; in any case he made extremely thorough preparations for their completion. Both were exhibited the following year at the Royal Academy under the titles "East Cowes Castle, the seat of J. Nash, Esq.; the Regatta beating to windward" (Collection of Mr. and Mrs. N. H. Noyes, Indianapolis; (fig. 1) and "East Cowes Castle, the seat of J. Nash, Esq.; the Regatta starting for their moorings" (Victoria and Albert Museum, F.A. 210; Colour Plate IIIa). In each of the paintings East Cowes Castle itself is to be seen on the hill above the River Medina, on which the Regatta was held during the first week in August. It is possible to trace in considerable detail the method by which Turner set to work to paint these sea-pieces.

Not only did he, as was his normal custom, make copious notes in his books of the scene; what was really unusual about his approach to the commission for Nash's paintings was that he set out to make a number of open-air sketches from the water's edge, or from a boat on the water, of the shipping in the river. This use of oil painting in front of the motif is rarely encountered in the build-up of Turner's mature canvases. One of his other main phases of open-air oil sketching is in fact assigned to the following year, when he was in Rome; others concern his early work on the Thames, in about 1807 and the Devonshire oil sketches of 1813.[5]

The disposition of the open-air sketches on his canvases was improvised. He divided up one of the six by four canvases sent to him by his father into two canvases, each measuring three feet by four feet. On one of these he painted five sketches and on the other, four sketches. These were not divided and stretched as individual pictures until 1906, and are now all in the Tate Gallery.[6] Turner spread his ideas for both his big pictures over each of these two fairly small, unstretched canvases. Of the sketches most closely related to the painting in the Victoria and Albert Museum in that they show the yachts at their moorings at the beginning of the Regatta, "A Regatta at Cowes" (fig. 2) (No. 1997) and "Shipping at Cowes I" (No. 1998) (fig. 3) are from one of the canvases, and "Shipping at Cowes II" (No. 2000) (fig. 4) from the other. Of these latter two have more the appearance of studies from nature and "A Regatta at Cowes," though closer to the final version, appears to have been worked up in Turner's painting-room at the Castle, to judge by the elaborate pains which he has taken to people the foreground with groups of spectators gay with summer dresses and sun shades. All three sketches share with the exhibited picture the Claudean group of trees on the right hand side; in two of them the Club House, West Cowes Castle, is to be seen in the immediate right foreground, and in each Turner has chosen his favourite view point, looking into the morning sun rising over the mouth of the estuary.

The oil studies of yachts actually under way in the race are even more closely linked to the exhibited version of the second painting, "East Cowes Castle; the Regatta beating to windward". Of these "Yacht Racing in the Solent I" (No. 1993) and "Yacht Racing in the Solent III" (No. 1995) were on one of the unstretched

67

1. EAST COWES CASTLE, THE SEAT OF J. NASH, ESQ.; THE REGATTA BEATING TO WINDWARD. Oil on canvas, $36\frac{1}{4} \times 48$ in. ($92 \cdot 1 \times 121 \cdot 9$ cm). Mr. and Mrs. Nicholas H. Noyes, Indianapolis.

2. A REGATTA AT COWES. Oil on canvas, 18×24 in. ($45 \cdot 7 \times 61$ cm). Tate Gallery, No. 1997.

IIIa. EAST COWES CASTLE, THE SEAT OF J. NASH, ESQ.; THE REGATTA STARTING FOR THEIR MOORINGS. Oil on canvas, $36 \times 48\frac{1}{2}$ in. $(91 \cdot 4 \times 123 \cdot 2$ cm$)$. Victoria and Albert Museum, F.A. 210.

IIIb. LIFE-BOAT AND MANBY APPARATUS GOING OFF TO A STRANDED VESSEL MAKING SIGNAL (BLUE LIGHTS) OF DISTRESS. Oil on canvas, 36×48 in. $(91 \cdot 4 \times 121 \cdot 9$ cm$)$. Victoria and Albert Museum, F.A. 211.

3. SHIPPING AT COWES I. Oil on canvas $18\frac{1}{2} \times 24\frac{1}{2}$ in. $(47 \times 62 \cdot 2$ cm). Tate Gallery, No. 1998.

4. SHIPPING AT COWES II. Oil on canvas, $17\frac{1}{2} \times 29$ in. $(44 \cdot 5 \times 73 \cdot 6$ cm). Tate Gallery, No. 2000.

5. BETWEEN DECKS. Oil on canvas, 12½ × 19 in. (31·7 × 48·2 cm). Tate Gallery, No. 1996.

canvases and "Yacht Racing in the Solent II" (No. 1994)[7] on the other. In the latter two a yacht in the foreground is prominent, as it is in the exhibited picture. These two sketches seem to have been painted with remarkable facility with only a close interval of time between, since the main difference is that in "Yacht Racing in the Solent III" the left hand group of yachts are no longer beating to windward but have changed tack. The chief contribution that "Yacht Racing in the Solent No. I" makes is in including the fully exposed mass of the guard-ship, which is seen unrigged in the centre of the exhibited composition.

Turner filled up the remaining space on these two canvases with sketches which he did not use for more ambitious pictures. "Shipping off a Headland"[8] shows an unrigged ship against East Cowes headland; "Study of Sea and Sky" is one of those almost abstract sea-pieces, with a minimal amount of coast visible at the junction of sea and coast, which have striking similarities to the sea-pieces which Constable was painting at Brighton almost at the same time, during the years 1824–8, and of which the tendency is to look forward towards later developments in painting rather than back into the past. The most unusual of the whole of this series of oil sketches is the interior "Between Decks" (No. 1996) (fig. 5), showing a jolly group of

sailors and their girl-friends grouped around a gun-port on the Mess deck of a man-of-war. All the sketches are characterised by a freshness of execution and a confidence of handling which make it all the more remarkable that Turner was so little addicted to painting such immediate impressions out of doors.

This particularly resolute intention to fix the moving image of the yachts in oil went hand in hand with extensive pencil sketching of the summary sort which was usually adequate to stimulate Turner's imagination. In the Print Room at the British Museum are two sketch books, and two groups of drawings on grey paper, which help to give further insight into his stay at East Cowes Castle.

One of the sketch-books (the "Isle of Wight" sketch-book, No. CCXXVII) was also used in Portsmouth and at London Bridge. Whilst it contains scenes on the Island, it has little of direct relevance to these paintings. It was in the other sketch-book ("Windsor and Cowes, Isle of Wight", sketch-book, No. CCXXVI) that Turner recorded many details which he might need for the finished oils. There are a few extraneous subjects but these, views of Windsor and Eton, are in harmony with the Gothic outline of Nash's own architecture. The remainder of the sixty-six leaves contain a great number of studies of yachts sailing, groups of figures on search for the aspect of ships under sail scribbled down with instantaneous haste. Ruskin characteristically described these as "rubbish" but few survivals from an artist's studio could give a more convincing illustration of the necessity he felt under to be exactly aware of the constantly changing aspects of objects in motion, and the labour he put into perfecting his knowledge of his subject-matter.

The other parcel of drawings on grey paper ("East Cowes Castle", No. CCXXVII (a)) reveals how much Turner was captivated by the Castle and its grounds. He was usually content with a quick impression of a place; on this visit he drew the fabric of the house from every aspect, frequently at night. Its recreation of the romance of the medieval past worked so powerfully on his mind that he peopled some of the drawings with lightly sketched-in figures of lovers embracing.[9] Other drawings are strictly records of the house and its

6. Sheet of studies of a yacht under sail. Pencil, $4\frac{3}{8} \times 7\frac{1}{2}$ in. ($11 \cdot 1 \times 19 \cdot 1$ cm). British Museum CCXXVI, p. 29a.

the shore, and of the profile of East Cowes Castle beyond the shipping. There are a few drawings of boat-loads of spectators, and of a buoy and an anchor. He has also noted on the back page of the book a list of the yachts taking part, with a note of their owners and their racing colours; these included the famous *Arrow* raced by Joseph Weld.

Some of these leaves have numerous profiles of yachts under sail, in the ungainly graphic shorthand which was sufficient for his own eyes (fig. 6). The parcel of forty-four sheets of grey paper ("Yachts etc. at Cowes," No. CCXXVIII) continues, in black and white chalk, this

7. EAST COWES CASTLE. Pen and white chalk on blue paper, $5\frac{1}{2} \times 7\frac{1}{2}$ in. ($13 \cdot 9 \times 19 \cdot 1$ cm). British Museum CCXXVIIA, 35.

8. EAST COWES CASTLE, LIGHTED INTERIOR. Body colour, $5\frac{1}{2} \times 7\frac{1}{2}$ in. ($13\cdot9 \times 19\cdot1$ cm). British Museum, CCXXVIIA, 14.

garden (fig. 7), and in yet others he anticipates the intimacy of his better-known Petworth scenes with views of the lights streaming from the Castle (fig. 8) and of the interior, with his host probably amongst the figures (fig. 9). Turner was a much travelled, hard-working man; in these revealing drawings we can sense what a refreshment it was to him to be part of a homely, domestic environment.

This haunting, enticing atmosphere of the recreated

9. EAST COWES CASTLE; THE DRAWING ROOM. Pen and white chalk on blue paper, $5\frac{1}{2} \times 7\frac{1}{2}$ in. ($13\cdot9 \times 19\cdot1$ cm). British Museum CCXXVIIA, 48.

10. BOCCACCIO RELATING THE TALE OF THE BIRDCAGE. Oil on canvas, 48×36 in. ($12\cdot9 \times 91\cdot4$ cm). Tate Gallery, No. 507.

past continued in his mind. At the Royal Academy exhibition, 1828, he showed with the two Regatta pictures a work entitled "Boccaccio relating the tale of the Birdcage" (fig. 10). It was a *fête champêtre* in which Turner entered into competition with Stothard, who had recently illustrated the Decameron and who himself had painted similar scenes in emulation of Watteau. The composition Turner chose is an elaboration of the idylls he had drawn on grey paper, and the form of the castle tower appears white and challenging in the distance. Here, as has been pointed out,[10] he is reverting to the eighteenth century theory that white can be used for a distant object. He returned to the theory in 1831 with a painting of an artist in his studio significantly called: "Watteau study by Fresnoy's rules", with the quotation from Du Fresnoy:

"White when it shines with unstained lustre clear,
    May bear an object back or bring it near",
in this case using white as a foreground colour. Perhaps more surprisingly he provided a paraphrase of Nash's towers and battlements as the Babylonian palace in the distance of his painting of "Shadrach, Meshach and

11. SHADRACH, MESHACH AND ABEDNEGO COMING FORTH FROM THE
BURNING FIERY FURNACE. Oil on panel, $36\frac{1}{2} \times 27\frac{1}{2}$ in. ($90 \cdot 2 \times 69 \cdot 8$ cm).
Tate Gallery, No. 517.

Abednego coming forth from the Burning Fiery Furnace", exhibited in 1832 (fig. 11).

But the Regatta pictures rely on none of this literary reference for their effect and East Cowes Castle plays a subordinate role in them. While the pendant, showing the race in progress, is a spirited action piece enlivened by the same fresh breeze that he had encountered when making his oil sketch, the Museum's scene of the preliminaries is a carefully worked out classical design into which Turner has introduced all his knowledge of the movement of water and of colour seen through lightly tinted mist. To his long-acquired facility he has added from the very substantial body of observation he recorded while at the Castle. The lively crowds on the shore, the boat-loads of spectators, the understanding with which the yachts are painted, depend throughout on truth in the presentation. The colour has that greater range which his palette underwent after his first visit to Italy in 1819, but lacks the garish dependence on yellows which makes some pictures of the same epoch, such as the "Cologne" in the Frick Collection, rather disturbing. Here the blues,

reds and greens are harmonised in a golden tone which is as true a tribute to Watteau as a deliberate pastiche such as "Boccaccio relating the Tale of the Birdcage".

This classic handling is not matched by an equal felicity in the conservation of the canvas. It is a work painted at a time when Turner was indulging in the perilous practice of "preparing his pictures with a kind of tempera".[11] Eastlake, who witnessed this procedure in Rome in 1828, comments that before the surface was varnished the pictures were not waterproof. Turner himself in one of his letters to his father from the Isle of Wight stated of another of his pictures, the "Cologne", "You must not by any means wet it, for all the Colour will come off . . . it must not be touched with Water or Varnish (only wiped with a silk handkerchief)till I return". Probably as a result of this method, "Starting for its moorings" has long been noted for the tendency of the oil to flake from the ground. The danger is increased by Turner's yielding to his fondness for putting the sun and its reflection frontally in his pictures, and adding layers of paint to increase the brightness of these sources of light. In fact, when the late Horace Buttery treated it in 1939 he described it as "a permanently ailing picture".[12] Since then, however, only a small amount of local attention has been needed.

The circumstances under which John Nash bought his third and last oil painting by Turner, the scene of a shipwreck off the coast at Yarmouth,[13] entitled "Life-boat and Manby apparatus going off to a stranded vessel making signal (blue lights) of distress" (Victoria and Albert Museum, F.A. 211; Colour Plate IIIb), are not exactly known. There appears to have been no second visit to East Cowes. Burnet in 1852 stated that it was painted for Nash, and Thornbury (1861) and Wornum (1862) make the same comment. There seems to be no earlier confirmation, and it is just possible that Nash bought it from the walls of the Royal Academy Exhibition in 1831, when it was shown as No. 73. Clearly rumours about its ownership, not altogether accurate, were circulating during the summer; Whitley quotes a letter from Westmacott saying "I think Soane bought it".[14]

That Turner should in this year have exhibited a picture with such a theme and title is an instance of his acute awareness of what was going on in the world, and of his sense of occasion. George William Manby, the inventor of the life-saving apparatus represented, had

12. SCENES ON THE SHORES AT YARMOUTH. Pencil, 4½ × 7½ in. (11·4 × 19·1 cm). British Museum, CCIX, p. 26a.

been barrack-master at Yarmouth since 1803, and it was witnessing a wreck there in 1807 which led him to develop his project. In 1831 his services to this and other forms of life-saving were recognised by his election as F.R.S. Accordingly Turner's theme was strictly topical. It should be noted that Turner did not give the location Yarmouth in his title. This identification of the spot had been made by the time the painting was sold from Nash's collection, and there seems no reason to doubt it. Turner first saw Yarmouth from the distance when he passed the coasts of Suffok and Norfolk on his way to witness George IV's visit to Scotland in 1822. He used a sketchbook (No. CC in the British Museum) on the voyage, but this only contains views of the shore from the coaster. His visit in 1824 is recorded in the "Norfolk, Suffolk and Essex" sketchbook (No. CCIX in the British Museum). This contains a number of slight sketches of the town and its shores (fig. 12). Nelson's monument appealed to him as a symbol of the place, and figures prominently in the engraving "Great Yarmouth" published in 1829 in "Picturesque Views in England and Wales". In a parcel of drawings in the British Museum (No. CCLXII) are some slight designs which have been associated with Yarmouth; in one (CCLXII, 10) is an indication of the old pier and of shipping reflected in the sands, which resembles FA 211. A painting in the Tate Gallery, No. 2065 "A Ship Aground", has been said to be "like a view of the 'Stranded Vessel off Yarmouth' (Sheepshanks Collection), seen from the other side of the pier",[15] but the resemblance is general rather than specific. More closely relevant is one of those remarkable water-colour sketches, called by Finberg "Colour Beginnings", in which Turner abandoned all reference to detail and isolated the colour structure of a scene. This work (CCCLXIV, 134: fig. 13) is more probably a design for the Sheepshanks picture than a memory sketch after it. In general the topographical indications of the picture are less precise than in those commissioned at East Cowes. The main identifiable ingredient is the old pier; the remainder is shore and sea. But the content was full of emotional significance for Turner. Themes of shipwreck figure prominently in British painting of the eighteenth and nineteenth centuries.[16] Turner himself had a natural affinity for the sea. He had sketched a storm off Dover around 1793, and made his first success in oils with a stormy seascape in 1796. G. D. Leslie described him as having the "indescribable charm of the sailor", and he reverted to nautical themes throughout his life. These were usually of tempest and disaster, in keeping with the gloomy forebodings of his mind. He reached an early peak of expressiveness in 1810 in the "Wreck of a Transport Ship" (Fundaçao Calouste Gulbenkian, Lisbon) and amidst his late paintings no work is more terrible than the "Slavers throwing overboard the dead and dying" of 1840 (Museum of Fine Arts, Boston). The "Lifeboat and Manby apparatus" is concerned with acute danger rather than realised disaster, though the violence of the on-shore sea is fully expressed. The hope of rescue is reflected in the beautifully handled contrast of weather, the black storm cloud over the ship, the sun breaking through to illumine with its irony the safety of the beach, where the watchers stand.

The full content of the painting might easily be missed without its original title. The Manby apparatus is a mortar whose firing has given rise to the puff of smoke in the middle distance on the right hand side of the painting. It has projected a stone to which a rope is fixed; this is seen just entering the black cloud above the wrecked ship. The vertical flares rising from the vessel are the blue lights of distress also referred to in the title. It was these blue lights which Turner made a main feature of the later "Rockets and blue lights (close at hand) to warn steam-boats of shoal water" (1840, now in the Sterling and Francine Clark Art Institute, Williamstown; fig. 14), in which the development of his sense of space and growing preference for convoluted curves is apparent. In the Sheepshanks picture one lifeboat is already approaching the ship and a second is being launched from near the mortar. The decorum of

13. FIRING ROCKETS AT YARMOUTH. Water-colour, 8¾ × 11¼ in. (22·2 × 28·6 cm). British Museum, CCLXIV, 134.

the painting was recognised by many contemporaries who could not understand Turner's bolder experiments. In the letter quoted above Westmacott said of his seven exhibits in 1831, "Only one was very mad—a Medea (Tate Gallery No. 513) raving in the midst of her bedevilments and incantations. You can conceive how Turner would out-Herod Herod in such matters. He had one very clever smaller work of a vessel in distress, in the distance blue lights, etc." Doubtless Nash and later Sheepshanks echoed this sense of the acceptability of Turner's vision in this case.

John Nash died in 1835. He was believed to be possessed of a vast fortune, but this was discovered to have disappeared, no one knows how.[17] Accordingly his collection was auctioned by Christie's on July 11, 1835, the sale "consisting of the two splendid and most interesting Pictures of the Cowes Regatta: and a third of the Blue Lights, by J. M. W. Turner, R.A.; a few Cabinet Specimens of West; and capital copies of celebrated Italian Pictures by Evans". There were

nineteen lots, removed from East Cowes Castle, five being copies by Evans after Raphael, Guercino etc. Lot 76, first described as a copy by Evans of Titian's Venus was corrected to "By West". There were four other modern copies of the Old Masters, four paintings by West and two attributed to De Witt and G. Dow. The copy of the priced catalogue in the National Gallery shows that all the works fetched low prices except the three Turners, which concluded the sale and were bought by Tiffin. Of these Lot 87, the "Regatta starting for their Moorings" fetched £283 10s. Lot 88, the "Regatta beating to windward" fetched £199 10s. and Lot 89, the "Life-boat and Manby apparatus" fetched £262 10s.

Tiffin frequently acted for Sheepshanks. Whether or not he was buying on commission on this occasion, Lots 87 and 89, the two most expensive, went direct into his collection.

The names of these paintings have undergone considerable modification, indeed degeneration, since they

14. ROCKETS AND BLUE LIGHTS (CLOSE AT HAND) TO WARN STEAMBOATS OF SHOAL WATER. Oil on canvas, 35×48 in. (88·9×121·9 cm). Sterling and Francine Clark Art Institute, Williamstown, Mass.

were first exhibited. No. 210 was called by Turner "East Cowes Castle, the seat of J. Nash, Esq.; the Regatta starting for their moorings". In Nash's sale it was described thus: "View of Cowes Harbour looking up the Medina, with East Cowes Castle seen on the left, and yachts preparing for the regatta, smaller boats and numerous figures—with a splendid effect of mid-day sun; a *magnificent specimen of the great artist*." In the first printed Sheepshanks list (1850) it was called: "Cowes, with Royal Yacht squadron." It was till recently labelled "East Cowes Castle, Isle of Wight. The regatta, with the Royal Yacht Squadron parting from its moorings." No. 211 was exhibited as "Life-boat and Manby apparatus going off to a stranded vessel making signal (blue lights) of distress". In Nash's sale it was described by the auctioneer thus: "Blue Lights off Yarmouth; a grand composition, painted with admirable effect." In the first Sheepshanks list it was "Vessel in distress off Yarmouth" and was till recently so labelled.

While in the former instance the change of action from "starting for" to "parting from" the moorings was comparatively venial, in the latter case the suppression of all reference to the Manby apparatus robs the picture of a great part of its significance. How easy it is to overlook this key to Turner's intentions is shown by the fact that there is no reference to the rescue apparatus in the long descriptive note which followed the title in the Museum catalogues from 1859 till 1907, and that R. Brandard, the engraver for the Turner Gallery failed to express the flying rope in his print of the picture.

Turner ensured that posterity should have every chance to comprehend the full range of his art by keeping together a large proportion of his important oils and almost all his working drawings. The great sources for the study of his mind are the collections of nearly three hundred oils in the National Gallery and the Tate Gallery and some twenty thousand drawings in the

British Museum. But there is a separate interest in seeing dispersed works of his which appealed to the collectors of his own lifetime and formed parts of a varied selection of contemporary British artists. When Sheepshanks presented his collection of two hundred and thirty-five oil paintings to the nation in 1857, one of the *fonds* which give the Victoria and Albert Museum its particular quality, these two works, which had originally been bought by John Nash, were amongst its finest examples of British painting.

Notes

1. John Summerson, *John Nash, architect to King George IV*, 1935, p. 155.
2. Joseph Farington, *The Farington Diary*, VIII, 1922–28, p. 300.
3. A. J. Finberg *The Life of J. M. W. Turner, R.A.*, 2nd edition, 1961 pp. 303–4.
4. It was not named the Royal Yacht Squadron till 1833 (information communicated by Mr. M. S. Robinson, National Maritime Museum, Greenwich.)
5. Sir John Rothenstein and Martin Butlin, *Turner*, 1964, pp.24, 38.
6. D. S. MacColl, *Catalogue: Turner Collection, National Gallery, Millbank*, 1920, pp. 31–3: Finberg, p. 304.
7. Sir John Rothenstein and Martin Butlin, *Turner*, 1964, pl. 70.
8. Rothenstein/Butlin, Colour Plate IX.
9. One such drawing, CCXXVII (a) 31, is reproduced in Jack Lindsay, *J. M. W. Turner*, 1966, p. 13.
10. MacColl, *op. cit.*, p. 14.
11. A. J. Finberg, *The Life of J. M. W. Turner, R.A.*, 2nd ed., 1961, p. 310.
12. Note in records of the Department of Paintings.
13. i.e. Great Yarmouth, Norfolk, not Yarmouth, Isle of Wight.
14. W. T. Whitley, *Art in England 1821–1837*, 1930, p. 212.
15. MacColl, p. 34: the sketch is reproduced Rothenstein/Butlin Plate 88.
16. T. S. R. Boase, *Journal of the Warburg and Courtauld Institutes*, XXII, 1959, pp. 332–346.
17. Summerson, *op. cit.* p. 274.

Charles VIII's Trojan War Tapestry

J. P. ASSELBERGHS

SINCE 1887, the Victoria and Albert Museum has had in its collections a Gothic tapestry depicting scenes of the Trojan War (6–1887), which dates from the last quarter of the fifteenth century.[1] This outstanding piece (fig. 1), currently one of the gems of the Gothic Tapestry Court (Room 38), was described in 1838 by Achille Jubinal in his important work, *Les anciennes tapisseries historiées*, following his purchase of the tapestry, the year before, from the painter Richard. The tapestry, at that time separated into three panels, had become the property of Richard after his discovery of it in 1807 at the château de Bayard. Jubinal had it restored and bequeathed it to the Bibliothèque Impériale in Paris on condition that it was hung on the great staircase. When the latter was destroyed, the tapestry was returned to the heirs of the donor and was sold to the Museum for the sum of £1,200.[2]

The tapestry represents three distinct episodes of the Trojan War as seen by the medieval poets and writers who neglected Homer because he lived in a later period and only gave credit to the forgers Dictys of Crete and Dares of Phrygia, so-called contemporaries of the famous siege.[3] On their writings was based the celebrated *Roman de Troie*, a poem of 30,000 octosyllabic lines, which was composed about 1184 by a Norman cleric, Benoît de Sainte-More, at the request of Eleanor of Aquitaine, wife of Henry II of England. The chief difference between Homer's poem and the story told by Dares and Dictys lies in the fact that the latter suppress the role of the Olympian gods. Benoît de Sainte-More naturally agrees with them in this, but he amplifies the intervention of Sagittarius—half man, half beast—and the part played by Penthesilea and her Amazons, elements congenial to medieval fantasy and the spirit of the *chansons de geste*, to which the *Roman de Troie* is closely allied by its blending of the customs of antiquity with those of the court of Henry II.

From the beginning of the 13th century, the poem of Benoît de Sainte-More was translated, copied, plagiarised and summarised in every European language. But it was eventually supplanted by the *Historia destructionis Troiae* (1287) of Guido delle Colonne, a judge at Messina, which, though a translation of the *Roman de Troie*, makes no mention of its author, and attributes all his inventions to Dares of Phrygia. Since Guido wrote in Latin it was long believed that his version was the original, and that of Benoît de Sainte-More, in the vernacular, merely a translation. Guido succeeded Benoît in popular favour and in his turn was translated and copied in every language.

When Raoul Lefèvre, chaplain to Philip the Good of Burgundy, was requested by his master to compile a *Recueil des Histoires de Troie*, it appears that he found time to complete, in 1464, only the first two destructions, by Hercules, and it was not until about 1467-68 that the copyists adopted the practice of adding to these one of the numerous French translations of Guido delle Colonne.[4] It was this *Recueil* which was translated by William Caxton between 1468 and 1471, at the command of Margaret of York, and published at Bruges in 1474 under the title *The Recuyell of the Historyes of Troye*, the first book to be printed in English.[5] Thus it was Benoît de Sainte-More who was the true, if remote, source for the events represented in the tapestries.

The tapestry in the Victoria and Albert Museum shows, on the left, the arrival of Penthesilea at Troy. The queen of the Amazons, bearing armour beneath a long robe, and wearing a high "hennin", is represented kneeling before King Priam who gestures that she should rise. Behind her are several mounted Amazons who have entered the city by the "Porte Imbrée". Aeneas, Antenor and other Trojans are witness to this meeting before the royal palace. Penthesilea, Philimenis and Polydamas are next shown leading Trojans and Amazons into battle through the "Porte Dardanide". The valiant queen has un-horsed Diomedes, whose steed is being led away by an Amazon, and is at grips with Ajax Telamonius. Polydamas is spearing a Greek warrior.

The third scene represents the arming of young Pyrrhus, son of Achilles, whom the Greeks had called to their rescue. Pyrrhus, with the Greek encampment as a background, receives the arms of his illustrious father from the hands of Ajax Telamonius in the presence of Agamemnon and other leaders.

The tapestry, which currently lacks a quarter of its width on the right hand side, originally depicted yet another battle scene. This is known to us by the "petit patron" or preparatory drawing (fig. 2), now preserved with seven others from the same series, in the Louvre.[6] Lacking also, this time at the top of the tapestry, are the French verses which are direct translations of the Latin ones which still exist inscribed on red banderoles at the bottom of the composition.

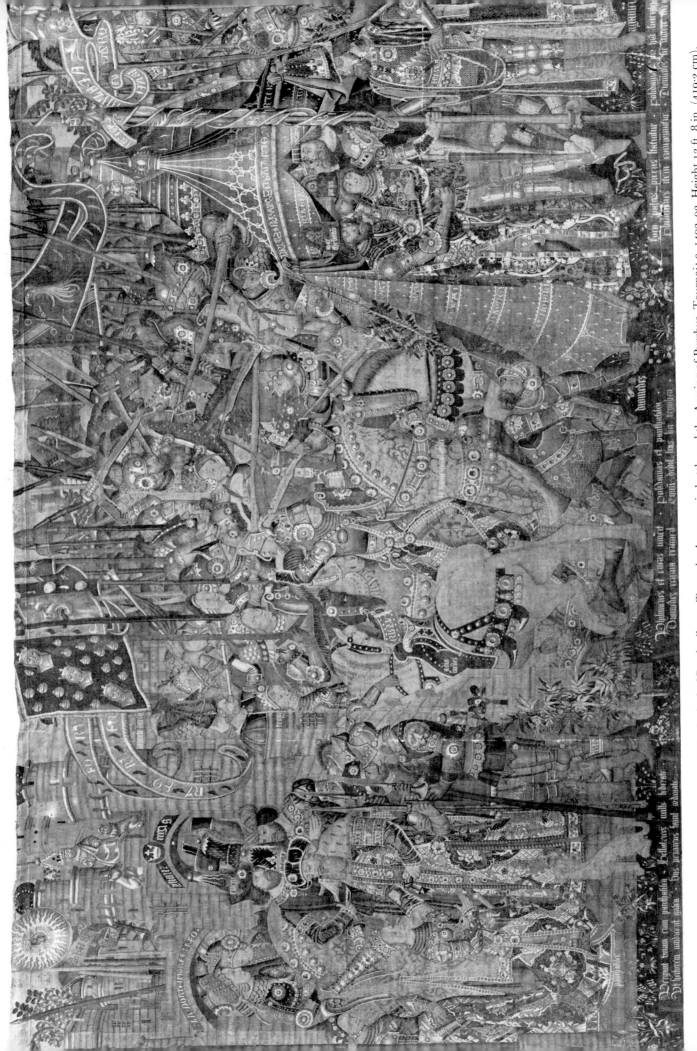

1. TAPESTRY WITH SCENES FROM THE TROJAN WAR: The Arrival of Penthesilea at Troy, the Amazons in battle and the Arming of Pyrrhus. Tournai; c. 1492–93. Height 13 ft. 8 in. (419·2 cm), width 24 ft. 2 in. (738·1 cm). Victoria and Albert Museum, 6–1887.

2. Fifteenth-century drawing for a tapestry with scenes from the Trojan War. Musée du Louvre, Paris.

Woven into the top left hand corner is a medallion (fig. 3) composed of four distinct elements. These comprise a Gothic "S" transversed by a diagonal bar and surrounded by the motto "plus quautre", twice repeated; the mottos are separated by a knotted girdle from a crown of sun or fire-rays. This medallion is not a later addition; but was, as Miss Nathalie Rothstein, after careful verification, kindly assured us, woven into the tapestry at the time of its fabrication. It is thus permissible to conclude that the tapestry was commissioned by the bearer of the device, so far unidentified.[7] The barred or shut "S" is none other than the "fermessa", a symbol of strength and fidelity, either political or amorous, which can be found on many works of art dating from the end of the fifteenth century or more notably from the sixteenth.[8] This "S" has been found at the castle of Amboise, as a decoration on small stone columns dating from the end of the fifteenth century and on the harness of St. Hubert's horse, on the tympanum of the chapel built by Charles VIII.[9]

The knotted girdle, or girdle of St. Francis, is equally well known since the end of the fifteenth century, when Anne de Bretagne, following the example set by her father, Duke François, introduced its use by the ladies. These two elements, combined, were also used to decorate the private apartments of Charles and Anne at Amboise, where the grey and yellow damask and satin draperies in their rooms were embroidered with grandes S.S. de velours noir et une cordelière à travers.[10]

During 1492 and 1493, the Queen commissioned Arnould de Vivier, her personal jeweller, to make her two necklaces and a gros sainct in the form of interlaced "S"s surrounded by girdles.[11] There is no reference to the motto "plus quautre" in any of the catalogues of heraldic devices, but the two known mottos of Charles VIII, "In medio splendor ignis, et de igne fulgor egrediens", and "Si deus pro nobis, quis contra nos" were usually accompanied, the first by a ball of fire, the second by a flaming sword.[12]

The evidence so far assembled does not allow any definitive conclusion to be drawn, for the barred "S", the girdle, and the sun or fire-rays are much too frequently met with to permit one to state categorically that the medallion is that of Charles VIII.[13]

Definitive proofs were found, with the kind aid of M. Jean Porcher, at the Bibliothèque Nationale, in Paris. Several manuscripts from its "Fonds français" belonged to Charles VIII and bear his arms and mottos.[14] Three among them are of particular interest. The first, an example of the Pèlerinage de vie humaine by Guillaume de Deguileville, has two barred Gothic "S"s in black upon a square grey background in the two upper corners of the frontispiece. The motto "plus quautre" is inscribed in the body of the "S" (fig. 4).[15] The second manuscript, Alain Chartier's Livre des quatre dames, bears the autograph signature of Charles VIII. The page facing the frontispiece is entirely filled by golden sun or fire-rays on a grey background, surrounding a barred Gothic "S" (fig. 5).[16] The last one,

. Detail from fig. 1, showing the device of Charles VIII.

4. Motto 'Plus Quautre' from Guillaume de Deguileville, 'Pèlerinage de vie humaine,' Bibliothèque Nationale, Ms. fr. 376 f. 1.

5. Device in Alain Chartier, *Le livre des quatre dames*, Bibliothèque Nationale, Ms. fr. 2235, f. 4v.

the *Ystoire du tres sainct Charlemagne*, has, above his signature, the motto *plus quautre* written by Charles VIII himself.[17] On this evidence I believe one can affirm that the Museum's *Trojan War* tapestry was ordered by Charles VIII.

On May 12, 1494, an inventory was made of the *Tapisseries à grands personnages* preserved at the château d'Amboise, where Anne de Bretagne, the young wife of Charles VIII, was resident at that period. That inventory specifically mentions *Listoire de troye contenant unze grandes pieces garnie comme la dessusdite tappicerie.*[18] In October of the same year these tapestries would have been hung to celebrate the visit of the duke and duchess of Bourbon.[19] Mention is made, in 1501, of a set of tapestries representing the *Destruction de Troie* at Blois when Louis XII and Anne de Bretagne received the visit of Philippe le Beau and his wife Juana on their way to Spain, and again at Amboise in 1518, when the castle was the scene of the baptism of the dauphin, son of François I.[20]

The inventory made between 1663 and 1716, during the reign of Louis XIV, of the *Mobilier de la Couronne* mentions, in the chapter concerning the *Tapisseries de haulte et basse lisse de laine et de soye*, the following set: *Une tenture de tapisserie de laine, haulte lisse, vieille fabrique d'Angleterre, figures gotiques, représentant l'Histoire de la Guerre de Troyes qui est expliquée dans des escriteaux qui sont au hault et au bas de chaque pièce sur des fonds rouges, sans bordure; contenant 93 aunes de cours, sur 4 aunes de hault; autrefois en unze pièces, et à présent mise en dix-sept pour la* *commodité de la tenture, doublée par bandes de toile blanche".*[21] That description and the measures given go very well with the Museum's tapestry, if we take into consideration that it has lost all the upper inscriptions and of a good quarter of its width.

Charles VIII married Anne de Bretagne in December 1491 and completely transformed and enlarged Amboise, which was to be their home, buying new furniture, tapestries, linen and silver.[22] One can reasonably assume that the *Trojan War* set, ordered on that occasion and present at Amboise in May 1494, was woven in 1492 and 1493.

As to the workshops which produced this most important series, one can only think of those set to work at Tournai by Pasquier Grenier and his sons, who owned the *Trojan War* cartoons, which had already been woven for Charles the Bold and Margaret of York about 1467[23] and for Henry VII of England about 1487.[24] Tournai was, at the time, a French town and, from the middle of the fifteenth century, Pasquier Grenier was providing tapestries for the French merchants.[25] An important citizen, he was, in 1479, in contact with Olivier le Daim, Louis XI's favourite. Two years later, the township of Tournai sent him to the French king as an ambassador.[26] After his death, his son Antoine sold, in 1495[27] and in 1508,[28] several series of tapestries to Cardinal Georges d'Amboise, counsellor of Charles VIII and favourite of Louis XII. No wonder that Charles honoured such a renowned family by his royal order!

Notes

1. A. F. Kendrick, *Catalogue of Tapestries. Victoria and Albert Museum*, London, 1924, pp. 25–27.
2. W. G. Thomson, *A History of Tapestry, from the Earliest Times until the Present Day*, London, 1930, p. 124.
3. A. Joly, *Benoît de Sainte-More et le Roman de Troie*, Paris, 1871.
4. A. Bayot, *La légende de Troie à la cour de Bourgogne (Société d'Emulation de Bruges, Mélanges I)*, Bruges, 1908, pp. 30–32.
5. A. Leroux de Lincy, *La vie et les ouvrages de William Caxton, premier imprimeur anglais*, offprint from *Revue britannique*, 1844, pp. 4–5, 14.

6. P. Schumann, *Der Trojanische Krieg*, Dresden, 1898.

7. A. F. Kendrick, *op. cit.*, p. 26.

8. G. de Tervarent, *Attributs et symboles dans l'art profane, 1450–1600*. (*Travaux d'humanisme et renaissance*, XXIX), Genève, 1958–59, col. 328–29.

9. *Amboise, le château, la ville et le canton*, Tours, 1897, p. 349.

10. A. Leroux de Lincy, *Vie de la reine Anne de Bretagne*, Paris, 1860, IV, pp. 83–84.

11. *ibid*, pp. 110 and 112.

12. A. Chassant et H. Tausin, *Dictionnaire des devises historiques et héraldiques*, II, Paris, 1878, pp. 491 and 656.
V. de Champeaux, *Devises, cris de guerre, légendes, dictons*, Dijon, 1890, p. 66.

13. Leroux de Lincy (*op. cit.*, I, p. 92, note) had already advanced that hypothesis: "quelle était cette devise assez courte pour qu'on pût la graver sur la vaisselle? Etait-ce celle que le père Ménestrier avait vue sur une menuiserie du château d'Amboise, au milieu d'une cordeliere, 'Plus qu'autre'? Le père Ménestrier l'attibue, à tort je crois, à François Ier".

14. L. Delisle, *Le cabinet des manuscrits de la Bibliothèque Impériale*, I, Paris, 1868, p. 96.

15. Bibliothèque Nationale, Paris, Ms. fr. 376, f.1.

16. *ibid.*, Ms. fr. 2235, f. 4v.

17. *ibid.*, Ms. fr. 4970, f. 47.

18. *ibid.*, Ms. fr. 22. 335, f. 147.

19. Francisque-Michel, *Recherches sur le commerce, la fabrication et l'usage des étoffes de soie, d'or et d'argent*, II, Paris, 1874, pp. 396–97.

20. J. Guiffrey, *Histoire générale de la tapisserie, France*, Paris 1880–81, pp. 67 and 69.

21. J. Guiffrey, *Inventaire général du mobilier de la couronne sous Louis XIV*, I, Paris, 1885, p. 344. The expression 'vieille fabrique d'Angleterre' is often used in the inventory and always is an attempt to establish the origin of Gothic series, without borders and bearing 'écriteaux'. These tapestries represent subjects often woven at Tournai in the second half of the XVth century or in the beginning of the XVIth., such as stories of *Hercules, Assuérus, Moyse, Jason, Sybilles, Boscherons* or *Vignerons* (pp. 344–47). Furthermore no important centre of tapestry production is known to have existed in England during the Gothic period and the 'vieille fabrique d'Angleterre' can only be attributed to the vivid imagination of the compiler of the inventory.

22. Leroux de Lincy, *op. cit.*, I, pp. 89–90.

23. J. P. Asselberghs, *Marguerite d'York, la nouvelle Hélène, et les tapisseries tournaisiennes de la Guerre de Troie*, in Catalogue of exhibition *Marguerite d'York et son temps*, Bruxelles 1967.

24. J. P. Asselberghs, *La tapesserie tournaisienne au XVe siècle*, Tournai, 1967, pp. 7–9.

25. E. Soil, *Les tapisseries tournaisiennes*, Tournai, p. 315.

26. *ibid.*, p. 316.

27. Comte de Laborde, *Les ducs de Bourgogne*, Part 2, I, Paris, 1849, p. XCIV.

28. A. Deville, *Comptes de dépenses de la construction du château de Gaillon* (*Collection de documents inédits sur l'histoire de France*, VI; *Publications archéologiques* no 5), Paris, 1850, p. 341.

Pugin's Marriage Jewellery

SHIRLEY BURY

A SET of enamelled and gem-set gold jewellery in the gothic style which was shown in the Medieval Court of the Great Exhibition of 1851 is said to have attracted the particular attention of Queen Victoria on one of her visits to the Crystal Palace.[1] The Court was the work of Augustus Welby Northmore Pugin (1811–1852), the son of the architectural draughtsman A.-C. Pugin[2] and himself an antiquary, architect, writer and designer. After his conversion to Roman Catholicism in 1835, the younger Pugin had set himself the task of imposing the gothic style upon his fellow countrymen as the only fit manner for a Christian nation. His phenomenal energy and complete dedication to what must have seemed to many at the outset to be a lost cause won him, nevertheless, an influential following in both the Roman Catholic and Established Churches. But as his Anglican admirers were frequently under attack by evangelicals within and without the Church of England, they were not always willing to worsen the situation by acknowledging their debt to their mentor. The Catholic Emancipation Act of 1829 had lessened the civil disabilities suffered by members of the faith; it had not made the protestant church-going public more tolerant. It is the more surprising that in 1851, despite the publicity that he had courted for his views, Pugin emerged as a genuinely national figure. The Queen, who deeply distrusted manifestations of Popery in the Anglican Church,[3] was quite undismayed by the tangible evidence of ritual and ceremonial in the Medieval Court at the exhibition. She noted in her diary for May 7, with every indication of approval, that she and the Prince Consort had visited "Mr. Pugen's [sic] Mediaeval room, full of church ornaments, beautiful mantlepieces, etc etc".[4]

Pugin's principal manufacturers, all represented in the Court, were John Hardman & Company of Birmingham,[5] who executed his designs for metalwork (including the jewellery), stained glass, embroidery and a variety of other media, J. G. Crace of Wigmore Street, London,[6] who specialised in furniture and furnishings, and Herbert Minton & Company of Stoke-on-Trent,[7] who made ceramics and tiles for him. His builder, George Myers of Ordnance Wharf, Lambeth,[8] contributed a single exhibit, a tomb designed for the Roman Catholic bishop, Thomas Walsh, who had died three years earlier and was buried at St. Chad's, Birmingham.[9]

Hardman's, who gained the highest distinction, a Council Medal, for their brass wares in the medieval manner,[10] were also awarded a Prize Medal for their church plate and metal furnishings, the workmanship of which was described by the jury of the goldsmithing section as "good, bold, and well defined".[11] The jury did not comment specifically on the jewellery, but Matthew Digby Wyatt,[12] who served as secretary to the Executive Committee of the 1851 exhibition, illustrated most of the set in his chromo-lithographed souvenir of the Great Exhibition, published under the title of *The Industrial Arts of the XIXth Century* in 1851–3 (fig. 1).[13] The names of the designer and manufacturer are acknowledged in the caption, but the jewellery is not discussed at all in the accompanying text. Digby Wyatt, spurred on by his pupil and friend William Burges, who assisted him in the task,[14] used most of the contemporary enamel work that he chose to illustrate as the pretext for a serial history of enamelling. The Pugin pieces provided the occasion for a survey of enamelled jewellery in the British Isles from the Roman occupation to the Middle Ages.

Three items from the Pugin set were acquired by the museum in 1962, the head-band by purchase, and the other two, a combined necklace and pendant-cross and a brooch, by gift (Colour Plate IV). It is fortunate that in view of Digby Wyatt's evasion of the subject there are other sources of information about the jewellery which make it possible to disentangle the complicated story of its origins. Benjamin Ferrey, Pugin's first biographer,[15] provided the most useful published material in his endearingly muddled *Recollections* of 1861.[16] His single direct statement about the jewellery is entirely correct, and can be confirmed by other documents: it was designed, he declared, "in anticipation of his [Pugin's] intended marriage with Miss L–" and subsequently exhibited in 1851.[17] Elsewhere, however, Ferrey made the egregious blunder of attributing the contents of the Medieval Court to the workshops of George Myers, including, apparently, "the wrought gold and silver ornaments" designed by Pugin "for the intended marriage with his third wife".[18] We need not pause to consider Myers as a metalworker, for there is every indication that this was a rôle to which he did not aspire. The mistake over Myers, so obvious to anyone acquainted with Pugin's work, perhaps contributed to the widespread misconstruction

85

1. The set of gold jewellery, enamelled and gem-set, designed by Pugin December 1847–January 1848 and shown in the Medieval Court of the Great Exhibition of 1851.

of the last part of this passage. Where Ferrey was simply making an oblique reference to Helen Lumsden, the unidentified Miss L– of his biography[19] whose broken engagement to Pugin will be discussed shortly, his words have been taken to mean that, whether or not the jewellery was designed for someone else, it was finally made for Jane Knill, who became Pugin's third wife on August 10, 1848. Pugin's descendants have certainly been under this impression: when some of them lent pieces from the set to the exhibition of Victorian and Edwardian decorative arts held at the museum in 1952, the catalogue descriptions reflected their belief.[20]

The touchstone to Ferrey is furnished by the surviving day books of the metalworkers, John Hardman & Company, coupled with Pugin's letters to Hardman

and to other participants in his compulsive correspondence, including his principal patron, John Talbot, 16th Earl of Shrewsbury.[21] The metal day book for 1845–49 establishes that with one exception the only gold articles in Pugin's account for the year in which his third marriage took place are the jewels designed and executed for the lady who jilted him, while the sole item of plate of any importance is a "Large Silver Dish in Florentine pattern".[22] The entry for the dish is dated April 18, 1848. The jewellery which, like the dish, was already completed by this date, was entered on the same day.

The appearance of these two items in virtual juxtaposition argues a connection between them, and so indeed there was, for the dish was presented by Pugin to his friend Henry Benson, who acted as an intermediary in the final stages of the stormy engagement between Pugin and Helen Lumsden.[23] Pugin, twice widowed and with a family of six children, had proposed to Miss Lumsden, who was not of the same faith as he, in November 1847. She accepted him informally shortly afterwards, and followed this with a formal letter in January 1848 confirming her promise to marry him, although she kept her family in ignorance of her betrothal. In March she secretly joined the Roman Church in preparation for her marriage. At this point, she confessed both her engagement and her conversion to her relations, who had already prevented her from entering the Church of Rome the year before, obviously regarding her predilections as evidence of the pernicious influence Pugin was already exercising upon her. Their reaction to her announcement was vigorously antipathetic; considerable pressure appears to have been put on her to induce her once more to renounce all connection with Pugin and the Roman Catholic faith. With Benson's assistance, Pugin made a last desperate attempt at reconciliation, but to no avail.

The unhappy suitor, balked at the last minute, was all the more embittered because he had already been at least twice frustrated in his search for a third wife by relations of the ladies to whom he attached himself.[24] But there is no doubt that he was genuinely in love with Helen Lumsden. He had spent a great deal of time and money in preparing for this marriage, designing the jewellery and the medieval costume that she was to wear on her wedding day,[25] as well as making extensive alterations to his house at Ramsgate for her sake. Characteristically, he found relief for his feelings of anguish and grievance in writing a pamphlet which he

IV. Brooch, head-band and necklace; part of the marriage jewellery designed by Pugin and made by John Hardman & Company of Birmingham. The brooch and necklace given in the name of Mrs. C. E. Gladstone. Width of brooch 2½ in. (6·3 cm). Victoria and Albert Museum (M20 & 21–1962). The head-band purchased separately (M.10–1962).

had printed for private circulation amongst his friends and acquaintances, recounting the whole history of the engagement. A letter to Hardman dating from this time contains the following reference to it: "I was up all night for 2 nights finishing my statement it is overwhelming I really think she must leave the country when it is published it keeps me in a dreadful state of mind".[26]

A copy of the pamphlet, entitled *A Statement of Facts*,[27] was despatched to Lord Shrewsbury with a covering letter from Pugin begging him to read it, "for a more cruel shameful case had never occurred I think I am the most unfortunate of men—this last business has completely upset me—I have no rest night or day"...[28] The *Statement* has not been preserved in any public collection, but fortunately Ferrey felt it necessary to publish the greater part of it in his *Recollections*, omitting only its conclusion, a diatribe directed at the Lumsden family, the language of which we may guess at from the term he employed in another letter to Lord Shrewsbury: "a complete body of Ultra Protestants".[29]

From the *Statement* as re-printed by Ferrey, we learn about the long courtship which began, to all intents and purposes, during the winter of 1846; how Helen Lumsden (referred to throughout as Miss L–) gradually became drawn to the Roman Church; and how her piety and interest were fed by Pugin's accounts of his visits to churches on the long tour of the Continent that he made in 1847, well before his proposal of marriage on November 26. Then follows that part of the story which we have already discussed. Pugin included extracts from their correspondence in his account, and one of his letters to Helen, dated February 7, [1848],[30] is worth noting, as it bears on the subject of the jewellery. He began by telling her how he was refurnishing his house in her honour, putting in panelling, inserting "new stained glass into the windows, redecorating the ceilings, and the three crosletts will not be forgotten". Pugin was following his invariable practice of displaying the armorial bearings of the owners in his domestic dwellings: in this case, he was adding Helen's arms.[31] The crosslets to which he refers were also used as the central motif of the head-band (Colour Plate IV). His letter continues: "I am fitting out in every department, and I do trust everything will please you. You have no idea of the work we have to get done by Easter. I have between thirty and forty people working different ways. There are five at your jewellery at Birmingham; of course I cannot pretend to vie in intrinsic value with thousands of people; but no woman, not excepting the Queen, will have better ornaments, as regards taste, than you will." The Hardman day book shows that the gold jewellery, with its casket (the latter not illustrated by Digby Wyatt) cost £255 9 6; Pugin himself claimed in his pamphlet that all his expenses over "this unhappy business" amounted to more than two thousand pounds.[32]

Ironically, the jewellery, and the dish for Benson, which Pugin had obviously hoped to bestow on his friend in recognition of his help in winning over Helen Lumsden's family, were finished at a time when virtually all hope had gone. He was being rigorously kept from her and it needed only Helen's final letter of renunciation, which seems to have arrived in May after three weeks of silence, for Pugin to be forced into accepting final defeat. But he had a mercurial temperament and the depths of misery into which he was cast were not to hold him long. In the summer he began to court Jane Knill, a Roman Catholic, twenty-one years old and a first cousin of Stuart Knill,[33] another of Pugin's devoted patrons. In accepting Pugin's hand, Jane came into possession of the jewellery which Helen Lumsden can never have seen. By a singular stroke of good fortune, her arms bore crosses crosslet fichée, as may be seen from the wedding card illustrated by Ferrey[34] (fig. 2), so that Pugin was spared the necessity of having a new central motif made for the head-band. However, the jewel casket was sent back to Hardman's for Jane's full arms to be substituted for Helen's. A day book entry dated August 8, two days before the marriage took place, records "Alterations to Jewel Case, including New Gilt & Engraved Circular Pieces and 2 New Shields, Enamelled etc", costing £4 8s.

Jane Knill became Pugin's wife at St. George's, Southwark, which was built to Pugin's design and opened only in the previous month.[35] Pugin was delighted with his bride, and in announcing his marriage to one of his few Anglican patrons at this time, J. J. Hornby, squire as well as rector of Winwick, Lancashire, he wrote that he had "got a first-rate Gothic woman at last, who perfectly understands and delights in spires, chancels, screens, stained windows, brasses, vestments, etc."[36] The presence of Jane in Pugin's household scarcely deflected him from his established practice of spending much of his time journeying round the British Isles in order to supervise the progress of his buildings, or travelling the Continent in search of models for his designs. Nevertheless, he

2. The wedding card of Pugin and Jane Knill, from a colour illustration in Ferrey's *Recollections* of 1861.

wrote continually to tell her of his unease away from her and of his anxiety to be home.[37]

Having considered the circumstances which prompted the making of the jewellery, we may now review it in the context of Pugin's work in the decorative arts. Pugin was venerated during his lifetime for his archaeological approach to design and manufacture. His letter to the French antiquary Adolphe Napoléon Didron,[38] first published in the *Bulletin Archéologique* in 1843[39] and cited almost as soon as it appeared in print,[40] was regarded as one of the most comprehensive statements of his Credo. As late as 1861, Ferrey thought it significant enough to transcribe (not absolutely accurately) in its entirety. The following passage concerns his metalwork: "J'ai fait copier ces objets d'après des modèles anciens, avec la plus grande exactitude, et je suis parvenu à former des ouvriers qui travaillent tout-à-fait dans l'ancien style" . . . "Je dois vous dire que ces objets sont executés dans l'ancienne manière: ils sont ciselés, gravés, émaillés, battus, et non pas coulés en fonte comme on a l'habitude de le faire aujourd'hui."[41]

Pugin reverted to this theme so often in his published work that his contemporaries came unhesitatingly to accept that all his metalwork was produced by methods used by medieval craftsmen. In practice, there was sometimes a wide discrepancy between vision and reality. The Hardman ledgers afford evidence of the employment of certain techniques for which no medieval precedent could be claimed: these included electrotyping and electro-gilding, both modern inventions.[42] Such new processes need not concern us, as they were often the means of cheapening production. There was no question of economy where the jewellery was concerned; it was made of precious metal and lavishly decorated in token of his affection, but there are anomalies about its execution which caused Pugin himself to despair and provoked a series of bitter letters from him to Hardman in the early months of 1848.[43] He was not given to introspection over his ability as a designer; when the quality of his finished work was questioned, as it sometimes was, he usually found factors other than his original conception to account for it: shortage of money or vacillation on the part of his patrons, or insufficiently skilled craftsmanship.[44] But we are entitled to discuss how closely he himself conformed to his own antiquarian standards before we can evaluate the extent to which he was ill-served by his manufacturers.

It must first be made clear that jewellery formed a very small part of Hardman's total output, and of this, the proportion of gem-set work was even smaller. The firm's chief trade in this line was in silver crosses which were sold at ten shillings each, finding an enthusiastic market amongst Roman Catholics and the more daring of Pugin's Anglican admirers. With the exception of a few pieces of gem-set jewellery which Pugin designed mainly for members of his immediate family, most of the elaborate and costly work was for ecclesiastical use. In January 1841, for instance, Hardman's completed a gem-set gilt morse, an episcopal ring, a gold seal with an amethyst, and two "Rich Gilt & enamelled Crosses & chains" as part of an order for the Mostyn family[45] which was destined for Francis George Mostyn, Vicar-apostolic of the Northern District, who was consecrated Bishop of Abydus on December 21, 1840. The secular jewellery that Pugin had made for his wives is closely related to such ecclesiastical work: the pendant cross of the museum necklace, with its quatrefoil ends, for instance, is remarkably similar in form to the illustration appended to the section on pectoral crosses in his *Glossary of Ecclesiastical Ornament*, 1844[46] (See fig. 3).

The sources of the illustrations in the *Glossary* were

PECTORAL CROSS.

3. Woodcut after a drawing made by Pugin to illustrate the section on Pectoral Crosses in his *Glossary of Ecclesiastical Ornament*, 1844, p. 91.

4. Part of a page from a sketchbook by taken Pugin on a visit to Italy in 1847. From S. Ayling's *Photographs from Sketches by A. W. N. Pugin*, 1865, II, 332.

the same as those for his designs; they included illuminated manuscripts, of which he had a collection, and the drawings he made in the course of his English and Continental journeys. Though he constantly visited ecclesiastical treasuries abroad he cannot have seen a representative range of the types of ecclesiastical jewellery produced in the Middle Ages, for comparatively few examples had survived. In this respect, the absence of a direct parallel between originals dating from the Middle Ages and his own designs indicates that he probably had recourse to secondary material. His sketches of statuary and paintings offered a rich store of information. He was clearly most influenced by the paintings he had seen in the Low Countries. So much of the statuary he designed for his churches looks like a three-dimensional rendering of a van Eyck painting that we may conclude that the jewellery also was in part inspired by such works as *The Adoration of the Holy Lamb*, the great van Eyck altarpiece in Ghent Cathedral.[47] In support of

this hypothesis, it may be noted that the angels depicted in this altarpiece wear head-bands, one of Pugin's favourite types of jewellery. As if to underline its ecclesiastical derivation, the museum head-band bears the inscription "Christi crux est mea lux". Pugin may well also have consulted some of Hollar's engravings after earlier masters. Dr. Phoebe Stanton has recently demonstrated Pugin's debt to Wenzel Hollar (1607–77) in the preparation of his *Contrasts* of 1836.[48]

From such disparate elements, Pugin absorbed the essentials and re-created them in his own idiom, which may perhaps best be described as archaeological in outline and personal in detail. Pugin's training as an architect had been primarily visual; his reputation as an antiquary, though notable for one with so little formal education, was largely based on his keen appreciation of things seen. He responded instantly to things which interested him, summarising their appearance in a quick sketch, rarely supplementing this first impression with more detailed studies (fig. 4). His

5. Borders for Altar Cloths. Detail from a chromolithographed plate in Pugin's *Glossary of Ecclesiastical Ornament*, 1844, 17, showing his use of the fleur-de-lys motif.

drawings were synthesised just as rapidly into designs. John Hardman Powell, Pugin's pupil and son-in-law, has left a graphic description of Pugin's method of working in an unpublished memoir written in 1889, *Pugin in his Home:* "The pace at which he worked would be incredible to anyone not seeing it. His few implements were at hand and his design was in his brain distinct even to the detail, so without hesitation he pencilled or penned or brushed it in; he never rubbed out or altered, all was as easy as talking."[49] To judge from the designs surviving in public collections, the details were sometimes drawn out as Powell implies, but more often they were merely indicated. Powell did not add, as he should have done, that Pugin could not have worked with such speed without the help of his manufacturers, who could usually be relied upon to interpret his designs in the way that he intended. On the occasions when they failed him, as with the jewellery, he expressed himself very forcibly.

The motifs used in the decoration of the jewellery were drawn from the same limited repertory that appears in all his work. The firm mouldings which reveal the thorough grounding in the Georgian gothick manner that he received from his father, the quatrefoil and the fleur-de-lys are the principal components of the set. Taking the fleur-de-lys alone, we can trace it in the *Glossary* (fig. 5), running below the encircling inscription on the bowl of the museum chalice of 1850

(fig. 6), and recurring in the brass fittings of the oak cabinet purchased, like the chalice, from the Great Exhibition (fig. 7).

One of the few solecisms in the jewellery, having regard to Pugin's antiquarian ideals, is the edging of half-pearls, countersunk in a fashion recalling the pearl

6. Chalice; silver, parcel-gilt, decorated with enamels and semi-precious stones. Birmingham, 1850. Made by John Hardman & Company from a design by Pugin. Purchased for the Museum of Manufactures, the ancestor of the V. & A., from the Great Exhibition of 1851. Height 10¼ in. (26 cm) (1327–1851.)

7. Cabinet of oak, with brass fittings. Made by J. G. Crace from a design by Pugin and purchased from the Great Exhibition of 1851. Victoria and Albert Museum (25–1852.)

decoration of late eighteenth and early nineteenth century mourning jewellery of classic inspiration (fig. 8). It is reassuring to discover from Pugin's letters to Hardman that this was a departure from his design.[50] The letters, as is customary with Pugin, are all undated, but it is possible from internal evidence to make a fairly accurate guess at their chronology. The first must date from the end of December or the beginning of January, as Pugin sent New Year greetings to his friend. By this time, he had already designed the head ornament and one of the crosses and promised to send the remaining drawings soon. The next significant letter was written just after he had received news that Paris was once more at the barricades, which dates it to the days immediately following February 23. He was immensely agitated by the Revolution, but even more by the sight of the museum brooch, the first piece to be completed and sent to him. Hardman had apparently made an attempt to justify its execution, which had

only served to arouse Pugin's passion of dislike still further. "I wonder you defend the Brooch," he wrote, "I think the half pearls execrable I won't have it, it is too horrid . . . it is a regular Houndsditch[51] affair poor and vulgar but I shall soon see you D.V. and then we can have it out . . . Only show me half pearls in the antient [sic] jewellery look at the illustrations in all books of . . . costumes etc . . ." His last statement was probably a reference to such publications as A. C. Stothard's *Monumental Effigies*, 1817–32, and Henry Shaw's *Dresses and Decorations of the Middle Ages*, 1843, which were much prized by antiquaries. A detail from one of the illustrations in the latter work is reproduced here (fig. 9) and shows Richard II wearing a gold and pearl pod collar and a jewel in the form of a white hart with pearl-set antlers. It was taken from the Wilton Diptych, which was then in the possession of the Earl of Pembroke and is now in the National Gallery. The same subject had been engraved in 1639 by Hollar.[52]

93

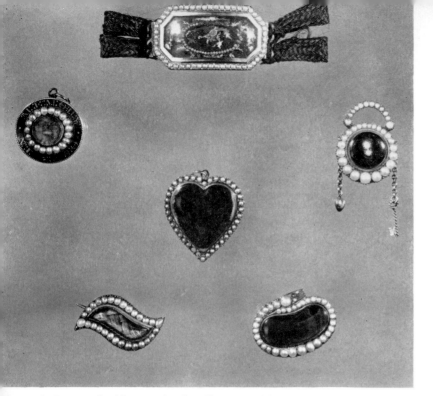

8. Group of gold mourning jewellery, set with half-pearls. Some of the pieces are enamelled. English, late 18th and early 19th century. Victoria and Albert Museum (928, 932, 933, 957, 972, 988–1888.)

Pugin had intended, as he described in a further letter elaborating his theme, that the pearls should be threaded individually on wires to form a kind of corona round the edge of the jewellery: "all the old examples show the pearls etc standing out fastened by gold wires". The colour of the gold, raw and bright also distressed him and he declared: "it is no use employing these men of *confirmed bad habits* . . . we must begin with a lad an uncorrupted person etc".

We may well ask who were these corrupted craftsmen employed by Hardman to make the jewellery. The answer is that they were almost certainly outworkers drawn from the mourning jewellery trade, which would account for the hateful half-pearls. Hardman was in the habit of using these jewellers, the only ones trained in the art of enamelling, to make the champlevé and translucent enamel plaques decorating the firm's church plate.[53]

In a third letter, written at almost exactly the same time, Pugin dwelt at length on the brooch. He had wanted it deeper in section so that the quatrefoil fell back from the central enamelled plaque, "then we should have had light and shadow . . . it is all flat no spirit no richness no life I fear it will all be a dreadful mull it is regular modern not a spark of the old spirit about it the fleur de lis [sic] are not like my drawing either". He concluded, ominously, "it is time I was with you". But, as we have seen, he lost heart in the next few weeks and there is little indication that the jewellery was drastically altered to meet with his criticisms. At this distance of time, and with none of his emotional involvement, we can appreciate the jewellery for what it is, a handsome exercise in the Victorian medieval manner by the prime master of the style.

In conclusion, it may be of interest to note the cost to Pugin of the individual items and to discuss the one outstanding problem posed by the day book entry. Taking the museum pieces first, the brooch, which is set with garnets, turquoises and pearls, and with a central plaque of translucent green enamel, was priced at £23 4 0; the necklace and cross, set with the same stones and enamelled in green and blue, £55 11 0.[54] The head ornament (which until the day books came to light has always been assumed to be a neck-band), is enamelled in green and white and set with diamonds, turquoises and pearls; the crosses crosslet are set against translucent green enamel. It cost £28 16 0.[55] Of the rest of the set illustrated by Digby Wyatt, the M monogram brooch was priced at £29 17 0;[56] the two bracelets (only one of the pair appears in the illustration) £72 0 0;[57] the small cross at the top of the plate, which was meant to be worn with a silk cord[58] £9 12 6; and the earrings £14 9 0. Only one ring

9. Richard II. Detail from a chromolithographed plate in Henry Shaw's *Dresses and Decorations of the Middle Ages*, 1843, I, 32.

corresponding to the illustration is listed in the entry: this was set with turquoises and cost £2 7 0. More seriously, there is no reference to a second necklace and cross such as appears in Digby Wyatt. The chain of this item may perhaps be identified with the piece described in a day book entry dated December 20, 1848 which was presumably commissioncd as a Christmas present to Jane. The entry reads: "A Gold Chain to order"; it cost £9 0 6. This leaves the large and elaborate pendant cross attached to it still to be accounted for, which is more difficult. "A Gold enamel chain & Cross" was supplied to him on December 21, 1843, when his second wife was still living. There is an ambiguous statement which might refer to this piece in one of Pugin's letters to Hardman, probably dating from late in January or early in February 1848. After giving instructions for the execution of the jewellery that he had just designed, he added: "I have disposed of the large necklace you made for me some time ago and it will require a little alteration". Perhaps—and we can only guess—the cross was detached from the necklace at this time, adapted and later given to Jane. As a coda, we may remark that the silver-gilt jewellery that Pugin also designed for Helen Lumsden, which included another head-band to hold her veil at their marriage[59] and a morse for fastening her cloak, has been excluded from discussion here. The museum, as yet, possesses no examples of this subsidiary set.

Notes

1. B. Ferrey, *Recollections of A. N. Welby Pugin, and his father, Augustus Pugin*, London, 1861, p. 221.

2. *Ibid*, pp. 1–101. A.–C. Pugin (1762–1832) came to England from France after the Revolution; he worked as a draughtsman for John Nash and later set up on his own account as an architect.

3. O. Chadwick, *The Victorian Church*, Part I, 1966, p. 166.

4. Quoted by gracious permission of Her Majesty the Queen. I am greatly indebted to Mr. Robert Mackworth-Young, M.V.O., Librarian at Windsor Castle, for providing this reference for me.

5. *Great Exhibition of the Works of Industry of All Nations*, 1851. *Official Descriptive and Illustrated Catalogue*, 1851, II, p. 761, Class 26, cat. no. 532.

6. *Ibid.*, cat. no. 530.

7. *Ibid.*, cat. no. 531.

8. *Ibid.*, cat. no. 533.

9. Thomas Walsh, consecrated 1 May 1825 as Bishop of Cambysopolis; afterwards became Vicar-Apostolic of the Central District. He was translated to the London District on 28 July 1848 and died 18 February 1849, aged seventy-three. It was Walsh who initiated the building of St. Chad's Cathedral, Birmingham, designed by Pugin and completed in 1841.

10. *Exhibition of the Works of Industry of All Nations*, 1851. *Reports by the Juries*, 1852 (single volume edition) pp. 497–498, 502.

11. *Ibid.*, p. 516.

12. Matthew (later Sir Matthew) Digby Wyatt (1820–1877), architect and writer on art, began as a Medievalist but ended as a protagonist of the Renaissance style. See *Dictionary of National Biography*, XXI, 1909, p. 1097.

13. M. Digby Wyatt, *The Industrial Arts of the XIX Century*, 1851–53, II, p. LXXXII.

14. *Ibid.*, II, 'Postscript', dated 7 March 1853, p. xii. 'From . . . Mr. W. BURGES, the Author has derived fourteen articles, among the most important of which may be pointed out . . . part of the series on Enamels . . . .' Burges later outstripped his master as an antiquary.

15. Ferrey, an architect, had been a fellow pupil with A. W. N. Pugin of the latter's father, A.–C. Pugin.

16. See Note 1.

17. Ferrey, *op. cit.*, p. 224.

18. *Ibid.*, p. 258.

19. The identity of Helen Lumsden was discovered by Dr. Phoebe Stanton while she was working on her Ph.D. thesis for the University of London, *Welby Pugin and the Gothic Revival*, 1950. Dr. Stanton, who is now preparing a critical biography of Pugin for publication, has most kindly given me permission to make use of her discovery.

20. *Victoria & Albert Museum. Exhibition of Victorian and Edwardian Decorative Arts. Catalogue*, 1952, C.22–26.

21. Shrewsbury (1791–1852) succeeded to the title and estates of his uncle in June 1827. Although his wealth has been exaggerated, he financed several major churches built by Pugin. See D. Gwynn, *Lord Shrewsbury, Pugin and the Gothic Revival*, 1946.

22. *Op. cit.*, p. 305. The dish cost Pugin £37 15s. It is in a private collection.

23. Ferrey, *op. cit.*, pp. 219–221.

24. M. Trappes-Lomax, *Pugin, A Mediaeval Victorian*, 1932, p. 280.

25. A sketch of the dress, taken from the Crace papers, is in the Drawings Collection, R.I.B.A. Library. V2/56(3).

26. Undated letter from Pugin to Hardman, from the 1848 letter box of Hardman & Company. Kindly lent to the present writer by Mr. Patrick Feeny of John Hardman Studios, Birmingham.

27. The full title was *A Statement of Facts relative to the Engagement of marriage between Miss Helen Lumsden and Augustus Welby Pugin, Esq., of S. Augustin, Isle of Thanet.* Apparently it was Ferrey who decided to omit Helen's name. Michael Trappes-Lomax had clearly seen a copy of the pamphlet in private possession when he wrote his biography of Pugin (*op. cit.*) for he gave the full title and part of the conclusion; pp. 281, 348.

28. Undated letter, from the collection of letters from Pugin to Lord Shrewsbury, and from Pugin to Jane Knill, presented to the V. & A. Library by Miss Eileen Riddell.

29. *Ibid.*

30. Ferrey, *op. cit.*, p. 213. The date is misprinted 'Jan. 25, 1843', a palpable error, as Pugin's second wife, Louisa Burton, was still alive at the time.

31. Helen Lumsden came from a Scottish family.

32. Ferrey, *op. cit.*, p. 215.

33. Stuart (later Sir Stuart) Knill, 1st Baronet (1824–1896); Wharfinger of the City of London. With his father, Knill was a generous benefactor of St. George's, Southwark.

34. Opp. p. 230. According to the Revd. W. A. Wickham, 'Pugin and the Re-building of Winwick Chancel', *Transactions of the Historic Society of Lancashire and Cheshire*, LIX, n.s. XXIII, 1908, p. 146, Pugin appears to have sent out the cards on his wedding day. An announcement of the marriage appeared in the *Morning Post*, 12 August, p. 8.

35. On 4 July 1848. See the *Tablet*, IX (9), no. 427, 8 July, p. 435.

36. Wickham, *op. cit.*, pp. 146, 147.

37. See note 28.

38. Adolphe Napoléon Didron (1806–1867) was an acquaintance of Pugin. He founded and directed the *Annales Archéologiques*, which ran from 1844 until 1872.

39. J. M. Guichard, 'Préliminaires', in Charles de l'Escalopier, *Théophile, prêtre et moine*, Paris, 1843, p. xii.

40. *Bulletin Archéologique*, publié par le Comité historique des Arts et Monuments, II, 1842–3, pp. 404, 405.

41. Ferrey, *op. cit.*, pp. 236–237. The quotation in this article has been taken direct from the *Bulletin Archéologique*.

42. S. Bury, 'In search of Pugin's Church Plate', *Connoisseur*, CLXV, May 1967, pp. 32–33.

43. There are seven of these letters, taken by J. H. Powell (see note 49) from the Hardman letter box for 1848 and forming part of the collection of Pugin-Hardman correspondence belonging to the estate of his son, the late Sebastian Pugin Powell. They were transcribed by Dr. Phoebe Stanton, who has very generously allowed me access to her transcriptions.

44. A. W. Pugin, *Some Remarks on the Articles which have recently appeared in the 'Rambler', relative to Ecclesiastical Architecture and Decoration*, 1850, pp. 6, 9–12, 15.

45. Hardman day book, 1838–44, 29 January 1841; the orders are in the names of Brown Mostyn, Miss Mostyn, H. Mostyn.

46. A. W. Pugin, *Glossary of Ecclesiastical Ornament and Costume*, 1844. The text was largely the work of the Revd. Bernard Smith (1815–1903), formerly Rector of Leadenham and a patron of Pugin, who was received into the Roman Church 15 December 1842.

47. Completed in 1432.

48. Phoebe Stanton, 'The Sources of Pugin's *Contrasts*', in J. Summerson, ed., *Concerning Architecture: Essays on Architectural Writers and Writing presented to Nikolaus Pevsner*, 1968, p. 129.

49. Typescript copy, p. 14, presented to the V. & A. Library by the late Lady Alford. The original manuscript was transcribed by Dr. Phoebe Stanton.

50. See note 43.

51. A synonym for cheap work.

52. G. Vertue, *A Description of the Works of . . . Wenceslaus Hollar*, 1759, p. 4, Class I, 72.

53. W. C. Aitken, 'The Revived Art of Metal-Working', in S. Timmins (ed.). *The Resources, Products and Industrial History of Birmingham and the Midland Hardware District*, 1866, p. 537; W. Burges, 'The Late Exhibition', *Ecclesiologist*, XXIII, 1862, pp. 338, 339.

54. Both these pieces had belonged to Mrs. C. E. Gladstone, who lent them to the Victorian and Edwardian decorative arts exhibition in 1952. See note 20. Mrs. Gladstone bequeathed the jewellery to her nieces, Lady Alford and Miss Eileen Riddell, who presented the two items to the museum in the name of their aunt.

55. The head-band and the pair of bracelets cited below were sold at Christie's on 28 February 1962 by the widow of Humphrey Watts, a great-grandson of Pugin. The head-band (Lot 104) was acquired by the museum from the sale.

56. Pugin visited Oxford on several occasions in the early 1840s (Trappes-Lomax, *op. cit.*, p. 138) and may have seen the mid-14th century example at New College (*ill.* E. Steingräber, *Antique Jewellery*, 1957, pl. 52).

57. See note 55.

58. This cross, set with a ruby, pearls and diamonds, was lent by Mrs. M. K. Riddell to the Victorian and Edwardian decorative arts exhibition. See note 20.

59. Lent by Mrs. R. Mugliston to the above exhibition: cat. no. C. 18.

Buddhist Porcelain Figures of the Yüan Dynasty

JOHN AYERS

THE porcelain figure in China has had a long, but somewhat intermittent history. Certainly there occurred no such large-scale extension of the art as was to take place in Europe during the 18th century; and there are few indications to suggest either that any sustained tradition was established in this form of manufacture, or that it acquired any particular cachet in the higher levels of patronage. A solitary exception, perhaps, are the refined, pure white *blanc-de-Chine* porcelains made at Tê-hua in the 17th century, which must surely have achieved a fame to match their distinction; and which indeed provided the model upon which some of the earliest European essays in the figure were based. No doubt this rather modest achievement is in part a reflection of the modellers' limited range of subject-matter. For throughout the Ming period (1368–1644) and into the 18th century, when a somewhat wider range of models were made—partly in response to the demands of a growing Western market—their craft was primarily concerned with subjects of a religious nature. These naturally included the more solemn deities of the Buddhist and Taoist beliefs; a relatively genial gallery of saints or "immortals"; and also a variety of auspicious beasts drawn from their mythology. But if it is only rarely that we encounter among these figures the true note of fresh artistic imagination, their execution nevertheless remains generally competent and effective; displaying that easy, inbred skill of handling that we have come to expect of the Chinese potter.

When we look back to the Sung period (960–1279) evidence for the production of figures, whether in porcelain or pottery, becomes harder to find. For while there are instances enough of figural work, particularly in the form of animals, this is almost invariably applied to the ornamentation of vessels and other objects, such as covers for jars or incense burners, writing table equipment, and even pillows, intended for practical use. There exist also a handful of religious images the Sung attributions of which must in most cases, however, be accepted with considerable reserve. A particular interest therefore attaches to a work recently acquired by the Museum (fig. 1),[1] which on present evidence it may not be overfanciful to suggest could represent the first of all serious ventures into the genre of the porcelain figure. It is a statuette of the Bodhisattva Kuan-yin (Avalokitesvara), measuring 11½ inches in height, and made of white porcelain covered with a *ch'ing-pai* ("bluish-or greenish-white") glaze: one of the classic ceramic types of the Sung period. For reasons which will be stated however, the piece may confidently be ascribed to the following dynasty of the Yüan (1279–1368). The evidence for this revolves round a larger group of related figures, possessing similar characteristics, the significance of which has only recently come to be recognised. A discussion of these will, it is hoped, serve not merely to illuminate an episode of absorbing interest in the history of the porcelain figure, but at the same time reveal a fresh approach to some of the more obstinate problems of general ceramic history in this period.[2]

The Yüan period is in effect one that students of Chinese art have come to recognise as a time of crucial change and development. The years of subjection that followed the gradual conquest of the Mongols in the 13th century bore heavily upon the social and economic order, forcing a transformation in both structure and outlook; the course of the older, "medieval" culture of China, which had reached its full tide in Sung idealism, was rudely arrested and its motive force diverted; after the Ming restoration in 1368, the arts appear re-channelled into new paths. A varied selection of material to illustrate the artistic aspects of these phenomena was brought together in a loan exhibition held at the British Museum in 1954 under the title "Art under the Mongol Dynasties of China and Persia";[3] and again in an even more comprehensive exhibition, "The Yüan Dynasty: Chinese Art under the Mongols", which took place at the Cleveland Museum of Art during October-November, 1968.[4] On both occasions developments in ceramics were well represented; and it was shown to what a remarkable extent post-war studies in this field have transformed our view of a period which in earlier days, had become something of a dumping-ground for the awkward and unidentifiable. Above all it has now emerged as the great formative period of painted porcelain, characterised chiefly by the rise of the porcelain manufactures of Ching-tê-chên, and by the all-important development of "blue-and-white". But in addition to this some headway has also been made in exploring the preceding phase: one showing a new mood of varied experiment in which the expiring Sung style was gradually superseded.

In Sung times this region had been the principal source of manufacture of the *ch'ing-pai* ware; and the intermediate *ch'ing-pai* of the Yüan essentially represents a transition in technique between this and the characteristic porcelain ware of the Ming. The new body material is generally heavier and more compact, while the glazes become somewhat "fatter", i.e., more viscous and often less translucent; evidently the ware was now fired at a somewhat higher temperature. As if reflecting the sad deprivations of the time the forms of vessels lose much of their former gracefulness and acquire a rather ponderous quality; some specific variations of older forms emerge, and some new ones are introduced. More striking still is the accompanying change in attitude towards decoration which as if in response to some deep-felt need now receives a marked emphasis, while there is also a move towards greater realism in representation. The designs, as in the coming blue-and-white, are disposed often in a series of horizontal bands with adjacent borders of conventional motifs. In one such class the designs are incised with a sloping stroke; in another they are applied in low relief, providing an alternation of panelled pattern with plain that creates an illusion of broken movement over the surface (figs. 16–19).

The Museum's Kuan-yin figure shares both in this general body of technical peculiarities and in the aesthetic tendencies just described. The glaze has a tinge of fresh greenish-blue that seems to emphasise the supernatural purity of the deity; the bejewelled ornaments, including strings of pearls—a feature to which we shall revert later—signify his nobility. As befits one whose mission is to assuage the sufferings of humanity, the expression of the figure is compassionate and approachable. By Sung times the Bodhisattva Kuan-yin had already become the most favoured of all Buddhist subjects for sculptural treatment. The identification is confirmed further by the pose, and also by the miniature lotus throne intended for a figure of Amida Buddha, now lost, which is set in the crown. The deity is seated in *maharajalila*—the pose of "royal ease", with the right arm resting lightly across the raised knee, and the left leg folded. Although otherwise bare to the waist it wears a mantle over the shoulders and upper arms, where it is shaped in characteristic scrolling projections at the ends; and folds of a long scarf hang down over the body and one arm. Both the body and the lower garment, or *dhoti*, are ornamented with elaborate chains of pearls and jewelled pendants.

The greatest attention, however, has been given to the treatment of the head which is modelled with considerably more care than the body, and to the minute elaboration of the head-dress. The hair is raised on top in a chignon, and fronted by a diadem of strung pearls bearing in the centre a lotus leaf with a jewel, with coiled filigrees on either side. This must originally have been somewhat more intricate, for parts have been broken off and are now missing. From it, side plaits, similarly dressed and bejewelled, descend to the shoulders where they are linked to two plaits from the back of the head, fanned out in wavy strands. The ears also are fitted with jewelled pendants. The rear view (fig. 2) shows a braided ribbon with tassels extending to the "collar", but apart from this detail the modelling of the back is rough and cursory.

From its relatively small size one might suppose this statuette to have been intended for use in minor, private devotions; and the same may also be said of another which is of broadly similar type, although less ornate in its treatment: the model of a seated Buddha, $10\frac{5}{8}$ inches in height, belonging to the Royal Ontario Museum in Toronto.[5] The six larger statues, all in the region of 20 inches high, may however be presumed to have occupied a prominent position in some communal place of worship; and are distinctly more imposing both in their overall presence, and detailed sculptural treatment. For sheer size and complexity they represent an undertaking for which no precedent springs to mind in the previous history of Chinese porcelain.[6] All have suffered damage in varying degree while some of them have been restored in such a way as to distort their former appearance. They include one Buddha figure, and five of Bodhisattvas, the iconographical character of which is however so much obscured in some instances that their identification remains in doubt. Some detailed description of their condition is therefore called for in the following analysis, even if this cannot be claimed to offer any immediate solution of the problems concerned.

Certainly the most significant from a documentary point of view, and in some respects also the most sculpturally impressive, is the Kuan-yin figure in the W. R. Nelson Gallery at Kansas City (fig. 3), with an inscribed date, a note on which was published by Laurence Sickman in 1961.[7] In its essentials the presentation of the deity is the same as that of the Museum's smaller statuette, although some minor differences may be pointed out. The diadem, which

1. THE BODHISATTVA KUAN-YIN. Porcelain with *ch'ing-pai* glaze. First quarter of 14th century. Height $11\frac{1}{2}$ in. (29·2 cm). Victoria & Albert Museum (No. C.30–1968).

2. Rear view of the Kuan-yin in fig. 1.

3. KUAN-YIN. Porcelain with *ch'ing-pai* glaze; the lower part unglazed. On the base is painted an inscription containing a date corresponding to 1298 or 1299 A.D. Height 20¼ in. (51.4 cm), W. R. Nelson Gallery of Art, Kansas City

includes much elaborate lotus foliage, must originally have been much more complex in design: virtually all its projecting parts, including the Amida figure, side ornaments and ear pendants which presumably belonged to it have been lost, with the result that the head has acquired a somewhat shorn appearance. The side plaits, if any, would seem not to have extended below shoulder level. Some evidence is provided by comparing the back view of the two figures shown, (figs. 2, 4). One feature unique to this particular figure is that the *dhoti* was left unglazed; and although no traces of pigment remain, we may reasonably assume that it was at one time painted or gilt. On the wrists and upper arms are jewelled bracelets, evidently mould-cast for the purpose, and contrasting with the simpler bangles worn by the smaller figure. These, together with anklets, are repeated on other members of the series. It will be apparent also that the pearl chain is both simpler and heavier in style, incorporating larger pearls of uneven size; although a smaller pearl-beading is to be found in the head-dress.

The peculiar documentary significance of the figure lies in the inscription boldly written in ink on the base, of which the still faintly legible part reads: *Ta Tê êrh* (or more probably, *san*) *nien pa yüeh*: "2nd or 3rd year of Ta Tê, 8th month . . .": i.e., 1298 or 1299 A.D. Sickman has argued effectively for the genuineness of

this inscription, and indeed it is difficult to believe it otherwise. There is conviction both in the bold, angular style of the script, and in its present physical condition. While the possibility of its having been added some short time after manufacture must be allowed for, its accuracy seems essentially supported by the strong circumstantial evidence of other porcelains related to it in style. With only minor reservations, we may feel justified in erecting this statue beside the celebrated blue-and-white temple vases of 1351 in the Percival David Foundation as the second major landmark in the ceramic chronology of the period.[8]

Apart from the damage it has suffered, the Kansas City Kuan-yin shows a variety of technical defects, such as the emergence of black specks in the porcelain due to oxidisation of impurities, noticeable particularly on the face; faults in the glaze, which shows a marked tendency to agglomerate in unsightly lumps or ripples, of a deeper greenish colour, the areas thus exposed turning to an orange-burnt "biscuit"; and also the development of rather frequent firing cracks in the porcelain itself. Even when allowance is made for the unusual difficulty of constructing and firing porcelain objects of this size, these might well be interpreted as evidence of imperfect preparation of the materials at a relatively untutored stage in technical production. A second Bodhisattva figure (fig. 5) which belongs to

. Rear view of the Kuan-yin in Kansas City.

5. A BODHISATTVA. Porcelain with *ch'ing-pai* glaze. About 1300. Height 20½ in. (52 cm). Museum Rietberg, Zurich.

the Rietberg Museum in Zurich[9] suffers in some measure from the same defects (in addition to which it shows other accretions resulting apparently from exposure or burial), and in other respects also may be placed rather close to the dated Kuan-yin in style. There are close resemblances in the modelling of the torso, the draperies, and the somewhat heavy jewellery. In this case the jewelled ear pendants have survived, also rather more of the lotus in the diadem; the curious top-knot of hair, however, is substantially restoration: perhaps originally it somewhat resembled the chignon of the Museum's figure. The subject was at one time identified as Kuan-yin but one must be permitted to doubt this if only on account of the wholly un-characteristic pose: the right hand rests palm downwards on the knee while the left hand lies open on the lap—originally perhaps to hold some attribute. One suggestion would identify it with the Bodhisattva P'u-hsien (Samantabhadra), sometimes in Chinese art represented holding a sceptre in this position; the remaining indications, however, are insufficient to confirm this.

To invert the figure in search of an inscription is to meet with disappointment, for the base plate, if it formerly possessed one, is absent: possibly it became detached during the firing. This has, however, revealed the cross-struts put in to support its weight—a feature present also, although in simpler form, in the small

Kuan-yin (see fig. 6), where a longitudinal strut within the body of the figure is also visible.[10]

At this point one may appropriately introduce the Buddha figure (fig. 7), belonging to a private collection in London, which reveals in its technique a rather similar primitive quality. The glaze covering the hard white body has a somewhat more positive bluish-green tint and appears more fluent, running here and there into relatively deep pools; a large fire-crack in the base,

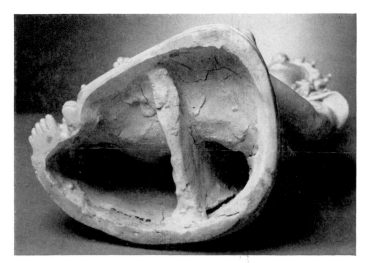

6. Base of the Victoria & Albert Museum Kuan-yin, showing strut support.

7. BUDDHA, perhaps Sākyamuni. Porcelain with *ch'ing-pai* glaze. About 1300. Height: 20½ in. (52·1 cm). Private Collection.

8. A BODHISATTVA. Porcelain with *ch'ing-pai* glaze. First quarter of 14th century. Height 20 in. (50·8 cm). Courtesy of the Metropolitan Museum of Art, New York. Gift of Judge Edgar Bromberger, 1951, in memory of his mother, Augusta Bromberger.

which has no vent-hole, has been filled up. The hands have undergone a certain amount of restoration.

As befits the subject, the sculptural treatment is more simple and jewellery is confined to bangles at the wrists and ankles. The back is plain but for the shoulder mantle which is folded in angular fashion over the left side, extending somewhat further down on the right. The elongated ears, pierced possibly for the insertion of real jewellery, and the treatment of hair, *usnisa* and *urna* are all appropriate to the subject. The right hand is disposed in the "wish-granting" (*vara*) mudra; that intended by the left hand however, with the middle finger crooked, is not positively clear. The facial features are rendered with marked refinement, and despite a certain crudity in the handling of the draperies the image achieves a presence of genuine distinction and power.

The Bodhisattva in the Metropolitan Museum of Art, New York (fig. 8),[11] is the only one of the group to be fully clothed, and also possesses the most extensive display of jewelled ornament. Here again restorations have in all probability greatly falsified its original appearance, for the entire bun of hair crowning the head, and also the left hand with its accompanying scroll (as well as the jewelled ornambets beside the right ear) are of plaster. The latter attrinute, perhaps,

is principally responsible for its traditional identification as Manjusrī and there is no indication of what other gesture the hand could originally have made, while the nature of the original head-dress can hardly be guessed at. The upper garment is a robe or jacket with long sleeves frilled at the cuffs. The mantle cast over it shows also the scrolled ends seen on the small Kuan-yin figure, although in more carefully delineated form; while the jewelled pearl-chains also repeat, with much greater elaboration, the same double formula.

If one can succeed in disregarding the various depredations and false additions to the heads of these four sculptures it is not difficult to recognise their close family resemblance; and this conclusion is one that may be extended equally to the Kuan-yin in the Museum when allowance is made for its smaller size and more summary execution. The oval faces, broad-browed, rather plump and square in the jaw, are at the same time curiously flattened, as shown in the side views (figs. 9–12), which also reveal the characteristic sag between protruding chin and neck. A common style is unmistakable also in the set of the small mouth, pursed upper lip, and long, sensitively-modelled nose; the high arch of the eyebrows, and the emphatic heaviness of the eyelids.

Other features in addition to these are characteristic

9–12. Side views of the heads of the figures shown in figs. 1, 3, 5 and 15.

of certain developments in sculptural style during the Yüan period: a subject to the study of which the Catalogue of the recent exhibition in Cleveland, with its thorough documentation and well-reasoned introduction, makes a fresh and valuable contribution. In their discussion of sculpture the authors emphasise as well as facial peculiarities such mannerisms as an unusually "long proportion in the body from the base downwards",[12] and "the schematic arrangement of the hair strands over the ears and shoulders"—features that may be observed, for example, in the important standing Kuan-yin from the Metropolitan Museum dated A.D. 1282 (*Catalogue*, No. 3). While no doubt of a Northern, Shansi origin, this impressive wood sculpture surely approximates in type to the southern sculptures in carved wood, now almost entirely lost, from which the porcelain modellers might have learnt their art.

And yet it is questionable whether their inspiration can have been wholly limited to this source. For while the relatively heavy pearl chains of the Kansas City Kuan-yin, for instance, could derive from sculpted works such as the dated Metropolitan figure, the crisp and refined treatment of the jewellery and beaded work on others spells out a technique beyond the scope of the wood carver. These ornaments betray a metal original; and perhaps the closest parallel for their execution, as well as their iconographical form, is to be found in a class of gilt bronze images, often relatively small in size, that were produced in China in the Tibetan/Nepalese style. Although the introduction of Tibetan Lamaist elements of iconography was certainly not new at this time their penetration was evidently much extended, owing in part to the direct support this form of Buddhism received from the Khan. Kubilai himself became an initiate in 1270; and it is shortly before this that the Nepalese master bronze-worker A-ni-ko, with other artists from Tibet, is reported to have arrived in Peking, where he is credited with important commissions.[13] While some progress has been made in tracing the evolution of this class of bronze images in Nepal itself during recent years,[14] however, the earlier development of the style in China still remains to be adequately studied. Thus while there exist a number of models which may be dated by their inscriptions to the 15th century,[15] those which may be ascribed with assurance to the 14th century are few. It may be, therefore, that the indirect evidence provided by this series of porcelain sculptures will prove to be of value in this connection also.

Of several such bronzes exhibited at Cleveland for which a 14th century date is contemplated it is the Tara (No. 16, lent by Usher P. Coolidge)[16] which most closely approximates to the porcelain figures in its treatment of the features we have described. But the force of the likeness is more strikingly demonstrated when yet another of the *ch'ing-pai* figures, that from the Porzellansammlung in Dresden (fig. 13), is compared with the bronze statuette shown in fig. 14.[17] The resemblance will be noted particularly in the shape of the head, the facial features, and even the blissfully withdrawn smile, but it extends also to the draperies, and to a lesser extent to the torso itself. The form of the crown and its jewelled ornaments are almost identical; and it is clear that the broken-off projections behind the prominent ears of the porcelain figure may be directly identified with the characteristic "wings" of the undamaged bronze head-dress. The chain of pearls, with its multiple pendants, is of a delicate complexity unmatched in any of the other figures. Indeed, the figure offers a remarkably complete presentation of the prescribed ornaments for a Dhyāni-Bodhisattva.[18] The period of this fragmentary, but very distinguished porcelain statue was perceptively diagnosed as Yüan some thirty years ago by Ernst Zimmermann,[19] who based his argument for the dating in part on its **103**

13. A BODHISATTVA. Porcelain with *ch'ing-pai* glaze; the lower part is a restoration in baked clay. First quarter of 14th century. Height (with pedestal): 26¾ in. (68 cm). Staatliche Porzellansammlung, Dresden.

14. A BODHISATTVA, seated on a lotus pedestal. Gilt bronze. In Nepalese style, but probably executed in China. ? 15th century.

strongly Tibetan/Nepalese style. While it has not been possible to examine it, his careful description is sufficient to confirm its evident association with the other figures of the series; although as he remarked, a proper identification of the Bodhisattva is made virtually impossible by the damage to the arms, which has destroyed any evidence that may have existed in the form of a mudra or attributes. The restoration of the lower part of the figure, which is in baked clay, would seem to have added disproportionately to the length of the body, and thus to have exaggerated its height.

The last figure in the group, the Bodhisattva in the Field Museum of Natural History, Chicago, (fig. 15),[20] possesses a certain facial resemblance to the image just described. He is again seated in the customary cross-legged posture and leans slightly forward to look down at the worshipper, supported from behind by a flat, shaped mandorla such as may still occasionally be found attached to Nepalese bronze statues.[21] Other points of note are the unusual pose of the hands which are raised, evidently to hold a loose drape of the scarf, in front of the body; the disposition of the curled strands of hair, which lie—as at Dresden—along the

line of the shoulder; and the curious, arrow-shaped *urna* mark applied to the forehead. The crown is virtually identical with that of the Dresden statue. The traditional description of the figure as Kuan-yin can hardly be correct; and at Cleveland its identification was given as Manjusrī. Its material characteristics are similar to those of the figures already described, and both glaze imperfections and fire cracks in the body are present: the glaze, however, is of a clearer and whiter tone than usual, running into a very light greenish-blue in its thicker accumulations.

Having regard both to the common sculptural style of this series of figures and to their material characteristics, there would appear to be the strongest case for regarding them as products of a single workshop. It must be allowed that the last two considered show an increased sophistication of manner, and also a degree of superiority in technique, which might be taken to imply a somewhat later date than that of the figure in Kansas City (1298/1299). The question: "how much later?" is an important one, for reasons that will become apparent. At Cleveland indeed, the Chicago figure was catalogued as "late 14th century": but it would seem permissible to doubt whether evidence is available to support such a late dating on purely sculptural grounds. As indicated in the case of the Dresden figure for example, the more harmonious result could be attributed at least in part to the copying of a superior model. The time-lag also seems larger than would be necessary merely to account for this degree of improvement in the preparation and firing of the porcelain. In this connection, therefore, we must consider the further evidence provided by porcelain vessels and other objects, the manufacture of which would appear to have been directly connected with that of the figures.

At this point our study of these statues leads directly to the central problem of ceramic development in the Ching-tê-chên area during the earlier part of the Yüan dynasty; i.e. that of the much-debated origins of painted blue-and-white. Of especial relevance also is the dating of that class of *ch'ing-pai* wares, essentially early in style, on which applied ornament in the form of strings of pearl-beading provides a major feature of the decorative scheme. Since the first study of these wares was made[22] a number of further examples have come to light: among them the missing "Gaignières-Fonthill" vase— the earliest surviving specimen of Chinese ceramics that can be shown to have been brought to Europe in medieval times—which was discovered,[23] now shorn of the enamelled mounts which once celebrated its ownership by King Louis the Great of Hungary (1326–82), in the National Museum of Ireland, some 8 or 9 years ago. A sizeable group of these pieces (represented here by the pieces shown in figs. 16, 17) was collected together for showing at the exhibition in Cleveland last year.[24] Their distinctive form of decoration is virtually without parallel in the history of Chinese ceramics; and that their production was linked to that of the figures can hardly be doubted. Moreover, certain pieces—notably the stemcup from Bristol with applied votive figures,[25] and the section of a pagoda from the Metropolitan Museum[26]—show an unusually direct association with Buddhist ritual. The pearl-beading so curiously draped over these wares corresponds exactly to that used, for example, to execute the prescribed ornaments of the Museum's Kuan-yin figure; and it would seem a very plausible hypothesis that the technique of producing it was evolved in the first place for the specific purpose of fulfilling these ritual requirements. Unlike the heavier pearl-chains that also appear on the figures these could not have been assembled from porcelain beads

15. A BODHISATTVA (perhaps Manjusrī), with shaped mandorla. Porcelain with *ch'ing-pai* glaze. First quarter of 14th century. Height 17⅜ in. (42·7 cm). Chicago, Field Museum of Natural History.

modelled separately: the tiny beads are virtually uniform in size and form continuous ropes, sufficiently cohesive not to fall apart during the firing. The secret of the technique must have involved the use of some form of thread. Possibly the "necklaces" were dipped in a liquid porcelain "slip", like the lacework on late "Dresden" figures in Europe; the base material then disappearing in the firing. There are instances in which the ropes are of twisted threads rather than beading.[27] In common with other *ch'ing-pai* wares of the period they show a considerable range in material quality. Pieces such as the octagonal bottle in the Museum (fig. 17),[28] for example, or the stemcup at Bristol show a distinctly rich and fluent glaze of good colour; while others such as the pair of vases with stands at San Francisco,[29] or the virtual twin to the Fonthill vase acquired by the British Museum (fig. 16),[30] are more thinly or imperfectly glazed. Yet the strictly limited style and highly idiosyncratic character of their ornament may be argued to preclude an extended **105**

16. BOTTLE, porcelain with *ch'ing-pai* glaze. The decoration is partly incised, and partly of moulded floral reliefs applied to hollowed-out panels, with applied strings of pearl-beading. The silver mount on the cut-down neck is perhaps Javanese. The piece closely resembles the so-called 'Gaignières-Fonthill vase' in the National Museum of Ireland. First quarter of 14th century. Height 10·9 in. (27·7 cm). British Museum.

17. OCTAGONAL BOTTLE, Porcelain with *ch'ing-pai* glaze and applied floral rel with pearl-beading. The gilt metal mount and cover on the cut-down neck probably German, early 18th century. Height 10⅞ in. (27·6 cm). Victoria a Albert Museum (No. C.68–1957). Given by Baroness Cassel van Doorn.

date-span. As a form of decoration for pottery the applied bead strings may fairly be censured as clumsy and naive; and sometimes—as Arthur Lane pointed out in the case of the Fonthill vase—their addition seems almost an afterthought, over-running a previously-executed scheme of incised designs. The panels of floral designs in applied relief which the beading was not infrequently used to frame (vide fig. 16) may perhaps be said to achieve a certain pictorial quality consonant with the changing aesthetic ideals of the period, and in this sense the style might seem directly to prefigure the introduction of painted decoration: it is difficult to believe, however that it can long have survived it.

Up to the present our only precise point of chronological reference has been the pair of blue-and-white vases in the Percival David Foundation dated in correspondence with 1351 A.D.:[31] hence the unusual significance of the Kuan-yin figure in Kansas City with its date of 1298/99. The remarkable *kuan* jar in the Percival David

Foundation here reproduced in figure 18,[32] which combines elements relating to both, is clearly therefore a key piece for study. For the panels of floral decoration, which are applied in relief on a hollowed-out ground, are not only framed in pearl-beading but coloured also in both cobalt-blue and copper-red, and accompanied by painted "blue-and-white" designs of some elaboration. Presumably it is its exceptionally ambitious character that leads Sherman Lee to express the view—while at the same time accepting that the Gaignières-Fonthill vase predates the development of painted decoration—that this jar represents a later development: ". . . It is as reasonable to suppose," he writes, "that the pierced and moulded decorative technique persisted into the second half of the fourteenth century as to assume that the underglaze blue technique, here well developed, should be pushed back in time."[33] It is arguable that the evidence tends to the contrary; and that to the measure that blue-and-white may have been made before 1351 it is correspondingly less probable that this earlier, obsolescent style should have persisted so far. On comparing the panelled decoration with that of the Fonthill type vase in fig. 16 one can hardly deny their appearance of close similarity. But in other respects also this *kuan* jar may reasonably be described as showing a relatively primitive character. In shape and size for example, its affinities are surely not, as suggested, with the type of jar to be broadly associated with the mid-14th century blue-and-white style:[34] they are rather with such pieces as the *ch'ing-pai kuan* with incised dragon decoration in the Brundage Collection at San Francisco (fig. 19),[35] or with the similar, covered jar in the Yamato Bunka-kan near Nara,[36] on which the incised phoenix design is reserved on a ground of unsuccessful copper-red: both characteristic products of what may be regarded as the earlier phase of varied experiment. As regards the painted designs, there is one feature which may prove to

be significant: the particular character of the asymmetrical, pendant scrolls which appear within the "lotus-petal" panels bordering the foot. A similar character in this motif is noticeable on many other blue-and-white pieces for which an early date has been suggested,[37] while it appears also in more primitive form in the pendant scrolls decorating the Fonthill-type pieces. Finally, in addition to certain crudities in potting and glazing, the David Foundation's *kuan* has in its base a major firing crack: a defect that in the mid-14th century would probably have caused it to be rejected. All these indications in fact lend support to the theory that this jar represents an intermediate stage: one at which the declining tradition of *ch'ing-pai* wares and that of the new painted style overlap. At the same time, the singular difficulty of establishing any extended sequence of stylistic development in early blue-and-white—one with which all serious students of the matter

18. JAR (*kuan*), porcelain with panels of applied floral reliefs framed in pearl-beading, and coloured in underglaze blue and red, with painting in underglaze blue. ?About 1325. Height 13 in. (33·0 cm). Percival David Foundation.

19. JAR (*kuan*), porcelain with incised design of dragons and waves, and floral scroll on the shoulder. ?About 1325. Height 12½ in. (31·7 cm). De Young Museum, San Francisco (Avery Brundage Collection).

will be familiar—leads to a further conclusion: that this development may well have been much more rapid than we have tended to believe. It is certainly a mistake to assume that any great number of years would necessarily be required to account for this level of accomplishment either in the techniques of blue-and-white, or in its design: and the ambitious complexity of this piece does not preclude its representing a rather early stage in such a short evolution.

Granted the speculative nature of these assumptions—they take only limited account, for example, of such factors as differences in style which may have emanated from various factories—it may nevertheless be of practical value to pursue their implications to the point of suggesting a loose, and highly tentative, chronological scheme. Thus the particular group of figures presented here, with their relatively wide variation in technical accomplishment, might be thought of as belonging largely to the period c. 1295–1325; while the "Fonthill vase" type of decoration would have reached its fullest development towards the end of that period. Allied to these, but perhaps requiring a slightly more extended timespan are the group of wares with incised designs alone,[38] which in some instances parallel those of the earlier blue-and-white wares. The introduction of painting in underglaze blue and red, perhaps occurring more or less simultaneously, may not in fact have taken place before the turn of the first quarter of the 14th century. This would allow for a development of hardly more than twenty years between the David Foundation's *kuan* jar and its temple vases.

The group of *ch'ing-pai* figures which have provided the occasion for this discussion extend even further the list of experiments and innovations that we can ascribe to this surprisingly fertile period of ceramic history; and as we have argued, they provide new points of reference in the charting of that history. Before concluding, however, mention should also be made of the fresh evidence now coming to light as a result of excavations, both controlled and uncontrolled, in the Philippine Islands. For here too *ch'ing-pai* figures of early type have been found during the last two years:[39] they are in general somewhat smaller than the Museum's figure, averaging perhaps six to eight inches in height, and include models of Kuan-yin, Lohans, and other deities and mythological subjects. The modelling is as a rule more free and rough than that described here but their character is none the less positive and appealing; in some instances they also have strings of pearl-beaded ornament. In the same graves as some of them, jarlets and other specimens of early blue-and-white or red-and-white were found. The proper dating of these pieces remains the subject of differing opinions, since in Manila the view is still held to that much of this body of varied material, including the painted wares, may be ascribed to the Sung period on the basis of archaeological findings.[40] The contrary opinion that would doubt this, and maintain that the developments concerned belong rather to the Yüan period, perhaps finds some further support in the stylistic arguments we have mapped out with reference to the dated Kuan-yin figure in Kansas City. The discovery of these *ch'ing-pai* figurines however, is not the least interesting aspect of the very important finds being made in this area, and provides an intriguing pendant to the picture of their production in so far as we have been able to trace it. It is much to be hoped that a comprehensive study of the series will be published.

Notes

1. Museum No. C.30–1968. Purchased at Christie's: see *Sale Catalogue*, May 20, 1968, Lot 124 (illustrated).

2. The present paper is in effect an expanded version of one delivered by the author to the Symposium held at the de Young Museum, San Francisco, on the occasion of the opening of the new Avery Brundage wing in August, 1966.

3. The exhibition was reviewed by Basil Gray in *Oriental Art*, N.S., I.4, 1955, pp. 3–11.

4. The assembling of this exhibition, together with its fully-documented and illustrated Catalogue by Sherman E. Lee and Wai-kam Ho, *Chinese Art under the Mongols: The Yüan Dynasty*, Cleveland, 1968, constitutes a major work of research. In the first of two long introductory essays Sherman Lee touches upon a number of the questions to be discussed in this article. This catalogue will be cited hereafter as *Cleveland Catalogue*.

5. Published by Henry Trubner, 'Two Examples of Ch'ing-pai Porcelain in the Royal Ontario Museum', *Archives of the Chinese Art Society of America*, XVIII, 1963, pp. 38–39; see also *Cleveland Catalogue*, No. 28.

6. Among earlier figures they are perhaps exceeded in size only by a well-known series of lead-glazed pottery statues of Lohans, which are also now widely scattered among Museums in the

United States and in Europe. The history of these much-discussed figures, which are now generally considered to date from the Liao period (10th–12th centuries), is conveniently summarised in a recent article by Marion Wolf, 'The Lohans from I-chou', *Oriental Art*, N.S. XV.1, Spring 1969, pp. 51–57.

7. L. Sickman, 'A Ch'ing-pai Porcelain Figure Bearing a Date', *Archives of the Chinese Art Society of America*', XV, 1961, p. 34, where the inscription is reproduced. The figure was acquired in China in 1935.

8. Mention should also be made of the valuable discovery recently recorded by Margaret Medley, 'A T'ien-shun Saucer', *Archives of Asian Art*, XXI, 1967–68, pp. 67–69, concerning a *ch'ing-pai* piece showing *shu-fu* type characteristics which may be dated by its moulded reign-mark to the period 1328–32.

9. See *Sammlung J. F. H. Menten: Chinesische Grabfunde und Bronzen*, Zurich, Kunstgewerbemuseum, 1948, (fig. 93).

10. This form of construction is probably common to all figures of the group: in the case of the Bodhisattva in the Metropolitan Museum, New York, for example, it is plainly visible through a break in the base.

11. From the collection of Judge E. Bromberger: Acq. No. 51.166.

12. *Cleveland Catalogue*, p. 4.

13. Douglas Barrett, 'The Buddhist Art of Tibet and Nepal', *Oriental Art*, N.S., III, No. 3, Autumn 1957, p. 95.

14. The catalogue of a recent and important exhibition, Stella Kramrisch, *The Art of Nepal*, New York (The Asia Society), 1964, publishes a long series of Nepalese bronzes, a number of which are ascribed to the 14th century.

15. Barret, *loc. cit.*

16. *Cleveland Catalogue*, No. 16: with the attribution 'late Yüan or early Ming dynasty', notwithstanding the inscription it bears reading: 'Bestowed during the Yung-lo era of the Great Ming'.

17. Present whereabouts unknown. Published in the review of a loan exhibition by H. d'Ardenne de Tizac, 'L'Art Bouddhique au Musée Cernuschi', *L'Art Décoratif*, No. 192, Paris, June 1913, fig. 39 (centre), where it is undated, and ascribed to Tibet. The highly traditional character of this type of figure renders a precise dating relatively unimportant for the present purpose.

18. Cf. Alice Getty, *The Gods of Northern Buddhism*, Oxford 1928, p. 46.

19. E. Zimmermann, 'Eine Porzellanfigur aus der Yüan-zeit in der Dresdner Porzellansammlung', *Ostasiatische Zeitung*, N.F., XIII, 1937, pp. 143–146, and Taf. 23.

20. *Cleveland Catalogue*, No. 24, According to information supplied by the Curator, Mr. Kenneth Starr, the figure was acquired in China for the Museum by Berthold Laufer during 1908–10.

21. Cf. S. Kramrisch, *op. cit.*, Nos. 39, 48.

22. John Ayers, 'Some Characteristic Wares of the Yüan Dynasty', *Transactions of the Oriental Ceramic Society*, 1954–55, pp. 78–80, fig. 17–25.

23. Arthur Lane, 'The Gaignières-Fonthill Vase: A Chinese Porcelain of about 1300', *The Burlington Magazine*, CIII, April 1961, pp. 124–32.

24. *Cleveland Catalogue*, Nos. 29, 107–11; and see pp. 17–18 of the Introduction by Sherman E. Lee.

25. Ayers, *op. cit.*, fig. 18; *Cleveland Catalogue*, No. 109.

26. *Cleveland Catalogue*, No. 29.

27. e.g. Ayers, *op. cit.*, fig. 25.

28. Ayers, *op. cit.*, fig. 21; *Cleveland Catalogue*, No. 107.

29. R.-Y. Lefebvre d'Argencé. *Chinese Ceramics in the Avery Brundage Collection*, San Francisco 1967, pl. XLVIII.B; *Cleveland Catalogue*, Nos. 111 a, b.

30. Basil Gray, 'Chinese Porcelain of the Fourteenth Century, III: Ch'ing-pai', *British Museum Quarterly*, XXV, Nos. 1–2, March 1962, pp. 29–31 and Plates VI–VII.

31. Percival David Foundation of Chinese Art, *Illustrated Catalogue, Section 3: Porcelains decorated in Underglaze Blue and Copper Red*, by Margaret Medley, 1963, pp. 46–47 and Frontispiece illustration; *Cleveland Catalogue*, No. 126 (with full bibliography).

32. Percival David Foundation, *op. cit.*, p. 58; Ayers, *op. cit.*, fig. 19. Of particular interest is the discovery in 1964 of a closely similar jar at Pao-ting in Hopei province, among a hoard of other 14th century wares: see the report in *Wen Wu*, 1965, No. 2, pp. 17–18. The jar still retains its cover, which is shallow and straight-sided, with a low domed top and lion knob finial.

33. *Cleveland Catalogue*, p. 18, and No. 39.

34. e.g. *Cleveland Catalogue*, Nos. 154–57.

35. *Cleveland Catalogue*, No. 98; d'Argencé, *op. cit.*, pl. XLVIII A.

36. *Sekai toji zenshu*, XI, Tokyo 1954, pl. 45, The comparison is reinforced by the similarity of its cover to that of the jar from Pao-ting referred to in n. 32 above, although in this case a simple knob replaces the lion finial. No covers for jars of the later type seem now to exist.

37. e.g., *Cleveland Catalogue*, Nos. 128, 129, 142. See also the remarks by Basil Gray, *loc. cit.*

38. Represented at Cleveland by Nos. 98–102 and 166 (with added ground of copper-red), and discussed on p. 17 of the Introduction. See also Ayers, *op. cit.*, figs. 16, 27, and pp. 75–83. Development of the *shu-fu* class of wares from about this time is also suggested by the evidence of the T'ien-shun marked dish published by Margaret Medley, *op. cit.*, (see n.8).

39. For the most part since the publication of Leandro & Cecilia Locsin, *Oriental Ceramics Discovered in the Philippines*, Rutland & Tokyo 1967, which provides a particularly informative and well-illustrated account of the more recent discoveries; see however the minor figurines shown on figs. 73 (left) and fig. 78; also fig. 136 for a small jar decorated with the characteristic pearl-beading.

40. See Rosa C. P. Tenazas, *A Report on the Archaeology of the Locsin-University of San Carlos Excavations in Pila, Laguna*, (Sept 4, 1967–March 19, 1968), Manila 1968; and the Introduction by Leandro & Cecilia Locsin, in which problems of dating are discussed. Students from many parts of the world attended a Seminar on Trade Pottery held in Manila during March 18–24, 1968 at which the new finds were examined; and it is anticipated that its proceedings will be published.

The Rood-Loft from Hertogenbosch

CHARLES AVERY

I. The Acquisition of the Rood-Loft for the Museum

THE importance of the rood-loft from the Cathedral of St. John at Hertogenbosch (Bois-le-Duc)[1] was justly emphasised by Sir Matthew Digby Wyatt in a report laid before the Board of the South Kensington Museum when they were considering its purchase in March 1869.[2] "It seems almost needless for me to assert," he wrote,

"1st that this from its bulk and splendour is a most important specimen of Architectural elaboration in marble.

2nd that its style is one regarded by many as *'impure'*—

3rd that it is only by extraordinary accident that any such specimen could be in the market. I do however make these assertions, because I would remark in reference to each of them,

1st that its very 'importance' seems to demand that it should be incorporated into the structure of the Museum buildings now in course of construction.

2nd Its style of 'impure' is full of grand intention, and illustrates a phase in the history of Art, comparatively unknown in this country, excepting by reflection through the Masons of the Jacobean age when the use of variously coloured marble monuments was common throughout England.

3rd I think *decidedly* that advantage ought to be taken of the extraordinary accident which brings this within reach and I most warmly recommend the purchase. With regard to price I am in nowise surprised at it— since its purchase by any dealer must have been a great speculation—its bulk—the hazard of removal—the cost of transportation and all the risks and costs of its exhibition and disposal certainly justify a large demand and handsome profit. It will no doubt be secured should the department decide upon its purchase upon the most favourable terms."

The rood-loft was at the time in the possession of the art dealer Murray Marks, who had purchased it as a speculation from the authorities of the Cathedral. "On many occasions," wrote Marks's biographer,[3] "it was his privilege to warn the officials at the Museum when special objects came into the market worthy of their possession, and he was responsible for advising them to purchase the magnificent rood screen, from the Church of St. John the Baptist, at Bois-le-Duc, North Brabant, which he eventually acquired and sold to the Museum."

Sir Matthew Digby Wyatt had been asked to report in his capacity of Art Referee on the merits of the prospective purchase from the evidence of a photograph. Fortunately, his remarkably perspicacious and cogent recommendation persuaded the authorities to secure the monument, despite a price which seemed high at the time.[4] In a letter of May 3[5] Marks formally offered to deposit the complex on loan at a rental of 5% per annum on the price of £900, which he had set upon it. This arrangement, which was not as unusual then as it might seem today, was confirmed by a contract signed the same day.[6] It was there stipulated that "the payment of this rental is not to be considered as binding the South Kensington Museum to the purchase of the objects, but the Museum is to have the right to purchase at the sum named during the period named". The period of rental was extended beyond the initial year, until in 1871 the authorities decided to exercise their option to purchase the rood-loft outright, at the original price.[7] Sir Matthew Digby Wyatt's suggestion that the rood-loft should be incorporated into the structure of the Museum buildings found acceptance, and by 1871 it had been rebuilt against the south wall of the Casts Court (Room 46 A), facing towards Trajan's Column. It was so placed that its central arch framed the doorway through which one actually entered the Museum from Cromwell Road for a period in the 1890's,[8] while the left hand arch sheltered part of a makeshift catalogue stall.[9]

The "extraordinary accident" whereby the rood-loft came into the art market in the first place was a rash decision by the authorities of the Cathedral of St. John to remove the loft from the crossing of their church on the grounds that it obstructed the congregation's view of the high altar.[10] One wonders if their real objection was not the inconsistency of its style with the Gothic architecture for which the Cathedral has always been justly famed. The monument was demolished in 1866 at a cost of 2000 francs and sold to Murray Marks for 1200 francs a year later.[11]

In the Netherlands the outcry was immediate: "Un acte que, à juste titre, on doit flétrir du nom de vandalisme, et stigmatiser de l'épithète de barbarie," was Charles Piot's outraged description of the affair, as early as 1867.[12] By 1873 Victor de Stuers could refer to

1. THE TOWN AND CATHEDRAL OF HERTOGENBOSCH, drawing by Pieter Saenredam, 1632.

it as "Het Bossche schandaal" in a highly emotional article which he wrote to incite public opinion against permitting further depredations on the national heritage of Holland.[13] The Hertogenbosch scandal was ultimately one of the prime reasons for the foundation of the Rijksmonumentenzorg, the Dutch equivalent of our Historic Monuments Commission.

The demolition and removal of the loft from its original site were criticized in this country too, soon after its reappearance in the Casts Court. In *The Builder* of January 7, 1871, the English public could read in the course of a general description of the Cathedral (which was little more than a vehicle for this complaint): "The furniture of this church is very rich and magnificent; and here we must protest against the removal of the rood screen, which was the finest example of Renaissance work in the whole of Holland. However much it might have been out of place in a Gothic church, its own immense value as a work of art and the intrinsic merit of the sculpture with which it was adorned, to say nothing of its costly material (black marble and alabaster), ought to have saved it from destruction; and we cannot but regret its removal." The fact that the rood-loft was rebuilt against a wall precluded a reconstruction of its rear façade, which had originally faced eastwards into the choir of St. John's, and this gave rise to a misapprehension that the Museum had purchased only part of the loft. Our anonymous correspondent in *The Builder* continues: "Portions of this noble screen have been purchased by the South Kensington authorities, and we regret that

the whole has not fallen into their hands, as in that case our readers might have judged for themselves of the great beauty of this work of art. However, enough is to be seen there to convince any man of taste of the correctness of our strictures upon those who removed this noble screen."

No official disclaimer was published by the Museum and the misapprehension was given general currency in the Netherlands by Victor de Stuers in his article of 1873,[14] where he surmised that the eastern façade was lost and might still be at St. John's or in private hands. Not until 1917 was the mystery solved. In that year Dr. P. Buschmann came to the Museum, after ascertaining that the missing elements were nowhere to be found in the Netherlands, and during an inspection of the rood-loft itself came across two or three baskets, lying forgotten on top of the structure. In these he found the important set of reliefs of the Corporal Works of Mercy and a jumble of decorative fragments, which had originally formed the rear façade.

This surprising discovery, published a year later in the Netherlands in the only definitive article ever written on the rood-loft,[15] persuaded the Keeper of the Department of Architecture and Sculpture to revive earlier proposals for removing the loft from the Casts Court into the East Hall (Room 50), where other original architectural specimens had long since been displayed.[16] In order to permit the reconstruction of the rear façade he selected the present commanding position across the length of this hall, which of course approximates to the original situation

2. The rood-loft from Hertogenbosch, in the Museum.

of the rood-loft (fig. 2). Unfortunately the hall is not wide enough to permit one properly to see the north and south ends of the structure, and therefore the statues of Justice and Peace and the reliefs from the ends are mounted under the side arches for the sake of visibility. The rebuilding took place in 1923–4 and was recorded by R. P. Bedford in a brief article for *Country Life*,[17] which constitutes the only previous publication on the rood-loft by an official of the Museum.

Presumably Murray Marks or agents of the Museum took the trouble to have working drawings made of the loft while still *in situ*, in order to facilitate its reconstruction at South Kensington. These no longer exist, but two 19th century photographs showing the rood-loft in its original position across the entrance to the choir of St. John's (possibly the ones from which Sir Matthew Digby Wyatt wrote his report) serve to confirm the accuracy of the present reconstruction (fig. 3). That this design was the original intention is proved not only by its close conformity with the details of the original specifications (see page 115) but also by a pen and wash sketch signed by P. J. Saenredam and dated July 3, 1632, which shows how the rood-loft

looked soon after its erection (fig. 4).[18] This charming sketch is sufficiently detailed to provide valuable information, for instance, about the position of the arms and hands of several of the statues, which have since fallen off, and about the function of the structure; for it plainly supported a pretty, 16th century organ, and was therefore presumably used by the choir as well. Even more evocative of the visual impression made by the rood-loft on the spectator as he looked down the soaring, Gothic nave of St. John's is a remarkable drawing made in 1777 by one Jacques Everts (fig. 5).[19] It combines a carefully projected cross-section of the whole width of the Cathedral, including side-aisles, flying buttresses and roof-timbers, with the typically Dutch genre of the church interior. Amazingly, the draughtsman succeeded in combining his archaeological interest in Gothic constructional methods, with an equally loving delineation of the late Renaissance furnishings of the interior, the rood-loft itself, the organ and the pulpit. He also included a number of captivating incidentals, such as a lady and gentleman about to make an offering in a heavily chained and padlocked alms-box, and a pair of gentlemen demonstratively admiring the nave. From this drawing can be seen what an important aesthetic role was played by the candlesticks, which punctuate the severely horizontal parapet, as well as by the pinnacled shape of the organ itself, in relating the incongruous, Renaissance forms of the rood-loft to its surroundings.

II. The Circumstances of the Commission and the Background to the Design

The Cathedral at Hertogenbosch, in common with practically every other major church in the Netherlands, had suffered severe damage during the second half of the 16th century, as a result of the prolonged and bitter struggle between the Spanish Catholic régime and the Calvinist insurgents. Quite apart from the normal hazards of war, one of the most extreme manifestations of the Protestant revolt was a wave of iconoclasm (aptly dubbed the *Beeldenstorm*, or "Storming of the Statues") which swept the Netherlands about 1566. The philistine frenzy of the movement may be judged from a later engraving by Gaspar Bouttats (1640–95) showing the sack of Antwerp Cathedral and the destruction of its rood-loft by a Calvinist mob (fig. 6).

An earlier, Gothic rood-loft in St. John's suffered precisely the same fate in the *Beeldenstorm*, and all hope of restoring it had to be abandoned in 1584, when a fire caused the partial collapse of the vault over the south transept and the fall of débris damaged the loft beyond repair. Not until the political and military situation had been stabilised temporarily by the signing of the Twelve Years Truce in 1609 could the citizens of Hertogenbosch think of undertaking an extensive programme of rebuilding. By that time, the division of the Netherlands into the Protestant United Provinces in the north and the Roman Catholic States General, or Spanish Netherlands, in the south had been effected. Hertogenbosch was the furthest north of the major towns under Spanish domination, being almost on the frontier established under the terms of the Twelve Years Truce. As such, it must surely have been regarded as a bastion of the renewed Catholicism of the Counter-Reformation, and it was in this atmosphere that the construction and decoration of the new rood-loft in the Cathedral were undertaken.

Soon after the end of the Truce in 1621, however, Hertogenbosch was captured by the Dutch in the last campaign before the frontier was finally stabilised (1629), and the Cathedral was taken over by the Protestants. Fortunately, by this stage the iconoclastic ardour of the Calvinists had lost its edge, and the newly-constructed rood-loft escaped the total destruction that had been the fate of so many similar complexes in the late 16th century. The puritan conscience of the invaders seems to have been salved by the removal of the figure of Christ the Saviour from the niche facing the choir and (possibly) by decapitating some of the images of the Virgin in the narrative reliefs. One might hazard a guess that the general toll of destruction was by this time so obviously appalling as to inhibit any inclination towards further wanton damage, especially in the case of so new and attractive a monument. The delicate sketch made some three years later by Pieter Saenredam shows the Nave side of the rood-loft in perfect order, though without a large, independent Crucifix which had hung above it, completing the iconography, since 1592 (fig. 4).

3. The rood-loft in St. John's, before 1867.

4. THE ROOD-LOFT IN ST. JOHN'S, drawing by Pieter Saenredam, 1632.

5. THE INTERIOR OF ST. JOHN'S (detail), drawing by Jacques Everts, 1777.

Violencias y Sacrilegios que los Herejes usaron contra las Imagines de Christo y de los Santos en la yglesia Cathedral de Amberez

6. THE SACK OF ANTWERP CATHEDRAL BY CALVINIST INSURGENTS, engraving by Gaspar Bouttats.

In September 1610, after reconstructing the vault of the south transept, the authorities began to cast round for a master and a design for the rood-loft. After that date, virtually every official decision affecting its reconstruction is recorded in the Municipal Archives at Hertogenbosch.[20] The documents preserved there provide a wealth of information about the circumstances of the commission; the alternative projects that were initially considered; the specifications of the subjects for all the sculpture; the progress of work; and the prolonged legal wrangles over additional payments. They are, however, disappointingly uninformative about the master to whom the whole scheme was entrusted, one Coenraed van Norenberch from Namur. From the wording of a document whereby he was granted the citizenship of Hertogenbosch in 1607–8, we learn that he came of the Van Norenberch family of masons which had been active at Namur and in the Meuse Valley throughout the 16th century.[21] His father, also called Coenraed, had been a master-mason at Namur between 1571 and 1595, the year of his death. The family had specialised in building rood-lofts as early as 1502, and this long-standing expertise, handed down from father to son, is the only explanation one

can at present offer for the choice of Coenraed the younger as entrepreneur at Hertogenbosch, which was a long way from his native Meuse Valley.

Whether his settling at Hertogenbosch in 1607–8 had any direct connection with the programme of restoring the Cathedral we do not know, but it seems far from improbable that he was involved in rebuilding the fallen vault, which was a necessary preliminary to erecting the rood-loft. No other name than his is ever mentioned in the documents concerning the loft itself and we have no evidence that the commission was ever put out to tender. Although two alternative projects were initially under consideration, it may have been a foregone conclusion that Coenraed would be the executant in either case. The more elaborate and expensive of these projects consisted of a rood-loft with five arches, a design for which there was no precedent during the Renaissance: it is described in great detail in a specification of September 22, 1610, and appears to have been presented in the form of a model too.[22] The cheaper alternative that was ultimately chosen was a design closely modelled on a rood-loft in Antwerp Cathedral.[23] This loft had only just been finished and was no doubt felt to represent the last word in modern design. As at

115

7. The rood-loft by Cornelis Floris. Cathedral, Tournai, 1571–74.

Hertogenbosch, an earlier, Gothic loft had suffered at the hands of the iconoclasts, and plans for replacing it were first considered in 1585.[24] The quarrying of stone began forthwith, but building operations were delayed until 1597, because of other subsidiary work in progress, including a series of marble screens to separate the choir from the ambulatory. In fact, the question of who was responsible for the design of the Antwerp rood-loft is obscured by the simultaneous execution of these other screens, for it is not always clear to which scheme the documented payments for drawings relate. Payments to Cornelis Floris in the late 1560's, for instance, have been mistakenly thought to refer to the rood-loft, which so obviously recalls his famous one at Tournai, when they are actually connected with the screens round the choir. The most promising candidate as designer of the architecture is Raphael Paludanus, an Antwerp sculptor, who in any case supervised its erection from 1597 until his death in 1599.[25] Work was not finished even then, and payments to the brothers Jan and

Robrecht de Nole for the decorative and figurative sculpture are recorded in 1605–6, while final payments are registered in 1608–9, only one year before the loft was chosen as a model for the one at Hertogenbosch.

Although the rood-loft at Antwerp was destroyed in the French Revolution (1798), its appearance is known from a number of paintings by Pieter Neefs,[26] from brief descriptions and from the engraving by Gaspar Bouttats (fig. 6).[27] For in his imaginary depiction of the *Beeldenstorm*, the engraver anachronistically showed the later rood-loft, which he himself knew, suffering the assault of the iconoclasts, instead of the Gothic one whose ruins it had replaced.

The name of the great architect, sculptor and designer from Antwerp, Cornelis Floris (1514–75), has been mentioned above in connection with the mistaken attribution of the design for the rood-loft in the Cathedral there. Although the interpretation of the documents in this case is demonstrably incorrect, and Floris was in any case dead by the time work was begun

8. Project for the rood-loft in Ste. Waudru, Mons, by Jacques Dubroeucq, 1545–48.

on the loft, the connection of the design with his name is symptomatic of its stylistic origins.[28] If Raphael Paludanus was indeed the author of the rood-loft, he was operating under the shadow of his greater fellow-citizen, whose scheme for Tournai Cathedral of 1571–4 (fig. 7) constitutes one of the masterpieces of the Renaissance in the Netherlands. It certainly provided the essentials of the composition for Antwerp, although the alterations embodied there were significant, and were absorbed into the stylistic vernacular of Netherlandish art in parallel with features of the Tournai scheme.

The feature of Floris's rood-loft at Tournai that distinguishes it from earlier Renaissance examples is the monumentality of the architecture. There is an almost Roman severity about the sonorous rhythms established by the pairs of massive, Doric columns and by the continuity of the architrave as it loops upwards, following the curves of the three, huge arches. By comparison, the most advanced earlier loft still looked decidedly Gothic in character: this was the one built between 1535 and 1548 by Jacques Dubroeucq in

Sainte Waudru, Mons. Although it has been demolished long since, its appearance can be reconstructed with the help of the original drawing (fig. 8) and the magnificent sculptures which survive.[29] The three deep, coffered barrel-vaults and many other architectural features of Dubroeucq's design made it the most thoroughly classicizing monument of its time, but there was still a pettiness in the distribution of additive details, such as clusters of tiny colonnettes and row upon row of miniature arcades, which represented the residual effect of the Gothic style upon Dubroeucq's understanding of classical art.

Quite apart from the fame of this loft at Mons, Cornelis Floris could have been influenced by his personal acquaintance with its designer, for in 1560 he had supervised the building of the Town Hall at Antwerp to designs that had been drawn up by a committee which included Dubroeucq. However, when he came to design his own rood-loft at Tournai, Floris swept away the last vestiges of the Gothic from his composition. He reduced his supports to single, plain columns and **117** disposed them so as to create trabeated bays which alternate with the arches. Though reminiscent in varying degrees of Roman triumphal arches, Jacopo Sansovino's Loggetta at Venice, and the arcades of certain Lombard cloisters in the style of Bramante, Floris' design is of great originality and admirably adapted to its position in the church. It is raised on three steps, two of which run its full length without interruption, and has two decorative friezes defining the attic storey which are punctuated only minimally and are emphasised by firm lines of moulding in black Tournai stone. The loft extends well to each side of the choir arch in front of the piers of the crossing and the total effect is to stress the horizontals, and not the verticals, as Dubroeucq had done at Mons.

The intervals between the arches of the Tournai loft are wide enough to accommodate large roundels with narrative reliefs instead of the single statues that had occupied the corresponding areas at Mons, and in the attic storey Floris introduced four rectangular reliefs immediately above them (see page 120). He relegated the smaller panels under the balustrades, which had contained narrative reliefs at Mons, to a purely ornamental function. Though on the one hand Floris reduced the decorativeness of the functional elements of his architecture, on the other he included a number of novel ornamental motifs, the most characteristic of which are the bosses in the form of baskets and composed of interlaced strapwork, all in stone.

When a rood-loft was commissioned for Our Lady's, Antwerp, it was inevitable that its designer should follow in the footsteps of Cornelis Floris, and the more so in view of the latter's earlier connection with the screens round the choir near the site of the new structure. Nevertheless, his design was by no means a servile imitation. Possibly because the width of the choir in Our Lady's was less than at Tournai and funds may have been more limited, the Antwerp loft was less elongated, and returned approximately to the proportions of the Dubroeucq scheme at Mons. The intercolumniations were narrowed as compared with Tournai, though the double columns were retained, and statues were reinstated between the arches. The colonettes used by Floris in the upper register to frame his narrative panels were brought closer together, such that there was room for only token niches between, too narrow even to be filled, if we are to trust the evidence of the Bouttats engraving (fig. 6). For the deep, barrel-vaults of Mons and Tournai, were substituted

ribbed cross-vaults in the Gothic manner, probably because this permitted an arch at each end of the structure instead of the low, straight lintel that had been necessitated in the earlier lofts by the springing of the vault behind. This gave a greater feeling of lightness to the end views of the loft and was copied at Hertogenbosch (fig. 3). In other respects the Antwerp scheme approximated to that at Tournai,[30] and hence acted as a faithful intermediary between Cornelis Floris and Coenraed van Norenberch.

Such was the background to the commission for the new rood-loft at Hertogenbosch. Its design was to be based in outline on the Antwerp loft, but Coenraed was free to alter or add to it at his own discretion, or so it seems from subsequent references to the original contract which has since disappeared. Whereas the Antwerp scheme had cost eighteen thousand guilders, it was evidently thought that the new project could be carried out for only eleven thousand. In the event, the elaborate sculptural programme and other subsidiary work which Coenraed found himself obliged to undertake cost a lot more. After the completion of the loft in 1613,[31] a dispute arose over the question of payment and lengthy negotiations ensued between Coenraed and his employers, the town-council of Hertogenbosch and the Masters of the Fabric of St. John's. Expense accounts have survived which record the quantity of wine consumed by these officials at two tiresome meetings with the architect on May 8 and September 15 and the costs of board, lodging and travel that were paid to two important sculptors who had to be called in as independent witnesses in the matter of valuation, Jerome Duquesnoy from Brussels and Hans van Mildert from Antwerp.[32] Even so, agreement could not be reached and Coenraed was forced to institute legal proceedings against his employers for the recovery of an extra two thousand guilders that he claimed as his due. In May 1616 he was awarded a total of six thousand guilders over and above the original eleven thousand, together with interest and legal costs, by the High Court of the Province of Brabant at Brussels.[33] In July 1618 seven hundred guilders were actually made over to him in part payment of a claim for over two thousand guilders for the costs of building materials. Nevertheless, Coenraed did not receive full satisfaction and registered a further claim as late as 1629, after the capture of Hertogenbosch by the Dutch. Although this claim was rejected, pressure was brought to bear on the town-council and the Masters of the Fabric, who were apparently obliged to realise some of their capital assets to settle their outstanding debts to the architect.[34] A rough calculation shows that the rood-loft ultimately cost nearly as much as its prototype at Antwerp, and in view of the considerable increase that was proposed in the amount of sculpture, both in the round and in relief, it is hard to understand how the original low estimate could ever have received credence. However, the actual contract has not survived with the rest of the documents, and it may be that this estimate was to include little more than the bare bones of a structure approximating to that at Antwerp and that any additional work was to be costed by mutual agreement during the course of construction. A dispute over extra payment could hardly have arisen had the original contract been precisely worded, for Coenraed would not have had a leg to stand on. There must therefore have been a clause which lent itself to widely differing interpretations on the parts of the executant and his employers respectively, and it may even be one repeatedly quoted in the legal proceedings of which we have records.[35]

A comparison of the rood-loft from Hertogenbosch with what we know of the one in Antwerp shows that both its architecture and its sculpture were distinctly more complex, and this was presumably the fundamental reason why it was so much more expensive than had been anticipated.

The façade of the loft is divided into three main horizontal zones by three bands of entablature with strongly projecting cornices which are broken forward at intervals to create a dramatic play in depth: the lowest is that above the columns, which has a canonical Doric frieze of triglyphs and metopes; the next runs the full length of the structure above the arches and is decorated with acanthus rinceaux, inhabited with mythological monsters; and the uppermost consists of a frieze decorated with masks, cartouches and strap-work designs in the manner of Cornelis Floris. These horizontals do not dominate the composition, however, because of the four emphatic vertical accents built up by the main pairs of columns, the statues above them, the niches flanked by colonnettes in the upper zone, and the brass candlesticks, which punctuate the silhouette of the top of the loft like pinnacles in Gothic architecture.

The effect is enhanced by a discerning use of different coloured stone as at Tournai and on some earlier lofts: the columns and colonnettes are of reddish jaspered marble with capitals of grey; the other architectural members are of black Tournai stone; and the sculptures are carved in alabaster, mostly the pink-veined, local variety, though the narrative reliefs are made of "good English alabaster", in accordance with the original specification, which is whiter and clearer in hue. The shiny, black Tournai stone, carved into sharply defined mouldings, is employed for the elements which articulate the scheme, such as the pedestals on which the columns stand, the lintels, cornices and arches, the frames round the reliefs and the niches of the shield-bearing figures. The main statues are all disposed against plain panels of this stone to emphasise their contours, while their height is so calculated that the heads all stand out against the black cornices behind.

Four of the statues stand between the spandrels of the main arcade on sections of cornice which are broken forward to form platforms: from left to right these are: St. Peter; the Virgin and Child; St. John the Evangelist; and St. Paul.[36] Directly above are four smaller figures supporting shields, who stand in front of shallow niches flanked by Ionic colonnettes. Though the coats of arms which were painted on their shields have long since disappeared, the identifications of the figures are in no doubt, owing to the precision of the original specification.[37] These statues represent an addition to the scheme laid down at Antwerp. On the same level but centred over each of the arches stand three more of the main statues, Faith, Charity and Hope. The cornice on which they are set projects in a semicircle under each and massive bosses of fictive basketwork hang beneath, functioning visually as keystones to the arches and compensating for their implied upward thrust. As the main columns are echoed above by the little, Ionic colonnettes, so these huge bosses are repeated in miniature below, under the four statues of the middle register. Justice and Peace (now exhibited below) occupied corresponding positions on the north and south ends of the loft (fig. 3). Flanking each of these five Virtues are two panels with scenes from the life of Christ, which reach about half the height of the statues, to the floor-level of the gallery behind. Above these panels small sections of balustrading support the upper cornice, and the whole is crowned with four pairs of large, brass candlesticks on moulded plinths, placed vertically above the main columns.[38]

The aesthetic success of the rood-loft results from the harmonious integration of the decorative and narrative sculpture into a subtly calculated architectural scheme.

The design succeeds despite its variety and complexity because of the logic and consistency with which the parts are interrelated: the plain lines of the architecture act as a foil to the intricate detail of the sculpture, while the ornamental motifs and religious statues articulate and enliven the basic composition.

III. The Narrative Reliefs and their Sources in Contemporary Engravings

Throughout their history rood-lofts had been adorned not only with statues of the Virgin, Christ, Apostles, Saints, Prophets or the Virtues, but also with narrative panels. These of course had a didactic as well as a decorative function, constituting part of the "Bible of the Poor" contained in the wall-paintings, altarpieces and sculpture of all great churches. A large Crucifix, sometimes with flanking figures of the Virgin and St. John the Evangelist, was often mounted on the rood-loft or on a rood-beam across the entrance to the choir (fig. 6), and consequently the imagery of the reliefs was normally selected from the Passion of Christ.

On the important rood-loft by Cornelis Floris at Tournai (fig. 7) large square reliefs in the upper register showing episodes from the Passion were supplemented by circular panels in the spandrels below with the scenes from the Old Testament which were regarded as their antetypes in mediaeval theology. Though its design was basically derived from the Floris loft, the rood-loft in Our Lady's, Antwerp, which formed the prototype for that at Hertogenbosch, apparently had no narrative reliefs. This was due simply to alterations in its proportions: the spaces where the Passion reliefs and roundels had been accommodated at Tournai were narrowed in the Antwerp design, as has been explained above, and were wide enough for only a niche above and a standing figure below (fig. 6). The horizontal division of the breastwork with an open balustrade above a series of decorative panels was, however, maintained. At Hertogenbosch these panels of ornament were replaced with a cycle of narrative reliefs on the standard theme of the Life and Passion of Christ.

The subjects of these ten panels were laid down in the original specification (except for the last two, which were omitted probably by a scribe's oversight)[39]: beginning on the end of the rood-loft that faced into the north transept, the series ran as follows: the *Adoration of the Shepherds* and the *Adoration of the Magi* (at present mounted below the left arch for visibility); and then from left to right across the front: the *Marriage at Cana*; the *Feeding of the Five Thousand*; the *Trans-figuration*; the *Betrayal*; *Ecce Homo*; and the *Nailing to the Cross*. On the south end were the *Resurrection* and the *Ascension* (now below the right arch). The absence of a scene of the Crucifixion itself was carefully explained in this document by referring to the prior existence of a large Crucifix which had hung above the entrance to the choir since 1592. The subjects of the eight panels on the choir facade were specified as the *Seven Corporal Works of Mercy* and the *Last Judgement*, a combination of iconography that was popular in contemporary cycles of religious art.

Throughout the Renaissance knowledge of major works of art had been disseminated over Europe by means of engravings: those by Lucas van Leyden or Dürer, for example, had been avidly studied in Italy, while those by Marcantonio Raimondi after Raphael or by Cornelis Cort after Titian had made available to artists in Northern Europe something of the style and some of the compositions of the High Renaissance. Such engravings were freely used as models by important as well as mediocre artists in an era when there was not such a premium on sheer originality as there has been since the Romantic movement.

The reliefs on the rood-loft from Hertogenbosch are a case in point: over two thirds of the total number can be shown to be based in a more or less servile fashion on contemporary engravings. The borrowing in this instance was on a domestic rather than an international level, for the prints that were copied came principally from nearby Antwerp, apart from a few published by an Antwerp firm temporarily in exile at Cologne.

Such engravings were produced and published by large family workshops operating on mass-production lines, either from their own designs, or more frequently from ones provided by well-known painters.[40] They appeared as small sets or bound together in the form of picture-books and provided a favourite vehicle for Counter-Reformation propaganda in the Netherlands, sundered as they were by internecine strife between Catholics and Calvinists. Antwerp was in fact the centre of the engraving and print-selling business, and not unnaturally the majority of the designs were supplied by local artists, working in the Late Mannerist style. The best and most famous was Maerten de Vos, a prolific artist, who must have run a well-organised workshop to produce the vast number of painted altarpieces and designs for engravings with which he is credited. Born in 1532, he had been trained by his father and Frans Floris, both strongly Italianate painters, and had then undertaken the journey to Italy that was *de rigueur* for any aspiring artist from the North during the 16th century. He formed a personal style by marrying his native expertise in rendering detail with the clear contours and lucid colouring of Italian Mannerist painting and with the compositional fluency and dramatic sense of Tintoretto. Returning to Antwerp, De Vos became a member of the Guild of Painters in 1558 and worked there until his death in 1603. He supplied designs to the famous publisher Plantin for book illustrations, as well as to the less distinguished firms which manufactured prints, thereby virtually monopolising the market. This is reflected in the selection of engravings used by the sculptor at Hertogenbosch; for all but one are after his designs. The single exception is a print after Stradanus (Jan van der Straet), a fellow-Netherlander and near-contemporary (1523–1606), who was currently enjoying great success in Italy itself.[41] Stradanus may even have been a formative influence on De Vos, and their styles become virtually indistinguishable once they have suffered the slight distortions that are inevitable in the process of interpretation at the hands of engravers. Although only two designers are represented in the engravings so far identified as having been used for the rood-loft, most of the main publishing houses operating about 1600 are involved: the *Betrayal* after Stradanus was part of a picture-history of the Passion of Christ published in twenty plates by Philip Galle (1537–1612), who had been established at Antwerp since 1564.[42] His son-in-law Adriaen Collaert (ca. 1560–1618) published a lavish exposition of the Life and Passion in fifty plates after De Vos, five of which were utilised on the loft.[43] The family firm of Crispijn de Passe (ca. 1565–1637) issued in 1608, during its period of activity at Cologne, a series of the Corporal Works of Mercy which provided inspiration and specific motifs for four of the corresponding panels on the back of the rood-loft, though, surprisingly, not for the rest of the set.[44] The same print-seller produced in 1599 twelve plates on the Life of Christ with designs in oval frames, set vertically;[45] from one of these relatively

unsuitable models the *Resurrection* panel at Hertogenbosch was derived. Two engravings by Jan Sadeler (1550–1600) after Maerten de Vos permit us practically to complete the roll-call of Antwerp print-sellers of the late 16th century: these are the *Ascension of Christ*, subtitled "Divitiae",[46] and a plate from the *Bonorum et Malorum Consensio*, a picture-book published at Antwerp in 1586 on the theme of the Creation and the Fall of Man. What can one deduce from this more or less haphazard selection of engravings for use as models? First, on account of the sheer variety of sources, it seems unlikely that a programme of copying particular designs chosen by the Cathedral authorities was involved. Had that been the case, one would surely expect the borrowings to reflect a logical system of selection from consecutive sets or books of engravings. One wonders instead if the selection reflects not so much the personal choice of the sculptor, as the rather muddled and tattered contents of his folio of designs. Hard use around the studio would account for some of the broken sets, for the processes of tracing or squaring for enlargement are inevitably destructive if frequently performed, while the bustle of activity in the studio, when many assistants were engaged on a major commission, would be fatal to the preservation of logically ordered sets of engravings. In the case of the prints of the Corporal Works of Mercy, dating from 1608, which had only just been published when copied by the sculptor, there is even a possibility that the engravings which he failed to use may not have reached him in time to be included in his series. It is in any case noticeable that the three panels in which it seems that he had to rely on his own invention, *Feeding the Hungry*, *Harbouring Pilgrims* and *Clothing the Naked*, are composed in an elementary symmetry that is quite out of keeping with the more sophisticated designs after Maerten de Vos. The panel with pilgrims looks suspiciously like an adaptation of a standard design for Christ at Emmaus, while the clothing scene contains figures of a naked woman with a baby and a man clutching a round, felt hat to his chest which seem to have been lifted from a totally unrelated source, an illustration to Genesis, Chapters 4 and 5, in the *Bonorum et Malorum Consensio*.

There are eighteen reliefs on the rood-loft and engraved prototypes have been discovered for twelve (not including the case just mentioned, where only two motifs are shared). In the cycle of the Life and Passion of Christ the sources of only two panels have so far defied identification. These are the *Ecce Homo* and the

Nailing to the Cross. The iconography of these scenes was fairly standard in contemporary paintings and engravings, as indeed was that of the *Last Judgement* (the most important scene on the back of the loft for which a model is missing), and practically all the individual motifs in the carvings can be paralleled, but not the compositions as a whole. Either the sculptor designed his own variations on these standard themes, or, as is more probable in view of his proven dependence on engraved designs, the particular prints on which he relied have simply not been located among the vast number of picture-books and illustrated Bibles published at the period.

As regards the reliefs for which engraved sources have been found, a discussion of the alterations that were made in every instance would be out of place in this context, where only a limited number can be illustrated. Therefore a representative selection has been made to demonstrate both the varying degrees of conformity to the models, and the wide variety of sources from which the engravings themselves came.

The *Betrayal* after Stradanus (figs. 9–10) is an example of how closely the sculptor sometimes adhered to his model: the main figures are virtually identical, even down to the play of folds on their garments, though the soldier at the right, carrying a fire-brand torch, has been brought into the foreground. Incidental details such as the broken lantern and the dock plant at the bottom edge, the palings and gate of the distant fence and the weeping willow tree in the centre background are all faithfully rendered in the alabaster. As in all the panels, it is mainly the subsidiary participants, often represented in the engravings by little more than their heads, that are suppressed. The *Adoration of the Magi*, the *Marriage at Cana* and the *Transfiguration* conform just as closely to their prototypes.

In the *Ascension* (figs. 11–12) and the *Resurrection* (figs. 13–14) the sculptor's fidelity to his patterns is of the same order, but he had to make allowances so as to accommodate the vertically biased designs to his horizontal, rectangular fields. In both cases he spaced the foreground figures out sideways and reduced the scale of Christ. In the *Ascension* this has the unfortunate effect of making the protagonist look dwarf-like by comparison with His majestic, almost Michelangelesque, proportions in the original design by Maerten de Vos. In the *Resurrection* the engraving suggests how we might visualise the head of Christ, which has been knocked off the relief. Again there is a distinct loss of aesthetic quality: the Christ no longer soars aloft amid a billowing shroud and in an aura of light, the sense of movement being enhanced by the vertical axis of the oval frame. Instead, banks of crudely stylised clouds dominate the composition, framing a Christ who looks diminutive beside the flanking warriors.

The engraving of the *Adoration of the Shepherds* (figs. 15–16), like that of the *Resurrection* (and the *Adoration of the Magi*, not reproduced), permits a mental reconstruction of some heads that have been lost from the relief. Although the general composition is the same, even down to details such as the ox, the ass and the pallet bed on which the Infant lies, an interesting regrouping of the shepherds has taken place, and the pair with one clutching the other's shoulders appears to be an interpolation, possibly taken from another representation of the same scene: it seems too effective to be regarded as an invention of our rather pedestrian sculptor.

Two panels from the cycle of the Corporal Works of Mercy show him at his best and most concise. In *Visiting the Sick* (figs. 17–18), a touching group of an invalid being fed gruel from a bowl is retained in the right foreground and reinforced by a male bystander with a bucket leaning solicitously over him, who has been transferred from the opposite side of the engraving. For the other corner, the sculptor's fancy was caught by a background group of a physician attending a couple of sick women in a double bed: here he used his imaginative powers, such as they were, to good effect, for he has enlarged the tiny vignette in the engraving to the scale of the foreground figures without any hesitancy. Details such as the rafters seen in perspective and the door flanked by roundels at the end of the hospital ward are summarily conveyed. An almost identical relationship exists between the relief and its prototype in the case of *Visiting the Imprisoned* (figs. 19–20). Here the main group of a cringing prisoner, whose release is being purchased, his benefactor, and a gaoler swinging open the door, is retained in its entirety. Otherwise, the motif of the naked, manacled prisoner has been brought into prominence in the right foreground. Again, summary details of the architectural setting, such as the two oculi in the vault and the pattern of bars in the distant grid are reproduced.

Obviously, the general principle that underlay the sculptor's adaptations of his models was simplification, both for ease of carving and, more important, for visibility from the point of view of a spectator at ground

Est animi exigui, atqȝ infirmi parua voluptas
Vltio, conueniens nec enim vindicta Tonanti

Vlla fuit, non liquit opem, famuloȝ reuulſam
Reddidit enſe Petri cunctis ſpectantibus aurem.

9. THE BETRAYAL OF CHRIST, engraving after Stradanus by Philip Galle.

10. THE BETRAYAL OF CHRIST, panel on rood-loft.

DIVITIAE.

11. THE ASCENSION, engraving after Maerten de Vos by Jan Sadeler.

12. THE ASCENSION, panel on rood-loft.

13. THE RESURRECTION, engraving after Maerten de Vos by Crispijn de Passe.

14. THE RESURRECTION, panel on rood-loft.

15. THE ADORATION OF THE SHEPHERDS, engraving after Maerten de Vos by Adriaen Collaert.

16. THE ADORATION OF THE SHEPHERDS, panel on rood-loft.

17. VISITING THE SICK, engraving after Maerten de Vos by Crispijn de Passe.

18. VISITING THE SICK, panel on rood-loft.

19. VISITING THE IMPRISONED, engraving after Maerten de Vos by Crispijn de Passe.

20. VISITING THE IMPRISONED, panel on rood-loft.

level. In most instances he was reasonably successful, though rarely, if ever, improving on his sources. One forms the impression of a competent but uninspired journeyman sculptor, who could work closely to what was set before his eyes, but who had few interpretative powers and no ambitions in that direction. All that can be said of his style, as distinct from that of his models, is that he employed a repertory of rather distinctive facial types (see page 130, section V).

It is a commonplace that engravings after Cornelis Floris, Cornelis Bos and Hans Vredeman de Vries had long supplied the masons and sculptors of the late 16th century with patterns for architectural details and ornamental motifs, and it now appears that engravings of figure-compositions could provide models for even those parts of a design which today we would most expect to bear the imprint of the artist's originality and imagination. Admittedly, the sculptors of the rood-loft may have been less inspired than some of their better-known contemporaries, but they may nevertheless be representative of the average standard of attainment during the Late Mannerist epoch.

IV. The Statues and their Authorship: the Roles of Coenraed van Norenberch and Hendrik de Keyser

Considering the vicissitudes which the sculptures of the loft have endured, including the Calvinist Dutch conquest of Hertogenbosch in 1629, the removal to London and the successive reconstructions even within the Museum walls, they are in remarkably good condition, apart from numerous slight damages. Especially to be regretted are the losses of hands, and sometimes whole arms, holding symbolic attributes, as in the case of Faith and Hope, Justice and Peace. These losses are in most instances the result of weaknesses in the dowelling together of separate pieces of alabaster, rather than of deliberate damage.[47]

However, in the course of a recent survey, it was noticed that the child standing beside the central figure of Charity (one of the several symbolic infants which customarily surround her) had been supplied with a loin cloth of plaster, cunningly modelled to reflect the drapery style of the other figures and pigmented to resemble alabaster (fig. 21). When this was removed, cruel damage was revealed round the little boy's loins, where the alabaster had been wantonly chipped to provide keying for the plaster drapery. Once this had been restored, the lively contours of his buttocks and stomach were revealed in their pristine nudity and the figure regained the innocent charm that had been the sculptor's original intention (fig. 22).

A further and even more ridiculous example of prudery was discovered on the figure representing Faith. Like the other Virtues, she is clad in clinging drapery that is distantly reminiscent of Hellenistic sculpture, and her navel is meant to be discernible under the material of her robe. The blatant sensuousness of this revelation so offended the susceptibilities of the ecclesiastics of Hertogenbosch that they caused the navel to be filled with the same sort of plaster that had served to render the infant morally inoffensive.[48] The removal of this plaster patch brought to light an unexpected subtlety in the suggestion of life and movement in the anatomical forms beneath the drapery. The head of the Faith has suffered real damage at some stage and has been reset on the shoulders in such a way as to give the figure an impression of woodenness and frontality that is foreign to the rest of the series. Serious losses around her left eye and cheek and on her chin had been restored in the coloured plaster, but so clumsily as to have raised the question whether she was even by the same hand as the other statues. These disfigurements have all now been removed and the eye and chin have been restored by reference to the other undamaged figures to give some semblance of her original appearance.

Nine alabaster statues just under life-size now decorate the rood-loft, the tenth, a statue of Christ the Saviour, having been destroyed in 1629, as mentioned above. Among these nine the St. John the Evangelist (to the right of the central arch) stands out as being far superior in quality and profoundly different in style (figs. 24–25). It was very perceptively attributed by Dr. Elisabeth Neurdenburg to the celebrated Dutch sculptor Hendrik de Keyser (1565–1621) on the grounds of its stylistic similarity to the bronze statues on his tomb of William the Silent at Delft, begun about 1614.[49] Since then, documentary evidence has been discovered which confirms her attribution and throws an interesting sidelight on the circumstances in which

21. CHARITY, on rood-loft.　22. LITTLE BOY, detail of CHARITY on rood-loft.　23. CHARITY, engraving after Maerten de Vos by Crispijn de Passe.

the statue was carved.[50] The evidence consists of two brief entries in the Minutes of the Consistory of the Reformed Church at Amsterdam for December 19 and 26, 1613. It had come to the notice of these Protestant authorities that De Keyser, the official city sculptor, was executing a statue of St. John for the rood-loft in the Roman Catholic Cathedral of Hertogenbosch. One of their number was delegated to remonstrate with the sculptor about this scandalous behaviour, and the latter obediently promised to desist. Whether or not he kept his promise, the statue was delivered to Hertogenbosch, presumably soon afterwards: the carving was probably well advanced before the authorities were alerted, and if another hand was employed to finish the work, it is not at all noticeable.

We have no indication of how this anomalous situation arose and can only suppose that Coenraed van Norenberch subcontracted the carving of the all-important statue of the patron saint of the Cathedral to Hendrik de Keyser as being the most talented sculptor whose services he could secure. The recent signing of the Twelve Years Truce between North and South no doubt encouraged a resumption of normal artistic relationships, in spite of the remaining political and religious differences.

Hendrik de Keyser was a native of Utrecht, only some thirty miles from Hertogenbosch, and he is likely to have had some indirect contact with that city through his own master, Cornelis Bloemaert, for the latter had been extensively employed there as recently as the 1590's.[51] De Keyser's is a highly idiosyncratic style,

formed without the customary journey to Italy, and apparently relying on a knowledge of the work of his contemporaries from the Netherlands, who were employed all over Europe as sculptors, painters and engravers.[52] The characteristic plasticity of his drapery style appears to have been derived ultimately from the technique of modelling figures in wax, as a preparation to casting bronzes. The similarity of the texture of polished alabaster to that of wax emphasises this link in the case of the St. John. This heavy, flowing drapery, with its broadly scooped out indentations, suggesting that the cloth is blown against the body and adheres in places, can be seen as foreshadowing or running parallel with the early Baroque style at Rome, while remaining utterly personal to its inventor. Perhaps this is what the writer of the Museum Guide of 1874 had in mind when he rashly wrote: "In the attitudes of the figures and the heavy distributions of drapery we trace debased imitation of the school of Bernini".[53] Its effect is quite the opposite of the tight contours and linear folds of the drapery in which the other statues on the rood-loft are clad. There, the gouge and the drill are employed as an equivalent to the engraver's burin or the draughtman's chalk, to render lines of shadow separating planes in highlight.

Although Neurdenburg's attribution of the St. John to Hendrik de Keyser has been confirmed by the new documentary evidence, a subsequent, ingenious theory of hers that some of the other statues might be by his chief assistant at the time, the Englishman Nicholas Stone, does not seem to be borne out by their style.[54]

127

There is no independent work by Stone in Amsterdam with which to compare them, and the sculpture which he is documented as having carved in and around London immediately after his return to England in 1613 is far closer than any of the figures on the rood-loft to De Keyser's style, particularly in the effect of the drapery.[55]

Stone's sculpture does, it is true, manifest many of the same characteristics as the statues on the rood-loft, especially the mannered exaggerations of their stances. But these traits are universal in Late Mannerist sculpture all over the Netherlands and so cannot be taken as proof of any direct connection between Nicholas Stone and the rood-loft.

One has only the name of Coenraed van Norenberch, the entrepreneur of the whole scheme, to fall back on as possible author of the sculpture.[56] It is by no means impossible that he was either a sculptor himself, and not merely a master-mason in the modern sense, or that his team of craftsmen included specialists in carving alabaster in a fairly consistent "house style". Several hands of varying ability are discernible, and even if the best figures are by Coenraed in person, he must have had assistants to whom the routine work could be delegated. The only other hypothesis is that, as in the case of the St. John, he subcontracted all the rest of the carving to an unrecorded sculptural workshop, on his own responsibility, such that no names appear in the documents. If this was the case, it was a workshop of which no other traces exist (except at Liège, see page 133, section VI), and whose style cannot be identified as that of any of the more important contemporary sculptors, such as the De Nole brothers, who had carved the statues on the Antwerp rood-loft a few years before. Provisionally, therefore, an attribution to Coenraed van Norenberch seems the more positive alternative as it has the weight of circumstantial evidence in its favour, but we should continue to bear in mind the possibility that behind his name there may stand an anonymous sculptor who remains to be identified.

In the case of the reliefs an intimate connection with engravings of the period has been proved, and through them with the fashionable style of Late Mannerism, which prevailed in the great centres of Brussels and Antwerp until the emergence of Rubens. This was the style that influenced the forms of the statues too. Although no direct prototypes have been discovered, series of engravings devoted to the "Virtues" or the "Gifts of the Spirit" give clear proof that the sculptor's

24. ST. JOHN THE EVANGELIST, by Hendrik de Keyser, on rood-loft.

25. ST. JOHN THE EVANGELIST, detail.

inspiration for the statues came from the same general sources (figs. 21, 23).[57] Of course a sculptor, when dealing with free-standing figures of almost life-size, could not benefit so directly from graphic models as when carving panels in low relief and on a small scale.

Furthermore, the master sculptor would normally be responsible for the major sculpture, and he would be the last person to need specific designs from which to work, assuming him to be the most imaginative and original artist in the studio.

V. The Style of Coenraed van Norenberch and Some Further Attributions to his Hand in St. Paul's, Liège

It has been remarked of the reliefs that the only trait which distinguishes their style from that of their engraved prototypes is an idiosyncratic repertory of facial types. These appear in the rest of the sculpture on the rood-loft as well, though with marked variations in the subtlety of interpretation. If one accepts Coenraed not only as designer but as principal sculptor, these idiosyncrasies must be the hallmarks of his style. The variations in quality can be accounted for by the difference between autograph work and carving executed by assistants.

For women, Coenraed favoured rather high cheekbones and almond-shaped eyes, which are sometimes slanted and narrowed to slits, giving a slightly oriental appearance. Among the reliefs examples can be found in the *Marriage at Cana*, *Giving Drink to the Thirsty* and *Visiting the Sick* (fig. 18). All the angels occupying the spandrels conform to this type and so do the statues of the *Virgin* (fig. 26) and, less markedly, *Justice*. *Faith*, *Hope* and *Charity* (fig. 21) have a slightly more classical type of face, though one which is still distinctly Netherlandish and not Italian in character. *Peace* is different again, with a less idealised, wider and heavier face, into which the eyes are unconvincingly integrated. For men, the sculptor preferred a facial type which superficially appears rather divergent: *St. Peter* and *St. Paul* (fig. 27), for instance, look very different from the *Virgin and Child*. This is so marked that it has even led to their being attributed to a different hand before now.[58] On closer examination, however, an intermediate type of youthful male face can be distinguished which provides the missing link. In this connection, the four minor figures with shields in the upper register are of interest:[59] the youth wearing a laurel wreath (who supported the coat of arms of the Archdukes Albert and Isabella) has high cheekbones and slightly slit eyes, a prominent chin and a recessive lower lip (fig. 28). He thus resembles the *Virgin and Child* extremely closely in facial appearance. On the other hand, he can equally be connected with his older neighbour in the ducal cap and cloak, representing Duke Godfrey (fig. 29). The latter's cheeks are beginning to hollow and his eyebrows to droop in a way that foreshadows the characteristics of the oldest type of male face that Coenraed uses, for instance on the Wild Man of Hertogenbosch, at the far right of the series of shield-bearers (fig. 30). There a further hollowing of the cheeks has occurred, which together with "crows' feet" round the eyes, wrinkles on the forehead and the long, flowing beard, suggests the pathos of old age with considerable skill.

Once we have comprehended this process of transition in facial type with advancing age, a glance at *St. Peter* and *St. Paul* will suffice to show where they fit into the scheme and how they are ultimately related to the type of the *Virgin*. All the stages of transition can also be traced in the reliefs, but with less precision, partly owing to the reduction in the amount of detail that is permitted by their small scale, and partly because they were almost certainly carved by an inferior hand.

An interesting piece of evidence has recently been brought to bear on the problem, and provides independent confirmation, if any be needed, of this underlying connection between the female and male types. For the two types appear in close conjunction on a commemorative altar of roughly contemporary date in St. Paul's, Liège (fig. 31).[60] This altar was dedicated to the memory of a certain Peter Oranus (D'Heur, in French) and his wife, who died in 1618 and 1595 respectively[61]. Apart from the inscription on the altar, which implies that it was erected by relatives after the husband's death in 1618, there is no documentary information, and the name of the sculptor is not known. Three alabaster statuettes crown the altarpiece

26. VIRGIN AND CHILD, on rood-loft.

27. ST. PAUL, on rood-loft.

28. Supporter of coat of arms of Archdukes Albert and Isabella, on rood-loft.

29. Supporter of coat of arms of Duke Godfrey, on rood-loft.

30. Supporter of coat of arms of Hertogenbosch, on rood-loft.

and two of them, a *St. Paul* and a *Virgin and Child*, correspond closely to the statues on the rood-loft, though reduced to about half their scale. The third figure, a *St. Peter*, differs from his counterpart on the loft only in pose: he brandishes his symbolic keys instead of permitting them to dangle at his waist and raises his book to read, like the *St. Paul*, instead of resting it closed on one knee. His drapery style and facial type are still intimately connected with the *St. Peter* at Hertogenbosch. The other main difference between the saints at Liège and their counterparts on the rood-loft is that the former are posed frontally, while the latter, which are on the two salient angles of the structure and can be seen from a wide arc of vantage points, are given a distinct twisting movement (fig. 3). The two groups of the *Virgin and Child* are almost identical: the folds and contours of their draperies match, and the pose of the Christ Child, the profile of His face and the unusual line of His hair are the same in each case. The attitudes and style of the statuettes are, in short, so close to those on the rood-loft as to render an attribution of the Oranus altar to the same sculptor or workshop absolutely inescapable.

This attribution can in turn be checked by comparing a related monument to another member of the Oranus family, Canon François (d. 1636), who was buried in the actual family chapel, some way from the altar (fig. 32).[62] A comparison of its architectural and decorative details, as well as its crowning statuettes, with those of the altar proves that they are both from the same workshop, as one might expect.[63] The figures of *St. Catherine* and *St. Barbara* standing at each side of the lower broken pediment are posed and draped in a style entirely consistent with that of their counterparts on the altar, while the *St. Barbara* is also very like the statue of *Peace* on the rood-loft. However, the most

significant feature of this monument is an allegorical relief showing St. Francis, the patron saint of the deceased (who kneels at the left in prayer), interceding on his behalf before Christ and the Virgin. This it is that most strikingly corroborates the connection between the group of sculpture at Liège and the rood-loft, for the unusual subject is treated in a style which is identical to that of the narrative panels of Hertogenbosch. In fact its composition and several specific motifs might almost be copied from the scene of the *Ascension* (fig. 12), while the treatment of the architecture, landscape and figures in the background can be closely paralleled among the *Corporal Works of Mercy*. From our point of view the most interesting implication that can be drawn from this new attribution concerns the crowning figure of the second monument, *Christ the Saviour*. He is almost nude and raises the cross in His right hand. In view of the other parallels between the Oranus statues and the rood-loft figures, may He not provide us with an idea of the appearance of the one statue that is now missing, the "Salvator", which we know stood in the central niche facing into the choir until the Calvinists conquered Hertogenbosch?

Research among the fragments of sculpture at Liège which have survived the onslaught of the French Revolution has failed to reveal any further sculpture belonging to this group, apart from an anonymous, badly damaged, kneeling figure from a relief, which has the same distinctive facial type and arrangement of drapery (Musée Curtius, Liège). The destruction of sculpture in Liège has been so extensive that extreme caution must be exercised when drawing conclusions from the paltry remnants, but it would be fair to say that the style does not appear to be that of either Thomas Tollet (ca. 1545–1621) or Elias Fiacre (1587–1664), the principal Liégeois sculptors operating at the

132

31. Altar of Peter Oranus. St. Paul's, Liège.

32. Monument of Canon François Oranus. St. Paul's, Liège.

period in question.[64] The discovery of the stylistic analogies of the Oranus sculptures with the rood-loft does not therefore clarify the problem of identifying the artist. On the other hand, the supposition that Coenraed van Norenberch might have been active at Liège receives some support from its proximity to Namur, his birthplace, and to the quarries of the Meuse Valley, the traditional haunt of his family. The dating of the Oranus monuments in the 1620's and 1630's means that they are later than the rood-loft and represent the only sculptures from later in his career that have so far been identified.[65]

VI. Conclusion: The Place of the Rood-Loft in Netherlandish Art

In view of the prevailing ignorance about art in the Netherlands in the years around 1600, it is not easy to assess the precise position of the rood-loft in terms of quality or of stylistic development. The heavy reliance of the sculpture on contemporary engravings, though no doubt symptomatic of the condition of the arts in the strife-ridden Netherlands, might seem at first sight to detract alarmingly from our estimation. Nevertheless, it would be a mistake to dismiss the rood-loft on these grounds as second-rate or uninteresting. For, as has been suggested, the sculpture was not meant to stand up in detail to critical scrutiny. The statues and reliefs constitute only one element in an ensemble, which should primarily be viewed as a whole.

Even in its present location in the Museum, the all-important side and three-quarter views of the rood-loft are drastically curtailed, and one cannot form a proper impression of how sumptuous and imposing it must have looked when it appeared principally in the role of architecture, dominating the wide spaces of the crossing and transepts of St. John's, and punctuating the vista down the nave. It is for this reason that the marvellous drawing by Jacques Everts (fig. 5) and the old photographs (fig. 3) are invaluable, for they permit one to visualise the original appearance of the rood-loft in its intended setting.

Seen in these terms, the rood-loft appears as the very climax of the development during the Renaissance of this peculiarly Netherlandish type of structure. Deriving inspiration in almost equal proportions from his two most influential predecessors, the sculptor-architects

Jacques Dubroeucq and Cornelis Floris, Coenraed succeeded by a judicious process of revision and innovation in producing a work of art which stands comparison with their masterpieces, and constitutes virtually the last major monument in the Renaissance style.[66] For by the time that the loft was complete, the young Rubens, who had recently returned from Italy, and the sculptors in his immediate circle had already made a considerable impact on art at Antwerp with schemes in a thoroughly new style, the Baroque.

Notes

1. Museum no. 1046–1871, located in Room 50. Hertogenbosch is in the Province of North Brabant, Netherlands. The general view by Saenredam (pl. 1) is reproduced by permission of the Bibliothèque Royale, Brussels. The principal literature on the Cathedral is: J. C. A. Hezenmans, *De St-Janskerk te 's-Hertogenbosch en hare geschiednis*, Hertogenbosch, 1866; C.F.X. Smits, *De kathedraal van 's-Hertogenbosch*, Brussels, 1907; J. Mosmans, *De St-Janskerk te 's-Hertogenbosch*, Hertogenbosch, 1931. On the rood-loft itself, the only definitive study is: P. Buschmann, 'Het Oxaal van 's-Hertogenbosch', in *Onze Kunst*, XXXIV, 1918, pp. 1–35. On rood-lofts in general, see: J. Steppe, *Het Koordoksaal in de Nederlanden*, Brussels, 1952.

2. Art Referees Reports, I, no. 10159, 1869.

3. G. C. Williamson, *Murray Marks and His Friends*, London, 1919, p. 50.

4. A comparable complex of architecture and sculpture, the Cappella Maggiore and High Altar of Santa Chiara, Florence (7720–1861), had cost as little as £386, in 1861.

5. Victoria and Albert Museum Registry.

6. Board Minutes, South Kensington Museum, Vol. D.2., p. 104, no. 20804, May 5, 1869 (Deposited at Public Record Office). The Museum undertook to pay £150 to cover the expenses of carriage.

7. Department of Art and Science Minutes, Vol. F.2., p. 162, no. 28095, July 20, 1871 (Deposited at Public Record Office).

8. Baedeker, *London*, 1892, p. 282, plan (brought to my attention by Charles Gibbs-Smith).

9. Museum photograph 14575.

10. Charles Piot, 'Le Jubé de la Cathédrale de Bois-le-Duc', in *Bulletin des Commissions Royales d'Art et d'Archéologie*, VI, 1867, p. 46.

11. P. Buschmann, 'Het Oxaal van 's-Hertogenbosch,' in *Onze Kunst*, 1918, p. 10, n. 1.

12. Charles Piot, *loc. cit.*, p. 50.

13. Victor de Stuers, 'Holland op zijn smalst', in *De Gids*, 1873, pp. 366–373 (quoted by Buschmann, *loc. cit.*, p.1).

14. Victor de Stuers, *loc. cit.*

15. Buschmann, *loc. cit.*

16. Even before 1908 there had been some question of moving the rood-loft from the Casts Court so that it might take its place alongside the collection of originals. In the *Report of the Committee of Re-arrangement, Presented to Parliament by Command of His Majesty*, and published for the Board of Education by H.M.S.O., 1908, p. 26, appeared a definitive statement which temporarily put an end to speculation: 'The Committee, after exhaustive discussions covering a long period, and having considered various alternative proposals, recommend that this object be left in its present position, where it will be in close juxtaposition to the other original European architectural specimens in the East Hall' (brought to my attention by Charles Gibbs-Smith).

17. R. P. Bedford, 'A 17th Century Rood-loft from Bois-le-Duc,' in *Country Life*, XV, 1924, p. 511.

18. British Museum, Department of Prints and Drawings, no. 1883. 7. 14. 102. Reproduced by kind permission of the Trustees.

19. In the Gemeente Archief, Hertogenbosch. Pen and ink with grey wash (49·5 × 54·4 cm), signed, dated and inscribed by Jacques Everts. Thanks are due to Mr. P. Th. J. Kuyer, Keeper of the Archives for providing information on this drawing.

20. R. A. van Zuijlen Jr., *Inventaris der Archieven van de Stadt 's-Hertogenbosch*, 1863–66, vol. II, p. 1175 *sqq*. The relevant extracts quoted by Buschmann, *loc. cit.*

21. J. Steppe, *Het Koordoksaal in de Nederlanden*, Brussels, 1952, p. 167 *sqq*.

22. Buschmann, *loc. cit.* p. 30, Appendix II.

23. Buschmann, *loc. cit.* p. 32, Appendix III.

24. For the Antwerp rood-loft see: M. Casteels, *De Beeldhouwers De Nole te Kamerijk, te Utrecht en te Antwerpen*, Brussels, 1961, pp. 141–143; and Steppe, *op. cit.* pp. 274–279.

25. Paludanus was the Latin form of the Dutch name Van den Broeck; for details of his biography see: Thieme-Becker, *Künstler-Lexicon*, s.v. Broeck.

26. Wallace Collection, London, no. 152; other versions in Brussels, Madrid, Cassel, see: Steppe, *op. cit.* p. 278 and fig. 99, repro.

27. Steppe, *op. cit.* p. 277, ns. 51, 52, quoting early sources. The Bouttats engraving is reproduced by permission of the Bibliothèque Royale, Brussels.

28. R. Hedicke, *Cornelis Floris und die Floris-Dekoration*, Berlin, 1913.

29. The drawing is reproduced by kind permission of M. A. Louant, Keeper of the Archives at Mons. See also: R. Hedicke, *Jacques Dubroeucq von Mons*, Strassburg, 1904.

30. The designer dispensed with the ornate, projecting pulpit incorporating a niche for the Virgin and Child that formed the central feature of Floris' design.

31. The workmen were about to leave Hertogenbosch on September 28, when their request for the customary 'tip' was entered in the accounts: see Van Zuijlen, *op. cit.* p. 1212.

32. Buschmann, *loc. cit.* p. 9.

33. Buschmann, *loc. cit.* p. 34, Appendix VII: extracts from the sentence.

34. Buschmann, *loc. cit.* p. 10.

35. See n. 33; the phrase reads: 'tot het voorschreven pourtraict bijgevueght ende verandert waeren' i.e. 'additions and alterations to the prescribed model'.

36. In the first instance, a statue of the Saviour was planned for the position occupied by the Virgin, and She was to have stood in the niche over the central door, facing into the choir. By the time that the actual specification of the sculptures was drawn up (January 27, 1611), it had been decided that these two statues should change places. The statue of the Saviour seems to have been destroyed in 1629.

37. Buschmann, *loc. cit.*, p. 33, appendix V. In R. P. Bedford's translation: 'The first of these persons shall be a man dressed in classical costume and on his shield the arms of Brabant; the second person shall be a figure of duke Godfrey, founder of this town of Hertogenbosch, having his arms on his shield; the third person shall be a man with a laurel wreath on his head, in classical costume, having on his shield the arms of the Archdukes Albert and Isabella; item, the fourth or last person shall be a wild man, having on his shield the arms of the town of Hertogenbosch'. These characterizations were strictly adhered to by our sculptor.

38. The candlesticks are 19th-century copies of the original set, two of which, engraved with the arms of Hertogenbosch and the date 1613, are exhibited on the stone beam in the archway. Wooden gates with elongated brass balusters hung in this arch (pl. 4). Under the arcade at each side stood an altar: an inscription dedicating one to St. Cosmas and St. Damian and bearing the date 1625 can be seen under the northern arch: this altar was originally on the south side and one dedicated to St. Servatius of Maastricht stood where the inscription now is.

39. Buschmann, *loc. cit.* p. 33, Appendix V.

40. See A. M. Hind, *A History of Engraving and Etching*, 1923, chapter IV. and F. W. Hollstein, *Dutch and Flemish Etchings, Engravings and Woodcuts*, Amsterdam, 1949–64.

41. Stradanus worked for instance with Vasari on decorations in the Vatican (1550–53), and subsequently became the principal designer for the Medici tapestry manufactory at Florence, supplying over 130 cartoons, many of which were subsequently re-used on a smaller scale as designs for sets of engravings. His style was based on that of the second generation of Italian Mannerists, Bronzino, Salviati and Vasari.

42. Philip Galle and other engravers after Stradanus, *Passio, Mors et Resurrectio D. N. Nostri JESV CHRISTI*, Antwerp, no date; Department of Prints and Drawings, Victoria and Albert Museum.

43. Adriaen Collaert after M. de Vos, *Vita, Passio et Resurrectio Iesv Christi, varijs Iconibus a celeberrimo pictore Martino de Vos expressa, ab Adriano Collart nunc primum in aes incisa*, Antwerp, no date. Hollstein, *op. cit.*, IV, p. 202, nos. 65–115. Plate 13 is reproduced by permission of the Bibliothèque Royale, Brussels.

44. Hollstein, *op. cit.*, XV, p. 186, nos. 471–77. These were brought to our attention by Mr. J. P. Ballegeer of Ghent University. Plates 17 and 19 are reproduced by permission of the Rijksmuseum, Amsterdam.

45. Hollstein, *op. cit.*, XV, p. 135–36, no. 79.

46. Jan Sadeler after Maerten de Vos, Print Room, British Museum, no. D. 6–154; reproduced by permission of the Trustees.

47. The drawing of 1632 by Saenredam (pl. 4) clearly shows the outstretched arms of Faith and Hope, and so the losses cannot have been caused by the Calvinists, and must have occurred later through deterioration in their dowellings.

48. An attentive examination of the old photographs showing the loft *in situ* proves that the plaster additions were made before it was dismantled. They were removed by Kenneth Hempel, Conservation Department, who also carved the new parts of the face of Faith in alabaster.

49. E. Neurdenburg, 'Hendrick de Keyser en het Oxaal van Coenraet van Noremberg', in *Bulletin van den Ned. Oudheidk. Bond.*, 1920, pp. 1–7.

50. J. Z. Kannegieter, 'Het St. Jansbeeld van het Bossche Oxaal', in *Oud-Holland*, LIX, 1942, pp. 110–11.

51. E. Neurdenburg, *loc. cit.*, p. 5.

52. E. Neurdenburg, *Hendrick de Keyser*, Amsterdam, 1930.

53. J. H. Pollen, *A Description of the Architecture and Monumental Sculpture in the South-East Court of the South Kensington Museum*, London, 1874, p. 35.

54. E. Neurdenburg, 'Het Oxaal van de St. Janskerk te 's-Hertogenbosch en Nicholas Stone,' in *Oudheidkundig Jaarboek*, VII, 1938, pp. 38–44.

55. W. L. Spiers, 'The Note-book and Account book of Nicholas Stone', in *The Walpole Society*, VII, 1918–19.

56. As Buschmann originally suggested.

57. One example is reproduced for comparison, the *Charity* from a series of the *Seven Virtues*, engraved by Crispijn de Passe after De Vos (Hollstein, XV, nos. 426–32). The general similarities in style and treatment are too apparent to warrant enumeration. There are equally striking similarities between the other Virtues on the rood-loft and other engravings.

58. The *St. Peter* and *St. Paul* have always been regarded as the best statues after the *St. John*, and superior in handling to the remainder (cf. E. Neurdenburg in a postscript to the article cited in n. 49). Neurdenburg gave them to Nicholas Stone in the later article cited in n. 54 and felt that the *Virgin*, though possibly to his design, was by an inferior hand.

59. See n. 37.

60. The author would like to record his gratitude to Prof. J. Philippe, Director of the Musée Curtius, and to M. L. Dewez for their cooperation at Liège.

61. Photo Copyright A. C. L. Brussels. L. Dewez, *La Cathédrale St. Paul à Liège*, one of *Feuillets Archéologiques de la Société Le Vieux Liège*, p. 14; and Thimister, *L'Eglise de St. Paul, Essai Historique*, Liège, 1867, p. 89.

62. Photo Copyright A. C. L. Brussels. L. Dewez, *op. cit.*, p. 10; Thimister, *op. cit.*, pp. 96 and 181–82. There is also a third monument to a member of this family, Pierre-Ernest (d. 1637), next to the second one. Although it is executed in roughly the same style as the others, its motifs are more Baroque, except for two little crowning statuettes. It looks like a later product of the same workshop, but is not immediately relevant.

63. The architectural details and the use of different coloured stones on both the altar and the monument are, needless to say, entirely consistent with the work of Coenraed van Norenberch on the rood-loft.

64. For Tollet see: J. Moret, 'Henri de Borset et Thomas Tollet, sculpteurs liégeois du XVIe siècle, leurs travaux dans la cathédrale de Nevers,' in *Bull. Inst. archeol. liégeois*, XLVIII, 1923, p. 85 *sqq.* Moret ascribed the splendid sculptures that survive from a rood-loft of 1602 in St. Jacques, Liège, to the hand of Tollet, but there are no documented sculptures for comparison Steppe, *op. cit.*, pp. 339–40, supports this thesis. Tollet was described in a legal deposition of 1662 as 'le meilleur sculpteur qu'il y eut dans Liège et par tout le pays', and these sculptures are the best that survive in Liège from the relevant period. Although related in general style to the Oranus monuments, and to the rood-loft, the statues and reliefs are not by the same hand, and are superior in expressive quality. For Elias Fiacre, his relationship with Tollet and Borset, and an alternative attribution of the sculptures in St. Jacques to his workshop, see: J. Yernaux, 'L'atelier Italo-liégeois des Palardins et des Fiacres, sculpteurs aux XVIe et XVIIe siècles', in *Annuaire Comm. commun. de l'ancien Pays de Liège*, I, 4, 1935–36, pp. 268–92.

65. Buschmann, *loc, cit.*, p. 10, mentions that the memorial to Bishop Gisbertus Masius (d. 1614) in St. John's, Hertogenbosch, might be by Coenraed. This has since been attributed to Hans van Mildert, the Antwerp sculptor who was called in to assess the extra sum due to Coenraed for the rood-loft, and who was subsequently responsible for the High Altar of St. John's (1619): see: Is. Leyssens, 'Hans van Mildert, 158?–1638', in *Gentsche Bijdragen*, VII, 1941, pp. 73 *sqq.*

66. See Steppe, *op. cit.*, chapters 5, 6 and 7.

Some Lithographs by Odilon Redon

FRANK DICKINSON

THE various demands of observation, intuition and intellect, the continued fight between realism, romanticism and classicism, brought a particular tension to the works of the great innovators of the late nineteenth and the early twentieth century. Odilon Redon, in his lithographs, a fine example of which was recently purchased by the Museum, clothed fantasy with a logic of the imagination. He made the imperceptible visible in concise chiaroscuro. Balancing such extremes resulted in works of great originality as well as in periodic failure. In his writings, discussing the indeterminate and equivocal drawings which inspire rather than define, he asks us to imagine arabesques unfolding and meandering in profound and indeterminate space, the play of lines combined with the most diverse elements including a human face with all the particularisation of one seen in the street. He goes on to state that this kind of juxtaposition, found in many of his drawings, is the force which incites the spectator's imagination according to his sensibility and depth.[1]

A poetic and articulate writer, he records the haunting images carried from childhood, the various influences of teachers, painters and poets, and sets out his aims and means: "My originality consists in bringing to life, in a human way, improbable beings and making them live according to the laws of probability, by putting, as far as possible, the visible at the service of the invisible."[2]

Dangerously, Redon pursued a lonely course outside the main flow of realism and impressionism. He might have become a completely isolated eccentric or a literary illustrator of the gruesome, but he succeeded brilliantly in his finest lithographs by finding a language appropriate to his suggestive art. The form and structure of these lithographs carry a compound of fantasy and reason, set in consistently simplified space, making a significant contribution to Post-Impressionism and the art of the twentieth century.

Redon's introspective character and uneven training to some extent isolated him from the influence of Impressionism and conditioned his late start; his first set of lithographs was published when he was almost forty years old.

At fifteen in Bordeaux his first drawing-master was the water-colourist Stanislas Gorin, who encouraged him to preserve his individuality and never to draw a line without sensibility and *raison*. He was introduced to the paintings of Corot, Millet, Gustave Moreau and Delacroix, whom he venerated and whose "Lion Hunt" at the Bordeaux Museum he later copied.

His friendship with the botanist Armand Clavaud in the late 1850's acquainted him with the processes of life on the frontiers of animal and plant, flower and being. The erudite Clavaud also introduced him to the first volumes of Flaubert, to Poe and to Baudelaire's *Les Fleurs du Mal*. But he thought Redon would do better as a writer than as an inventor of forms.

In Paris at seventeen, following the wishes of his family, he began studies in architecture. The study of geometry and especially the projection of shadows on solids he found useful later. However, he failed the examinations to the École des Beaux-Arts and returned to Bordeaux, where he studied sculpture for a year, copying casts of antique fragments in clay which he enjoyed handling. Then in about 1863 he met Rodolphe Bresdin, who taught him etching and pen-lithography. This romantic genius revealed to Redon the greatness of Rembrandt and the power of Dürer and the Northern engravers. Redon must have been deeply impressed by the swarming detail of Bresdin's compositions, moving and transforming itself under the eye of the spectator, and by the juxtaposition of real and imagined, of light and darkness, life and death.

In 1864 he entered the *atelier* of Gérôme at the École des Beaux-Arts. This proved an unhappy period, which hardened Redon's attitude to the sterile academic tradition. A friendship with Corot no doubt restored his balance between observation and imagination, and helped him to a sense of tonal values in landscape.

But the 1860's were not very productive years for Redon and the Franco-Prussian War, declared in the summer of 1870, proved a turning point in his career. The stress of the brutal conflict heightened his perceptions; indeed, he maintained that the War had made him conscious of his individuality and natural gifts. On release from the army in January 1871 he increasingly used the medium of charcoal, usually on toned paper. This medium lends itself to mystery and suggestion, allowing broad tonal effects to be quickly achieved and the image to be dusted off, leaving a residue of the original conception to be worked over and transformed. Almost all of his charcoal drawings were made at Peyrelebade, the sixteenth-century house in the Médoc, surrounded by vineyards and marshes, to which he

1. ARBRE. 1892. $18\frac{3}{4} \times 12\frac{1}{2}$ in. $(47 \cdot 6 \times 31 \cdot 7$ cm)

returned each summer. It was the setting of his lonely, ailing childhood, and, after the death of his father in 1874, the source of years of dispute in the family. He also found that making a careful study of some natural object stimulated his imagination. He records that he felt an ebullition, a ferment of the mind, and that this infusion was the source of his true inventions.[3] The perception that went to produce this "boiling" of the mind presumably comprised profound order as well as variety and mystery. "Arbre" of 1892,[4] a large lithograph derived from a drawing, still shows this kind of response to nature. Every contour, every leaf, has been seen intensely and realised faithfully without generalization or facility (fig. 1).

Redon did not often use the conventional symbols of mythology and Christianity. He did not need to find an expressive motif like the painters of romantic landscapes. He did not work by assemblage and elaboration like Moreau or by simplification of traditional compositions like Puvis. But given the chance to re-commence his education as a painter, he made it clear that he would have studied the human figure and its anatomy thoroughly, dissecting, analysing and modelling, in order to recreate it easily from memory in profusion.[5] Writing in 1890, the critic Arthur Symons perceived the weakness in Redon's Art: "The drawing of Redon, like that of Blake, is only too often faulty; his men and women are only awkward spectres, his human faces lack the very elements of beauty."[6] But of course Redon, since youth, had known the expressive deformations of Delacroix. Clavaud had extolled the great painter's passionate unity, in which a hand conjures the whole figure, achieved through legitimate distortion.[7] As Redon's style matures, gauche drawing becomes more and more inseparable from intuitive and structural deformations.

Though Bresdin had introduced Redon to etching and pen-lithography, it was after 1871 that he met Fantin-Latour, who showed him the technique of crayon-lithography and the use of transfer paper. This was a perfect means of translating and multiplying the charcoal drawings.

Huysmans, in *A Rebours*, 1884, described some of the drawings and prints by Redon of the late 70's and early 80's in the esoteric collection of the modern hero Des Esseintes, which included works by Gustave Moreau, Bresdin, Jan Luyken and El Greco. They induced in Des Esseintes a reverie ranging through the terrors of monstrous pre-history, optical distortions, the nightmares of typhoid fever, and prompted comparsion with Goya's *Proverbios* and the stories of Poe, which produced in him a similar malaise. This controversial novel, in which Huysmans moved from Naturalism to Symbolism, established Redon as a maker of monsters, and though he was flattered by this attention he was later to note that Huysmans' understanding of his art was incomplete and that he had, he believed, taken a part in Huysmans' evolution.[8] However, the sale of sets of lithographs to a small number of collectors became possible.

Redon's complete *oeuvre* in lithography, about one hundred and seventy images, comprises individual subjects, frontispieces, portraits and thirteen sets or series from *Dans le Rêve* of 1879 to *Apocalypse de Saint-Jean*, published by Vollard in 1899.

The fifth set, *La Nuit* of 1886, is still rather dependent on the raw, visionary stuff of the charcoal drawings.[9] Six strikingly individual images, realised with a variety of tone and texture, combine gauche drawing with an insistence on odd relationships or "plastic rhymes". There is a conversation between the classic contours and planes of the head in "A la Vieillesse" (fig. 2), between tree trunk and man (fig. 3), between the features of "L'Ange Perdu" and his basalt wings (fig. 4), and between the eye and the bald pate of "Le Chercheur", his bowl and the round arch (fig. 7). The rhyming repetition intensifies the mood of each individual image, and each in turn behaves as a contrast to the others, almost an irritant rubbing against its fellows. Symons wrote of Plate II (fig. 3) "There is another landscape, a primeval forest, vague and disquieting, and a solitary figure, the figure of a man who is half a tree, like some forgotten deity of a lost race: the forest and man are one, and hold converse".[10] The Chimera is the only monster to survive in this set (fig. 5). The traditional conception of such a monster as an assemblage of parts is replaced here by the shifting metamorphosis of animal, serpent and human characteristics which affects individual features. Such deformation, combined with gauche drawing and mysterious tone, gives the whole image a peculiar, pathetic power. The shimmer of light which terrorises the monster evoked for Jules Destrée "la possible silhouette d'une petite princesse lumineuse, élevant les bras et se pament de terreur devant le giroiement rugissant de cette chimère issue des empires de la viscosité".[11] The more objective Mellerio simply saw ". . . une phosphorescence vague scintillant dans la nuit".[12]

In *La Nuit* the deformations are subjective, intensely personal and various. In the set *Songes* of 1891[13] each image has a structure which has grown out of the juxtaposition of particular forms and is like a stanza in the sequence of a poem. There is a balance between subjective and objective deformation. The essential frontality of Redon's vision has been expressed in the simple geometry underlying these compositions, usually making use of the square as a division of area and placing focal points centrally or on diagonals. On this aspect Redon wrote: "It is nature also who ordains that we shall obey the gifts that she has given us. Mine led me into the dream; I suffered the torments of the imagination and the surprises which it gave me under the pencil; but I guided and controlled these surprises according to the laws of the organism of Art which I know, which I feel, with the sole end that they should exercise on the spectator, through a process of attraction, all the evocation, all the charm of the uncertain that lies at the boundaries of thought."[14]

Songes was dedicated to the memory of Armand Clavaud, who died in December of 1890. The simple designs make an obscure apotheosis. The napkin bearing the imprint of the face of Christ is inset, the depth of the border places the image at one remove from the spectator and underlines its visionary nature "...c'était un voile, une Empreinte..." (fig. 8). The dominant left eye is central laterally. A similar frontal, framed image "Le Jour" closes the series with trees seen through a window from a dark interior, in which float small creatures not dispelled by the light of day (fig. 13).

The sequence progresses from the familiar Christian apparition to a gigantic sagittarian figure in a broken sphere "Et là-bas l'Idole Astrale, l'apothéose" (fig. 9), and then to a profile of light suspended in a lantern over a desolate landscape with the dark bulk of a mountain in the distance "Lueur Précaire, une tête à l'infini suspendue" (fig. 10). The figure of the archer is cut rather than contained by the sphere, and this gives the feeling of a glimpse into another dimension of superior reality. A certain interpenetration takes place at the edges of the broken shell; sources of light seem to shift mysteriously, and carefully realised textures contrast with broad free contours. The profile compressed into the lantern is a variant of the window into another reality, it is also a source of light shed on a foreground of indeterminate scale.

The fourth plate "Sous l'Aile d'Ombre, l'être noir appliquait une active morsure . . ." (fig. 11) appears to be touched by satanism and eroticism but without the stifling, lush décor of Symbolist poetry.[15] Pictorially the theme of an eclipse is suggested, and perhaps the embrace is that of the powers of light and darkness. But the figures are reminiscent of the allegories of death and corruption found in the work or Rops and Besnard. Are we seeing a brisk love bite or the sting of death? The shadowed moon lies in front of the horizon, its shape rhyming the vortex of cloud and its tone the wings of the "black being".

The fifth plate "Pélerin du Monde Sublunaire" (fig. 12) shows a lonely pilgrim riding into the blackened radiance of a moon. The whole composition is dominated by diagonally opposed elements in reverse of

139

2. A LA VIEILLESSE. *La Nuit* I, 1886. $9\frac{5}{8} \times 7\frac{1}{4}$ in. (24·5 × 18·4 cm)

3. L'HOMME FUT SOLITAIRE DANS UN PAYSAGE DE NUIT. *La Nuit* II, 1886. $11\frac{1}{2} \times 8\frac{3}{4}$ in. (29·2 × 22·2 cm)

those in the third plate (fig. 10). The horse and rider, entering from the left, are cut by the edge of the image in the manner of Degas.

The monumental lithograph "Lumière" of 1893 (fig. 14) recently acquired by the Department[16] has many of the qualities found in *Songes* simplified and intensified; the framed image, the manipulation of space and scale, the splendours of tone and the simplicity of structure. Shapes in the drawing of the large hand rhyme with the plain geometry of the setting and more abstrusely perhaps, with the arms of the minuscule figures in the foreground. The play of semi-circle and rectangle appears to be carried through to the asymmetry of the flanking pilasters which may even suggest that this bay is the first of several.

The creative climate of the years 1886–1893 spanned by these lithographs and the events which might have touched Redon's working life are worth a brief examination. The older, traditionally symbolic art of Puvis de Chavannes and Gustave Moreau and the mature art of the Impressionists co-existed with that of the Post-Impressionists and the richly various manifestations of Symbolism. While the Impressionist revolution was being transformed by further heightening of colour and the introduction of new structures, moves against Naturalism were made in literature and philosophy. Intuition was admitted as a means to

discover a superior reality; a new kind of order, a new elevation was sought.

In 1886 Redon had participated in the eighth and last Impressionist exhibition along with Degas, Gauguin, Pissarro and Seurat, who showed his uncompromising "Un dimanche d'été à la Grande Jatte". The publication of Zola's *L'Oeuvre* had estranged the naturalist from Cézanne, Manet and the Impressionists. The conflict centred on these works contributed to the dissolution of the Impressionist movement. Jean Moréas in "Le Symbolisme" urged that in Symbolist poetry the idea must be clothed in form which remains subservient and that it "must not let itself be deprived of the sumptuous robes of exterior analogies; because the essential character of symbolic art consists of never going straight to the centre of an idea".[17] In the same year Redon also exhibited with *Les Vingt* in Brussels and came to know Mellerio, who introduced him to some of the *Nabis*, and subsequently wrote the definitive catalogue of his graphic work. 1886 also saw the birth and death of Redon's first son at Peyrelebade.

In 1887 Renoir exhibited his monumental "Les grandes Baigneuses" at Petit's, another demonstration of a return to structure. Mallarmé's *Poésies* were published in this year and about this time Redon began to spend his summers at Samois on the Seine near to Mallarmé

4. L'ANGE PERDU OUVRIT ALORS DES AILES NOIRES. *La Nuit* III, 1886
$10\frac{1}{8} \times 8\frac{3}{8}$ in. $(25 \cdot 7 \times 21 \cdot 3$ cm$)$

5. LA CHIMERE REGARDA AVEC EFFROI TOUTES CHOSES. *La Nuit* IV,
1886. $9\frac{3}{4} \times 7\frac{1}{4}$ in. $(24 \cdot 8 \times 18 \cdot 4$ cm$)$

6. LES PRETRESSES FURENT EN ATTENTE. *La Nuit* V, 1886. $11\frac{1}{4} \times 8\frac{3}{8}$ in.
$(28 \cdot 6 \times 21 \cdot 3$ cm$)$

7. ET LE CHERCHEUR ETAIT A LA RECHERCHE INFINIE.
La Nuit VI, 1886. $10\frac{7}{8} \times 7\frac{1}{8}$ in. $(27 \cdot 6 \times 18 \cdot 1$ cm$)$

8. . . . C'ETAIT UN VOILE, UNE EMPREINTE . . . *Songes* I, 1891. $7\frac{3}{8} \times 5\frac{1}{4}$ in. ($18 \cdot 7 \times 13 \cdot 3$ cm)

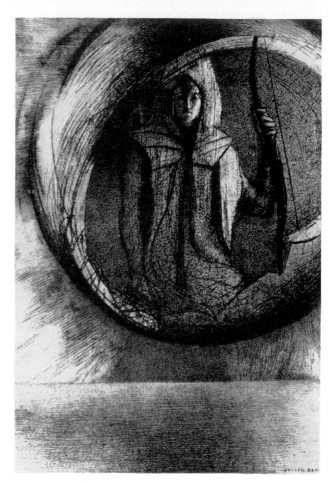

9. ET LA-BAS L'IDOLE ASTRALE, L'APOTHEOSE. *Songes* II, 1891. $11 \times 7\frac{5}{8}$ in. ($28 \times 19 \cdot 4$ cm)

at Valvins. Huysmans had introduced him to the poet earlier in the decade and Redon had been drawn into the circle of Mallarmé's famous *Mardis*, which included some of the most perceptive writers in the history of criticism as well as a range of painters such as Manet, Monet, Degas, Puvis, Vuillard, Gauguin, Munch, Rops and Whistler. In the general atmosphere of toleration generated by the poet, mutual influences were no doubt as oblique as the new Symbolism itself.[18] Certainly Redon suffered a loss of innocence through contact with writers; his interpretations of Picard's *Le Juré* of 1887 and two of his series for Flaubert's *Tentation de Saint Antoine* of 1888 and 1889 lack the intense simplicity of his earlier work and seem, in parts, uneven and literary compared with the almost classic *Songes*. But from his deep friendship with Mallarmé Redon must have found confirmation in poetry of many of the aspects of his own art, in the secret harmonies, the radical manipulation of syntax in simile and metaphor, the analogies of words, forms, colours and sounds.

1889 brought the birth of Redon's second son Ari; Eiffel's stupendous imaginative engineering was to be seen at the Paris World's Fair. In the following year Redon participated in another exhibition with *Les Vingt* along with Cézanne and Van Gogh, Impressionists and Neo-Impressionists; Clavaud died in December.

Seurat's aggressively structured "Chahut" was shown in the Salon des Indépendants in 1890, and his "Cirque" in 1891, followed by his sudden death. In 1891 Jules Destrée's catalogue of Redon's lithographs was published in Brussels; Durand-Ruel exhibited Monet's paintings of Haystacks, the ultimate development of Impressionism. The departure of Gauguin for Tahiti had been preceded by a farewell banquet, which Redon attended; a Symbolist programme for his benefit was given at the *Théatre d'art* in which Redon collaborated.

In 1892 there was the Seurat memorial exhibition and Péladan organized the first *Rose-Croix* Salon. There were major exhibitions of paintings by Renoir, Pissarro and Gauguin, and the first *Nabi* exhibition.

The 90's saw the Toulouse-Lautrec posters for the Moulin Rouge and the beginning of a "renaissance" of colour lithography stemming from Chéret, Bonnard and Vuillard and fostered by Roger-Marx's *L'Estampe Originale* and Vollard's *Les Albums des peintres-graveurs*, though Redon, like Carrière and Fantin-Latour, continued to develop the medium in monochrome.

Against this rich background it appears that Redon's art ran a parallel course with literary Symbolism while keeping its extraordinary individuality and gaining in subtlety. In the more mature *Songes* and in "Lumière" his imagination seems increasingly tempered with

10. LUEUR PRECAIRE, UNE TETE A L'INFINI SUSPENDUE. *Songes* III, 1891. 10⅞ × 8¼ in. (27·6 × 21 cm)

11. SOUS L'AILE D'OMBRE, L'ETRE NOIR APPLIQUAIT UNE ACTIVE MORSURE . . . *Songes* IV, 1891. 8⅞ × 6⅞ in. (22·5 × 17·5 cm)

12. PELERIN DU MONDE SUBLUNAIRE. *Songes* V, 1891. 10⅞ × 8⅛ in. (27·6 × 20·7 cm)

13. LE JOUR. *Songes* VI, 1891. 8¼ × 6⅛ in. (21 × 15·6 cm)

14. LUMIERE. 1893. 15⅜ × 10¾ in. (39 × 27·3 cm)

reason. The juxtapositions and deformations had remained more or less constant but they were expressed in terms of fine tone and structure which might be seen as sharing in the classical revival, the return to form, with Cézanne, Gauguin and Seurat.

Notes

Catalogue raisonné
Mellerio, André. *Odilon Redon*, Société pour l'Etude de la Gravure Française, Paris, 1913.

1. O. Redon, *A Soi-Même*, introduction by J. Morland, Paris, 1922, pp.28, 29.
2. *Ibid.* pp. 29–30.
3. *Ibid.* p. 30.
4. Arbre. 1892. Printed in an edition of 25 by Becquet, Paris. (Mellerio 120) *Lithograph.* E.20–1894.
   The Museum bought this lithograph and 'Pégase captif' (Mellerio 102) for £1 4s. in 1894; impressions of these sold for £1900 and £1300 respectively at Sotheby's, 26 March 1968.
5. *A Soi-Même*, p. 18.
6. Arthur Symons, 'A French Blake: Odilon Redon', *The Art Review*, I, No. 7, July 1890, p. 207.
7. 'Ah! cette main dramatique et disproportionnée du père de Desdémone, et qui maudit! Combien souvent m'en a-t-il montré avec exaltation la beauté, la légitimité de sa deformation. Le style de cette main, en sa hardiesse, fut, je crois bien, l'initiale essence et la cause de beaucoup de mes premiers travaux.' (*A Soi-Même*, p. 20).
8. 'Huysmans ne me comprit qu'incomplètement. Je crois avoir aidé à son évolution, mais je suis resté sur le sol.' Redon's annotation on p.234 of a copy of Emile Bernard's article in *L'Occident*, Mai 1904, reprinted in *Odilon Redon*, by Roseline Bacou, Genève 1956, pp. 274–284, and reproduced in J. Rewald, 'Quelques Notes et Documents sur Odilon Redon', *Gazette des Beaux-Arts*, XLVIII, November, 1956, pp. 101–112.
9. La Nuit. 1886. Set of six lithographs published by L. Dumont, Paris, in an edition of 50 printed by Lemercier et Cie. (Mellerio 62–67). Given by Mr. A. G. B. Russell. E.2694–2699—1908.
10. Symons, *loc. cit.*
11. Jules Destrée, *L'oeuvre lithographique de Odilon Redon*, Bruxelles, 1891, p. 34.
12. Mellerio 65.
13. Songes. 1891. Set of six lithographs published by Dumont, Paris, in an edition of 80 printed by Becquet. (Mellerio 110–115). E.52–57—1961.
    Songes was among the works exhibited at the famous 'Armoury Show' in 1913, when 'Redon went over big' (see Milton W. Brown, *The Story of the Armoury Show*, New York, 1963, p. 108).
14. *A Soi-Même*, p. 27.
15. Sven Sandström, *Le Monde Imaginaire d'Odilon Redon*, Lund and New York, 1955, pp. 101–104 and figs. 80, 81, demonstrates the relationship between this lithograph and an earlier drawing.
16. Lumière. 1893. Printed in an edition of 50 by Becquet, Paris. (Mellerio 123) *Lithograph.* E.102–1968.
    Formerly in the collection of André Mellerio, this lithograph was bought by the Museum for £1000 at Sotheby's, 26 March 1968, from the collection of Stephen Higgins.
17. Jean Moréas, 'Le Symbolisme', *Figaro Littéraire*, 18 September 1886.
18. Mallarmé's circle is discussed in the catalogue of an exhibition 'Les Mardis', held at the University of Kansas Museum of Art, 1965–66.

The Mural from 44 Grosvenor Square

DESMOND FITZ-GERALD

SOME years ago, when alterations were being carried out in the first floor front drawing-room of 44 Grosvenor Square, a large mural was discovered behind its Edwardian "Adam" decoration. Number 44 stood on the south side of the square and was basically an early eighteenth-century brick house, which had unfortunately been much altered internally. The house was one of the last Georgian examples left standing amidst the red-brick and stone-dressed monotony of the polite neo-Georgian flats and offices that today form the North, South and East sides of the square, but it too was finally demolished in 1968, to make way for a new luxury hotel. The mural was undoubtedly the most important feature of No. 44 and, owing to the fact that it was painted with oil on plaster, posed considerable removal problems. However, through the combined generosity of the Duke of Westminster (the landlord), the Grosvenor Estate Company and Mr. Maxwell Joseph, the developer of the hotel, the mural was finally presented to the Victoria and Albert Museum, where it has been erected on the stairs leading up from the Raphael Cartoons Court into the English Primary Galleries. This article attempts to trace the history and possible authorship of the painting and explains why it is such a welcome addition to the Museum's collections of early eighteenth century English decorative art.

The building of Grosvenor Square started about 1721, when Sir Richard Grosvenor leased sites to various speculative builders under the direction of his lawyer-agent, Robert Andrew.[1] In 1725 a newspaper records that "There is now building a square called Grosvenor Square which for its largeness and beauty will far exceed any yet made in and about London".[2] We are only concerned with the south side, of which unfortunately, there is no contemporary engraving. Nicholl's bird's eye view of 1731[3] shows the other three sides with their rather more elaborate mansions, but most of the houses on the south side seem to have been of a uniform type with four bays, a basement and three floors including an attic story, all built of brown brick with red dressings and a stone cornice. A line drawing (fig. 1) based on the façade of No. 44 appears in Sir John Summerson's *Georgian London*,[4] and he has credited the building of Nos. 43 and 44, the only ones that survived until 1968, to the master-builder Thomas Barlow.[5] However, the lease for No. 44 (originally No. 39), preserved in the Middlesex Land Registry for the years 1726–8,[6] shows that Sir Richard Grosvenor leased this site and another next door (that of No. 45, originally No. 40) to one Thomas Richmond, who appears to have been a carpenter living in the parish of St. Anne, Soho. From about 1725 onwards, Richmond indulged in various speculative building enterprises mainly in the parishes of St. Anne and of St. George, Hanover Square.[7] The new houses he built in Grosvenor Square in about 1728–9 were of a standard London plan but, owing to the later alteration of No. 44 in 1908 for the Dowager Duchess of Devonshire,[8] it has been necessary to make a conjectural reconstruction of the ground plan and the hall (figs. 2–3). At this time

1. No. 44 Grosvenor Square—the exterior reconstructed before its later alterations. (Reproduced by kind permission of Sir John Summerson).

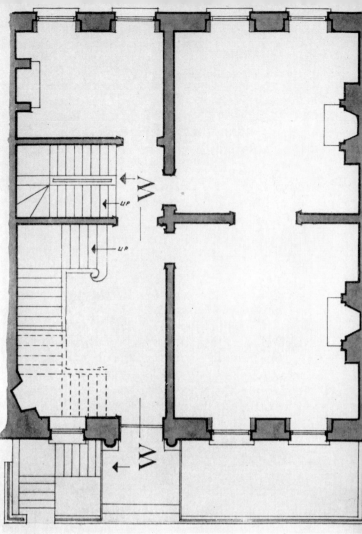

2 & 3. The section and ground plan of the staircase hall of No. 44 Grosvenor Square. Further decoration occurred below the arcade, and traces of it shown here were found during the demolition of the house. (By courtesy of the Historic Buildings Section of the Greater London Council).

the original staircase well was reduced to one story in order to form a new long Drawing Room on the first floor with all four windows facing the square. A new flight of stairs was erected behind the original staircase well, in the place of the original service stair.

The most grandiose feature of the house was the old hall with its staircase ramp leading up towards the front of the house. The walls of this staircase were painted in *trompe l'oeil* to represent groups of figures in contemporary costume, looking down over the balustrade from an arcaded gallery (fig. 4). Before discussing the authorship of these murals, it is necessary to mention another house built by Richmond, the speculator-builder—No. 75 Dean Street, Soho. This was one of four similar houses, all assessed for rates by 1735.[9] The ground plan[10] of No. 75 was of almost identical cast to 44 Grosvenor Square (fig. 3), before its alteration. But what really concerns us here is that the hall with its staircase was also decorated with *trompe l'oeil* murals of figures in contemporary costume leaning over a balustrade (figs. 5 and 6), all in very much the same manner as those at Grosvenor Square. It would seem very likely that Richmond employed the same artists and craftsmen in both these building enterprises. The first occupant of Grosvenor Square was an Irish M.P. for Dungannon, Oliver St. George,[11] and there seems

to be no connection between him and Dean Street's first tenant, Bulstrode Peachey Knight, M.P. for Midhurst,[12] so the choice of the painter-decorator may well have been Richmond's own. The murals in Dean Street were long attributed to Thornhill as he was said to have lived in the house—an assertion not confirmed by the rate books.[13] Thornhill's son-in-law, Hogarth, was also credited with their authorship as early as 1833,[14] again with no foundation, although there is a tenuous connection with Hogarth as we shall see later.

75 Dean Street was demolished in 1919 and the stairs eventually found their way to the Art Institute of Chicago. Unfortunately the murals, though carefully restored and removed, were damaged in transit and were finally broken up. Luckily old photographs of the staircase exist,[15] and through them it is possible to get a very good idea of how the Grosvenor Square staircase hall originally looked. Presumably the Corinthian-pilastered arcaded architectural backdrop continued all the way round the first floor. The hall at Dean Street was ceiled by a *trompe l'oeil* dome apparently opening to the sky with figures looking down over a balustrade. It is more than likely that the ceiling at Grosvenor Square was treated in a similar way. But who was responsible for this baroque theatrical extravaganza?

. The mural from Grosvenor Square. It originally formed the upper storey of the hall, and is shown in place in Fig. 2. Victoria and Albert Museum.

5 & 6. The decoration of the staircase hall at No. 75 Dean Street before its restoration. The area below the murals was painted to simulate ashlar blocks.

7. William Kent's *trompe l'oeil* decoration on the King's Staircase at Kensington Palace. The immediate prototype for the work at Dean Street and Grosvenor Square.

8. Louis Laguerre's staircase at Petworth showing Borrominesque capitals comparable to those at 44 Grosvenor Square.

The convention for this type of decoration, as Mr. Croft-Murray points out,[16] goes back to the Sala Regia at the Quirinal in Rome by Lanfranco, Agostino Tassi and Carlo Saraceni, and the idea was re-used by Le Brun in his famous *Escalier des Ambassadeurs* at Versailles, a work destroyed in 1752. In England the two most important examples are Louis Laguerre's Saloon of about 1720 at Blenheim Palace, which was directly inspired by Le Brun, and the King's Staircase at Kensington Palace (fig. 7), executed by William Kent before 1727. Kent, remembering his Roman education, based the Kensington scheme on the Quirinal work, adapting the *trompe l'oeil* vaulting with its grotesque ornament above the figures. The Grosvenor Square mural must date only a year or so later than the Kensington staircase. It would therefore have been a new and highly fashionable feature at this date and is just the sort of decorative element that might have appealed to the builder of the two houses and to his clients.

If one compares the figures in the Kensington painting with those at Dean Street, we find an identical lady touching her lips with a fan. Also the interplay of arches behind the basic colonnade is reminiscent of Kensington, and finally Kensington has a *trompe l'oeil* ceiling not unlike the one originally at Dean Street. From this, it would seem that William Kent could have been the author of the work at Dean Street and Grosvenor Square. Unfortunately two objections can be raised against such an attribution. Firstly the quality of the paint-work in the two houses, even taking into consideration the lamentable condition of the Dean Street work, seems freer, sketchier and in a sense considerably livelier than Kent's smooth, competent but uninspired composition at Kensington. Secondly, Kent was an important man in 1727—busy with commissions for Lord Burlington, fresh from work at Chiswick, Ditchley, Cannons and Houghton,[17] besides his influential decorations in the royal palace of Kensington. He surely would not have deigned to decorate the staircases of a speculative builder like Richmond.

9. A detail of Louis Laguerre's decoration in the Saloon at Blenheim Palace. The wigged gentleman above Louis Laguerre's signature may be a self portrait.

Mr. Croft-Murray considers the mural from No. 44 Grosvenor Square to be closer to the work of Louis Laguerre at Blenheim (the Blenheim Saloon dates from about 1720, and the inscription "L. Laguerre F." under a portly wigged man may well suggest that it is his self portrait [fig. 9]). There is another connection between Grosvenor Square and Laguerre, for the Borrominesque Corinthian capitals in the former are very close to the capitals of the painted columns that flank Laguerre's *Triumph of Elizabeth, Duchess of Somerset* at Petworth (fig. 8), which dates from after 1714. However, Laguerre died in 1721,[18] which rules him out for the work we are investigating. Vertue notes that he had a son called John, and it is worth quoting his obituary of 1748 in full:

(In March) dyd John Laguerre painter (son of Lewis Laguerre, history painter). This man, indolent and careless of his studyes when young and his father was living, he had a strong impressed natural genius from his father—but not cultivating it he took to singing and playres stage. Therein got reputation and money but heedless and careless had ups and downs at great difficulty to live but at last ageed and want, dyed in poor circumstances. (of his paintings and drawings for the playhouses—his designs of Hob in the Well—those prints were remarkable and many were sold).[19]

What is more likely than that he should have worked in his father's manner and that his connection with the world of the theatre should have led him to scene-painting.[20] He is known to have painted a mural, a "Bacchanalian procession on the walls of a tavern in Drury Lane where a club of Virtuosi met",[21] and "Honest Jack Laguerre"[22] had close connections with Hogarth during the very period under review, for he was a witness with Thornhill, King and Vanderbank in 1728 in Hogarth's law case with the tapestry weaver Joshua Morris,[23] and a benefit ticket for John Laguerre signed "W. Hogarth In" is in the British Museum.[24] Furthermore Hogarth represented Laguerre's satirical etching *The Stage Mutiny* as a show cloth in his famous print *Southwark Fair*[25] and Bryan bluntly comments, though one does not know on what authority, that Laguerre worked under Hogarth.[26] All these points suggest that the traditional Hogarth attribution at Dean Street can be seen to have some substance. Decorative paintings such as those in the halls at Dean Street and No. 44 Grosvenor Square are very likely to have been the work of a scene-painter influenced by Hogarth. Fortunately Laguerre's paintings for John Hippisley's ballad opera *Hob in the Well*[27] have recently come to light[28] and are now in the collection of Mr. and Mrs.

149

10-11. HOB TRIUMPHS OVER SIR THOMAS; HOB WELCOMES MR. FRIENDLY TO THE WAKE; two scenes from John Hippisley's opera comedy *Hob in the Well* painted by John Laguerre (From the collection of Mr. and Mrs. Paul Mellon). There are various points of similarity between these paintings and the murals at 75 Dean Street and 44 Grosvenor Square.

Paul Mellon. Laguerre, it is amusing to note, himself played the part of Hob on Thursday, April 17, 1729, and his wife acted with him.[29] Comparing two of the opera paintings with our murals is not unrewarding for in three of them and in a fourth engraving[30] we find the same odd mannerism of figures incongruously leaning over walls and looking at the absurd antics of Hob, Mr. Friendly and Sir Thomas. In the painting *Hob triumphs over Sir Thomas* (fig. 10)—the duel scene—the two pale ladies watching are not unlike the couple with fans in the Dean Street painted balcony. In another, *Hob welcomes Mr. Friendly to the Wake* (fig. 11), the lady in the straw hat holding a basket of flowers might well have walked outside from her place in the centre arch of the Grosvenor Square mural. The brush-work of the figure of Mr. Friendly in his tricorne hat seems also very akin to the elderly bewigged and tricorned gentleman who converses with two Poles in the right-hand arch at Grosvenor Square. This portly figure is also similar to the doctor, who appears to be dealing with the scalp wound of his companion, on the extreme left of Hob's duel-scene already alluded to.

Hippisley's opera was first performed in 1729,[31] so the paintings could have been executed at about this time or a few years later, in fact very close in date to our murals. The attribution is, however, by no means a certainty, for no doubt there were many other artists capable of executing this type of decorative work; but it does not seem unreasonable to suggest that these charming wall-paintings were by the younger Laguerre.

The technical problems of moving the Grosvenor Square murals to the Museum have been discussed elsewhere[32] but considerable tribute should be given to Professor and Mrs. Eve Baker and their team, for their skill and patience has saved a notable work of decorative art from crumbling into dust, and it is particularly fitting that the mural is to be erected on a staircase that leads from the Raphael Cartoons into the English Primary Galleries. For in this way the murals will again be seen in their proper perspective, looked up at and not seen too closely, and surely underlining in a visual manner the links between seventeenth-century Italian wall-decoration and that of our own brief era of Baroque Art.

Notes

1. See John Summerson, *Georgian London*, London, 1945 pp. 86–87. For a convenient history of the square and a complete account of the occupants of all the houses down to 1934 see Arthur L. Dasent, *A History of Grosvenor Square*, London, 1935.

2. *The Daily Journal*, July 12, 1725.

3. Reproduced in Hugh Phillips *Mid-Georgian London*, London, 1964 fig. 347.

4. Summerson, *op. cit.*, p. 88, fig. 13. Drawn by Alison Shepherd, A.R.I.B.A. and reproduced by kind permission of Sir John Summerson.

5. *Ibid.*, p. 87.

6. I am much indebted to Mr. Walter Ison and the Greater London Council for this information and other assistance over the preparation of this article.

7. Information from Mr. Walter Ison.

8. Directed by Frederick Wheeler, F.R.I.B.A. At the same time the ground floor front room was altered. The brick bay window added to the exterior of the ground floor may well also have been built at this time.

9. For a full description of this house and Richmond's other building enterprises in Dean Street see F. H. W. Sheppard (editor), *Survey of London—The Parish of St. Anne, Soho*, London, 1966 XXXIII, p. 221ff and XXXIV, pls. 102, 104–5.

10. Reproduced in Sheppard, XXXIII, p. 225.

11. Dasent, *op. cit.*, p. 225.

12. Sheppard, XXXIII, p. 221.

13. *Ibid.*, p. 224.

14. *Ibid.*

15. Cited in note 9.

16. MS. note prepared at the time of the demolition of No. 44.

17. For a list of his works see Howard Colvin, *A Biographical Dictionary of English Architects* London, 1954 pp. 343–4.

18. See Edward Croft-Murray, *Decorative Painting in England, 1537–1837*, London, 1962, I, 250ff.

Mr. Croft-Murray lists the Dean Street work tentatively as being by Kent in Vol. II of *Decorative Painting in England* London, 1969 p. 234a. He discusses Grosvenor Square on p. 303a. I am indebted to Mr. Croft-Murray for letting me see the page proofs of his second volume.

19. *The Walpole Society*, XXVI, Vertue V, p. 68.

20. D. N. B., XI, p. 397.

21. Ronald Paulson, *Hogarth's Graphic Works*, Newhaven, 1965, I, p. 301.

22. K. A. Esdaile in *Thieme Becker*, XXII, p. 222.

23. Austin Dobson, *William Hogarth*, London, 1891 p. 26.

24. Paulson, I, *op. cit.*, p. 318. This is one of the 'Joseph Sympson Jr' etchings, and is not accepted by Paulson as Hogarth's work. For further information about Laguerre's connection with Hogarth *Ibid.*, p. 156.

25. *Catalogue of Prints and Drawings in the British Museum—Political and Personal Satire*, London, 1873, II, pp. 794 and 835.

26. *Bryan's Dictionary of Printing and Engraving* London 1904, III, p. 163.

27. Known also as *Flora, An Opera . . . Made from Hob, or, The Country Wake*. Mentioned by Vertue.

28. I am much indebted to Mr. Bill Drummond of Messrs. Sidney Sabin for bringing his discovery to my attention.

29. Emmett L. Avery (editor), *The London Stage 1660–1800*, Carbondale, 1960 pt. 2, p. 1026. See also Allardyce Nicholl, *A History of Early Eighteenth Century Drama, 1700–1750*, Cambridge, 1925, p. 336.

30. A set of 8 engravings for the Opera were signed 'Laguerre Inv and Delin-Claude du Bosc Sc.' and are in the British Museum.

31. See note 27.

32. S. Mackenzie, 'Problems of Preserving Art', *Journal of the Institute of Clerks of Works*, December, 1968, 86, pp. 236–238.

John Lochée, Portrait Sculptor

TERENCE HODGKINSON

IN 1772 a student of sculpture at the Royal Academy Schools was enrolled under the curious name Joannes Carolus Lochees, rendered in the Council minutes as John Charles Lochée.[1] From the enrolment we know that he was born on November 4, 1751; but the place of his birth and particulars of his parentage are unknown. Lochée's career as a sculptor seems to have lasted for only fifteen years, from 1775 until 1790. In 1791 he was declared bankrupt and nothing more is heard of him. Even the date of his death has not been discovered.[2] Although the majority of his sculptures were in the smaller forms—wax portraits, Wedgwood medallions and Tassie gems—Lochée executed a number of portrait busts, which until recently have passed unrecognised. That it is possible to identify some of these busts, all unsigned yet all accomplished and characteristic, provides the reason for writing about him now.

In 1776 Lochée exhibited at the Royal Academy for the first time, his two works being described as "Bust of a gentleman" and "Bust of a boy" and his address being given as 17 King Street, Soho.[3] Eight years passed before he exhibited again, by which time he had moved to 11 Rupert Street, Haymarket. Two of his contributions in 1785 are described as "Portrait of a gentleman", a third as "Portrait of a lady" and a fourth as "Model of Lord Hood". Almost certainly the "model" was a wax relief, a form of portraiture in which Lochée excelled. In 1786 he exhibited "H.R.H. the Prince William Henry; a model" and it must be at this date that he began to describe himself as "Portrait modeller to Prince William Henry". A trade card, bearing this description is fixed to the back of a wax portrait of an unknown man in the Mary Bate Collection, which is on loan to the Victoria and Albert Museum. (figs. 1 and 4). In 1787 he exhibited a "Bust of H.R.H. Frederick Duke of York and Bishop of Osnaburg", "H.R.H. the Prince of Wales; a model" and also three works of art described only by their subjects, but which were presumably wax reliefs: "His Serene Highness Prince Charles of Mecklenburgh", "His Serene Highness Prince de Ligne" and "H.R.H. Prince Edward". His address at this time was 13 Poland Street, and he was living here at the time of his bankruptcy.

A collection of eight wax reliefs by Lochée in the British Museum[4] includes versions of the Prince William Henry (fig. 2), the Prince of Wales (fig. 3) and the Prince Edward (fig. 5). On the back of the relief of Prince William Henry is a trade card (fig. 6), in which the sculptor is described as "Portrait Modeller to T.R.H. Prince William Henry, Prince Edward, Prince Ernest Augustus and Prince Augustus Frederick". These were the third, fourth, fifth and sixth sons respectively of King George III. In the same year a payment to Lochée, recorded in the royal archives,[5] supports this new and more elaborate description:

His Royal Highness
George Prince of Wales
To John Lochée

1787				
April 2	To a Bust of His Royal Highness Prince William Henry	10	10	0
May 7	To an Original Model in Wax of your Royal Highness	6	12	0
May 8	To the Models of the Royal Princes	29	8	0
June 9	To a Copy of Your Royal Highness in Wax	4	4	0
		£50	14	0
	To a Cameo of His Royal Highness Duke of York Mounted in Gold	3	13	6
		£54	7	6

The receipt, dated August 5, 1790, is signed: John Lochée. The waxes and the bust of Prince William Henry mentioned in this account appear to be no longer in the royal collections.

In the last three years that apparently remained to him as a sculptor, from 1788 to 1790, Lochée exhibited six busts in the Royal Academy and one "Portrait of a clergyman". No "models" are listed in these years and it is possible that his career was taking a turn away from the smaller forms, by which he must have previously earned his living. But before giving particulars of his busts, some mention must be made of his work for Josiah Wedgwood and James Tassie.

Even before he first exhibited in the Academy, Lochée had been employed by the Wedgwood factory as a modeller. Josiah Wedgwood wrote to Thomas Bentley on September 11, 1774:[6] "I am glad you have given

1. WAX RELIEF OF AN UNKNOWN MAN, with Lochée's trade card on the back of the frame. Mary Bate Collection, lent to the Victoria and Albert Museum. H. 3¼ in. (8·26 cm).

2. GEORGE, PRINCE OF WALES. Wax relief in the British Museum. (87, 12–16, 24) H. 3 5/16 in. (8·42 cm).

3. PRINCE WILLIAM HENRY DUKE OF CLARENCE. Wax relief in the British Museum. (87, 12–16, 26) H. 2 11/16 in. (6·84 cm).

4. Trade card on the back of the relief shown in fig. 1.

5. PRINCE EDWARD DUKE OF KENT. Wax relief in the British Museum. (87, 12–16, 27) H. 3 5/16 in. (8·42 cm).

6. Trade card on the back of the relief shown in fig. 3.

Lochée something to do. We want a great deal of modeling, having many things before us within a little of being capital. The small Bass relief Heads of Eminent Men, Greeks &c, should be made more complete and extensive. If Lochée is capable of anything in that stile you may venture to engage him for a time. We could employ him here for a year or two repairing Busts & Figures if we durst have him in the country for Hackwood is of the greatest value and consequence in finishing fine small work, and of this kind we have and shall have enough to employ him constantly." Lochée seems to have given satisfaction, for we hear of him thirteen years later, in December 1787, still employed by Josiah Wedgwood, copying gems in the collection of the Marquess of Buckingham at Stowe. In the following year he is again at Stowe, this time accompanied by Charles Peart, an assistant.[7]

No doubt a great deal of Lochée's work for Wedgwood 153

7. FREDERICK AUGUSTUS DUKE OF YORK. Wax relief in the British Museum. (87, 12–16, 25) H. 2½ in. (6·35 cm).

consisted in making copies of antique gems, which were immensely popular at the time; but he also played an important part in creating the great series of contemporary portraits, in jasper ware, called by Wedgwood *Heads of illustrious moderns* in his catalogue of 1787. A number of artists were engaged in this enterprise, including John Flaxman R.A; but Lochée was certainly one of the principal modellers.[8]

Another source of employment for artists of Lochée's attainments was provided by James Tassie, whose contemporary portraits and copies of gems in glass paste won a large public response. Ten portrait heads by Lochée are listed in Raspe's catalogue of the Tassie gems, dated 1791 and there were probably more. Many are of the same sitters as the Wedgwood portraits.[9]

Turning now to Lochée's busts, particulars of those with known subjects are as follows:

8. FREDERICK AUGUSTUS DUKE OF YORK. Marble. Windsor Castle. H. 26¾ in. (67·94 cm).

9. FREDERICK AUGUSTUS DUKE OF YORK. Painted plaster. Lent to The Royal Pavilion, Brighton, by Lord Sherwood. H. 27 in. (68·58 cm).

10. PRINCE WILLIAM HENRY DUKE OF CLARENCE. Print dated 1788 after a drawing by Lawrence, based on a bust by Lochée. National Portrait Gallery.

11. SIR WILLIAM HERSCHEL. Plaster. National Portrait Gallery. H. 32½ in. (82·55 cm).

H.R.H. FREDERICK DUKE OF YORK AND BISHOP OF OSNABURG. Exhibited R.A. 1787. A wax relief of this subject by Lochée in the British Museum (fig. 7) and a Tassie medallion after a model by Lochée leave no doubt that the closely similar, unsigned marble bust of the Duke of York at Windsor Castle (fig. 8) is by this sculptor.[10] A pigmented plaster version belonging to Lord Sherwood is on loan at the Royal Pavilion Brighton[11] (fig. 9). The material of the version exhibited in the Royal Academy is not specified. There are two contemporary prints of the Duke of York after the Lochée portrait.[12]

PRINCE WILLIAM HENRY. Supplied to the Prince of Wales in 1787. Although this bust is unlocated, its existence is known from Lochée's bill in the royal archives and from a print published in 1788, which is inscribed "Drawn by T. Lawrance (sic) from a bust by J. Lochée"[13] (fig. 10). Such portrait drawings after busts sometimes depart a good deal from the sculptures; and the wax relief by Lochée in the British Museum (fig. 3) probably provides a safer guide to the appearance of the missing bust.

SIR WILLIAM HERSCHEL. Exhibited R.A. 1788 ("Bust of Dr. Herschell").[14] An unsigned plaster bust of the great astronomer in the National Portrait Gallery (fig. 11) had remained in the possession of his descendants until 1958[15] and can be confidently ascribed to Lochée. According to the Dictionary of National Biography, a

12. ADMIRAL LORD HOOD. Plaster. The Honourable A. L. Hood, Loders Court, Bridport. H. 31 in. (78·74 cm).

13. R. B. SHERIDAN. Marble. Victoria and Albert Museum. (A.44–1950). H. 31¾ in. (80·64 cm).

bust of Herschel by "Lockie" was commissioned in 1787 for Sir William Watson, who died in that year.

ADMIRAL LORD HOOD. Exhibited R.A. 1788. In 1785 Lochée exhibited "A model of Lord Hood" and he was the author of the Wedgwood medallion of this subject (see note 8). An unsigned plaster bust in the possession of his descendants can be ascribed to Lochée (fig. 12).[16]

RICHARD BRINSLEY SHERIDAN. Exhibited R.A. 1790. Although the sitter is not named in the printed catalogue, which gives only "Bust of a gentleman", the identity is provided by an annotated copy in the library of the Royal Academy. A print of Sheridan of 1794 is inscribed "From an original bust by Lochée".[17] Identical marble versions of a bust of Sheridan, all

unsigned, are at Windsor Castle, in the Victoria and Albert Museum[18] (fig. 13) and in the Museum of Art, Carnegie Institute, Pittsburgh.[19] A version formerly in the possession of the sitter's family was once ascribed to Nollekens;[20] but there is no evidence that Sheridan was portrayed by Nollekens or by any sculptor except Lochée, at this period. The print of 1794 departs a good deal from the busts and shows the subject wearing a stock. In Sir George Scharf's notebooks in the National Portrait Gallery is a drawing of the Windsor version, noted as being "in corridor" on November 4, 1881. Scharf drew another version, on February 20, 1862, which was in the studio of the sculptor Francis at 56 St. Alban's Street; he describes it as "a plaster cast from an original bust at Windsor".

14. GEORGE, PRINCE OF WALES. Print dated 1791 of a bust by Lochée.

15. GEORGE, PRINCE OF WALES. Marble. Wildenstein and Co. H. 32¼ in. (81·92 cm).

GEORGE PRINCE OF WALES. Exhibited R.A. 1790. The Society of Arts awarded a silver medallion to Lochée for his bust of the Prince of Wales in 1790 and published "a print from a Cast of that Bust" in 1791[21] (fig. 14). In terms of prestige this work must have been Lochée's highest achievement. The Prince is shown in Garter robes with the Star and the George clearly visible. The print, it must be stressed, represents a plaster version. The marble version, (figs. 15 and 16), which was acquired from Lady Sackville[22] by Wildenstein and Company before the First World War and which is still in their collection in Paris, lacks both the Star and the George. The only explanation that can be hazarded is that bankruptcy and perhaps ill-health or even death may have overtaken the sculptor before he

had completed the marble version and that it was summarily finished by another hand. On the separate rectangular block under the bust is incised "LOGEE SCULPTr". In view of the spelling, this can hardly have been carved by the sculptor himself. On the basis of the inscription, Louis Réau made a communication to the *Société de l'histoire de l'art français* on the sculptor Logée, known only from this bust.[23] The subject was thought to be the Duke of Berwick.

So much for the busts of known sitters, which, although all unsigned, can be ascribed with some supporting evidence to Lochée. They have a distinctive manner, curiously florid and rococo for the late 1780's. There is no sign of neo-classical severity in these gracious likenesses, with their frilled collars and fur-lined cloaks,

157

16. GEORGE, PRINCE OF WALES. Marble. Wildenstein and Co.

17. UNKNOWN LADY. Perhaps Mrs. Robinson. Marble. Ascribed to Lochée. Frick Collection, New York. H. 33 in. (83·82 cm).

their orders and medallions, the hair or wig rendered naturalistically and the drapery covering the truncations in opulent folds. The drapery devices are reminiscent of those employed by Roubiliac in some of his later busts; there is nothing to remind us of Wilton or of Nollekens, who, it is difficult to remember, was Lochée's senior by fourteen years.

With Lochée's idiosyncrasies in mind, it may be permissible to ascribe to him a marble bust of a lady (fig. 17), about which we have no evidence from contemporary sources. The bust was acquired by the Frick Collection, New York, from the J. Pierpont Morgan collection in 1915 as a portrait of Madame Roland by Augustin Pajou. The resemblance to Marie-Jeanne Roland, the leader of the Girondins, is not close and the elaborately fashionable hair style and the fur-lined cloak are uncharacteristic of her. The name was presumably suggested to explain the monogram MR or RM, which is carved on the medallion. The ascription to Pajou has never been argued and cannot be sustained. Yet it is easy to understand that no alternative was put forward until the publication of the Frick Collection sculpture catalogue of 1969,[24] as, without the clue provided by the Lochée busts, no suggestion presented itself. The bust in the Frick Collection bears in fact a close family resemblance to the busts and reliefs by Lochée. Hair and drapery are treated in a similar way; the medallion and the fur-lined cloak strongly recall the bust of the Duke of York and the frilled collar the busts of Herschel and Sheridan;

the eyes and eyebrows are treated as in the busts of Sheridan and the Prince of Wales. As to the subject, there is a strong presumption that she is to be found in London in the last quarter of the century and that she is a person of some renown. Of all the possible sitters with the initials RM or MR, who are listed in the catalogue of engraved portraits in the British Museum, the most comprehensive list of candidates available, by far the most likely is Mary (Perdita) Robinson (b. 1758; d. 1800), actress, writer and, briefly, mistress of the Prince of Wales. We know that she employed the monogram MR on her carriage; and it is noticeable that among Lochée's sitters for busts were the Prince of Wales and Sheridan, who was a close friend of Mrs. Robinson. Yet it cannot be argued that the features of the bust are particularly like those of Perdita, as she appears in painted portraits, and the suggestion that it represents her is put forward with a good deal less confidence than the attribution to Lochée.

The Academy catalogues record four busts by Lochée which cannot be identified: three that are described as "Bust of a gentleman" (one of 1776 and two of 1789) and one called "Bust of a boy" (1776). The same applies to contributions described as "Portraits": two of 1785 called "Portrait of a gentleman", one of the same date called "Portrait of a lady" and one of 1788 called "Portrait of a clergyman". It seems likely that these were busts, although we cannot be sure. He may also have executed a few busts that were not exhibited in the Royal Academy. Probably, therefore, some more works by Lochée remain to be discovered, elegant, accomplished, unclassical and almost certainly unsigned.

Notes

1. S. Hutchinson, 'The Royal Academy Schools 1768–1830' in *Walpole Society* XXXVIII, 1962, p. 138 (the year misprinted as 1774).

2. R. Gunnis, *Dictionary of British Sculptors 1660–1851*, London 1953, gives the date of the bankruptcy incorrectly as 1795. It is recorded in *Universal Magazine* 1791, p. 238. His Will is not at Somerset House and his death is not included in the records of the parish of St. Anne's Soho, in which he was living in 1791. I am grateful to Julian Litten for searching these records. Two other Lochées were of some importance in London towards the end of the eighteenth century: Lewis Lochée Esquire, described in the *Gentleman's Magazine* at his death in 1791 as 'late lieutenant-colonel of the Belgic legion and keeper of the Royal Military Academy at Chelsea', and his son John Lochée the auctioneer, who died in 1815; but their relationship, if any, to the sculptor is undetermined.

3. A. Graves, *The Royal Academy of Arts, a Complete Dictionary of Contributors*, London 1906. All quotations from the Royal Academy catalogues are derived from this publication.

4. The British Museum waxes by Lochée, presented by A. W. Franks in 1887, are of the following subjects: George III, George IV as Prince of Wales, Frederick Augustus Duke of York, William IV as Prince William Henry Duke of Clarence, Prince Edward Augustus Duke of Kent, Prince Ernest Augustus Duke of Cumberland, Prince Augustus Frederick Duke of Sussex and Prince Adolphus Frederick Duke of Cambridge. They are uniform is style. The frames are similar and three of them bear Lochée's trade card.

5. Royal archives Windsor, Georgian papers No. 26694. The text is made available by gracious permission of H.M. the Queen. I am grateful to Geoffrey de Bellaigue for supplying this information.

6. A. Finer and G. Savage, *The Selected Letters of Josiah Wedgwood*, London 1965, p. 165.

7. E. Meteyard, *The Life of Josiah Wedgwood*, II, London 1866, p. 507.

8. According to R. Gunnis, *op. cit.*, the Wedgwood archives attest Lochée's authorship of the following medallions: Prince Augustus, Prince Adolphus and Prince Ernest, Princesse de Ligne, William Pitt the Younger, Count Pinto the Portuguese ambassador, the Marchioness of Buckingham, Lord Hood, the Honourable Keith Elphinstone, Dr. Denman, Mr. Dennis O'Kelly and the Duke of Brunswick. According to H. M. Buten, *Wedgwood and Artists*, Merion Pennsylvania, 1960, p. 26–27, Lochée is also credited with medallions of Prince de Ligne, Prince William Henry, W. T. Franklin, the Marquess of Buckingham and Princesse de Lamballe. However, the Wedgwood literature contains no authoritative analysis of the various hands involved in the *Illustrious Moderns* and Lochée may well have executed more than these.

9. R. E. Raspe, *A descriptive catalogue of a general collection of ancient and modern engraved gems, cameos as well as intaglios . . . by James Tassie, modeller*, London 1791, gives Lochée's portrait heads made for Tassie as follows: Prince of Wales, Prince William Henry (two), Mrs. Barwell, Princesse de Lamballe, Count O'Kelly, Chevalier Pinto, the Duke of York, Mrs. Siddons and an unnamed lady. All these are described as cameos taken from models by Lochée, except the Princesse de Lamballe which is a cornelian. J. M. Gray, *James and William Tassie*, Edinburgh 1894, p. 115 lists (No. 188) a Tassie medallion of Major Henniker, which is inscribed: LOCHEE F.

10. Exhibited, R. A. *Bicentenary Exhibition*, 1968–69, No. 102 and Queen's Gallery, *Royal Review of the British Soldier*, 1966, No. 88.

The photograph is reproduced by gracious permission of H.M. the Queen.

11. Brighton Royal Pavilion, *Regency Exhibition Catalogue*, 1948, No. 1.

12. British Museum, *Catalogue of Engraved British Portraits*, II, London 1910, p. 253–54, Nos. 11 and 32.

13. British Museum, *op. cit.*, IV, p. 490, No. 36.

14. Another bust of Herschel by Peter Francis Chenu was exhibited in the same year.

15. Exhibited R. A. *Bicentenary Exhibition*, 1968–69, No. 103. Mrs. E. D. Shorland sale, Sotheby's, March 4, 1958, part of lot 466.

16. At Loders Court, Bridport. Collection of the Honourable Alexander Lambert Hood. Another bust of Lord Hood by 'Silvester' was exhibited in the same year.

17. British Museum, *op. cit.*, IV, p. 86, No. 2.

18. A.44–1950. Bought, without history, from Gerald Kerin.

19. Bought at sale of February 21, 1969, Parke Bernet, New York.

20. W. Sichel, *Sheridan*, II, 1909, p. 370.

21. Society of Arts, *Transactions*, VIII, 1790, Class 173 and X, 1792 frontispiece.

22. There is no evidence that the bust came from the Hertford-Wallace Collection, as did a number of Lady Sackville's possessions.

23. The communication is mentioned in Société de l'histoire de l'art français, *Bulletin*, 1924, p. 84.

24. More material on this bust is included in the catalogue of sculpture in the Frick Collection, New York, 1969.

Index